THE ART OF LANDSCAPE ARCHITECTURE

AMERICAN SOCIETY OF LANDSCAPE ARCHITECTS CENTENNIAL REPRINT SERIES

ASLA CENTENNIAL REPRINT SERIES

Country Life: A Handbook of Agriculture, Horticulture, and Landscape Gardening (1859)
Robert Morris Copeland

Landscape Architecture, as Applied to the Wants of the West (1873)
H. W. S. Cleveland

Charles Eliot, Landscape Architect (1902)
Charles W. Eliot

The Art of Landscape Architecture (1915)
Samuel Parsons Jr.

Prairie Spirit in Landscape Gardening (1915)
Wilhelm Miller

Landscape-Gardening (1920)
O. C. Simonds

The Spirit of the Garden (1923)
Martha Brookes Hutcheson

Book of Landscape Gardening (1926)
Frank A. Waugh

New Towns for Old (1927)
John Nolen

Landscape for Living (1950)
Garrett Eckbo

The series is underwritten by the Viburnum Foundation.

THE ART OF
LANDSCAPE ARCHITECTURE

SAMUEL PARSONS JR.

Introduction by Francis R. Kowsky

UNIVERSITY OF MASSACHUSETTS PRESS / AMHERST
IN ASSOCIATION WITH
LIBRARY OF AMERICAN LANDSCAPE HISTORY / AMHERST

This volume is reprinted from the 1915 edition of
The Art of Landscape Architecture by Samuel Parsons Jr.,
published by The Knickerbocker Press, New York.

Printed in the United States of America

LC 2008046553
ISBN 978-1-55849-695-8

Printed and bound by Sheridan Books, Inc.

Library of Congress Cataloging-in-Publication Data
Parsons, Samuel, 1844–1923.
The art of landscape architecture / Samuel Parsons Jr. ; introduction by Francis R. Kowsky.
p. cm. — (American Society of Landscape Architects centennial reprint series)
Originally published: New York : Knickerbocker Press, 1915.
Includes bibliographical references and index.
ISBN 978-1-55849-695-8 (cloth : alk. paper)
1. Landscape architecture. 2. Landscape gardening. I. Library of American Landscape History. II. Title. III. Series: Centennial reprint series.
SB472.P27 2009
712—dc22

2008046553

British Library Cataloguing in Publication data are available.

This volume is dedicated to

NANCY R. TURNER,
founding president of LALH,

whose generous spirit and love of American parks and gardens
are reflected in the expanding library of works
published by LALH.

Publication of *The Art of Landscape Architecture*
was underwritten by the Trustees of the
Library of American Landscape History.

CONTENTS

PREFACE

The ASLA Centennial Reprint Series comprises a small library of influential books about American landscape architecture. The ten titles were selected by a committee of distinguished historians and practitioners who identified them as classics, important in shaping design, planting, planning, and stewardship practices in the field and still relevant today. Each is reprinted from the original edition and introduced by a new essay that provides historical and contemporary perspective. The project was initiated by the Library of American History to commemorate the 1999 centennial of the American Society of Landscape Architects.

In his new introduction to *The Art of Landscape Architecture*, Francis R. Kowsky makes the case that Samuel Parsons Jr. (1844–1923) was a cultural soldier who, as one contemporary put it, "fought to a finish those who would destroy the Park." The park in question was Central Park in New York City, where Parsons served as superintendent for much of his active career. The fight was his near-continuous battle to fend off proposed incursions that ranged from automobile speedways to endlessly proliferating statues. Parsons battled entropy, too, arguing that the degraded state of the elms lining the Mall—"the few poor, dilapidated, moribund survivors"—was a disgrace. One year before his death, he chaired the Society for the Elms on the Mall, which managed to raise $40,000 to plant forty 50-foot trees. Preserving the integrity of Frederick Law Olmsted and Calvert Vaux's Greensward plan was Parsons's passion and professional mission, and, as Kowsky notes, he executed it with admirable success.

Parsons was also an accomplished landscape designer. Examples of his work can be visited throughout Manhattan, including several vest-pocket parks, such as De Witt Clinton, Thomas Jefferson, Hamilton Fish, and John Jay parks. In his various roles as landscape architect for New York City, Parsons also created redesigns for Union Square and City Hall Park, and he laid out the Broadway Mall. His most brilliant park design, for St. Nicholas Park, was a response to the dramatic, rocky topography of West Harlem. The design is currently undergoing a restoration that promises to renew a cultural treasure that had become derelict. Parsons maintained a national practice as well, executing projects ranging from smaller parks to cemeteries, planned communities, and campuses throughout the nation, from Birmingham to San Diego. He was also a key player in the creation of the American Society of Landscape Architects, whose inaugural meeting was held in his office. A prolific writer who contributed frequently to a range of professional and popular magazines, Parsons also wrote six books, the last of which was *The Art of Landscape Architecture*, published in 1915.

Parsons's engaging text promotes an approach to landscape design rooted in the Romantic tradition of his professional forebears, Calvert Vaux and Prince Hermann von Pückler-Muskau, whom he considered the two greatest exponents of his art. This assessment, published in a 1915 article on Italian villas in *American Architect*, pointedly ignores Vaux's better-known partner Olmsted, whom Parsons felt had unfairly overshadowed his mentor. Just before writing his book, Parsons visited Pückler's extensive park in Silesia, and in 1917 he supplied the introduction to an ASLA-sponsored reprint of the German prince's 1834 volume, *Hints on Landscape Gardening*. His allegiance to Pückler's Romantic principles is evident throughout *The Art of Landscape Architecture*, even as he wrestled with the scope of the emerging modern profession. At the core of Parsons's philosophy (and that of Pückler) was a conviction that landscape design should find inspiration in nature but should also clearly reflect the imprint of humankind. As Parsons wrote, "What would Wordsworth's descriptions of nature be without the human note?"

Copiously illustrated with images of Central Park, Goethe's cottage at Weimar, the Boboli gardens, Villa d'Este, Durham Cathedral, and several American estates, *The Art of Landscape Architecture* captures a heady moment in the emerging field. The century's second decade was a period of rapid growth in America and in the profession, too, owing to a burgeoning number of landscape commissions that included new towns, parks, and college campuses as well as residential estates. The pool of design ideas was also expanding, as landscape architects brought increasingly imaginative work into both the public and the private spheres.

Parsons's own designs were inherently conservative, and yet, as Kowsky notes, certain of them may have influenced later practitioners. He cites the similarity of Frank Lloyd Wright's Fallingwater, in Bear Run, Pennsylvania, to Parsons's work for John A. Staples in Balmville, New York. Parsons's dramatic and spare design for St. Nicholas Park is also exuberant in its celebration of natural forms, in this case the rocky cliffs that explode from the earth's surface at the northern end of Manhattan Island. Few city parks provide such bold encounters with Nature.

It is fitting that the ten-volume ASLA Centennial Reprint Series concludes with *The Art of Landscape Architecture*, a book whose comprehensive scope and title announced the legitimacy of the profession to the general public. The publication date of the original edition, 1915, falls midway between the earliest of the titles in the series, Robert Morris Copeland's *Country Life* (1859), and the latest, *Landscape for Living* (1950) by Garret Eckbo. New reprint editions of Copeland's and Eckbo's books are also coming out in 2009; the ambitious LALH initiative, begun in 1999, is thus complete.

Frank Kowsky's fine new introduction contains many insights into Parsons's background and the landmark book that helped authenticate the profession. These add immeasurably to the growing body of scholarship in the field, and I thank Frank for them. I am also grateful to Carol Betsch for her thoughtful editing and to Mary Bellino for her meticulous proofreading. I am grateful to Jonathan Lippincott for his imaginative book design and to Sara Cedar Miller for the transcendently beautiful photographs that appear on the book's jacket. Sally Nichols, associate production manager at University of Massachusetts Press, saw this book through its final stages. I thank her and all the members of the Press staff. My deepest thanks go to the Trustees of LALH and to the Trustees of the Viburnum Foundation, whose enthusiasm for the series made this new library of work possible.

Partial support for the reprint edition of *The Art of Landscape Architecture* was provided by the Trustees of the Library of American Landscape History. This volume is dedicated to Nancy R. Turner, the founding president of LALH, in recognition of her generosity, wise leadership, and love of the American landscape.

Robin Karson, Executive Director
Library of American Landscape History
Amherst, Massachusetts

LALH

Library of American Landscape History, Inc., a nonprofit organization, produces books and exhibitions about North American landscape history. Its mission is to educate and thereby promote thoughtful stewardship of the land.

Samuel Parsons Jr. (1844–1923). *National Cyclopedia of American Biography* (1906).

INTRODUCTION TO THE REPRINT EDITION

Francis R. Kowsky

FOR Samuel Parsons Jr., nature, the preservation of rural scenery, urban parks, and a faith in the common man were the major themes of a long career as a landscape architect. The place he cared for above all others was New York's Central Park. When Parsons was a young man, this first true monument of the American park movement was just taking form under the guidance of Calvert Vaux and Frederick Law Olmsted. Central Park would become for Parsons a classroom, a professional responsibility, and a celebrated cause. First as an apprentice to Vaux and then as superintendent of the park, Parsons devoted himself to safeguarding the Greensward plan—the name Olmsted and Vaux gave to their design of 1857—against those who sought to change it. He would be remembered always, wrote a close friend, as "a gallant soldier who for a lifetime fought to a finish those who would destroy the Park."[1] In the process, through his prolific writings, Parsons became a well-known advocate for the values of the Romantic tradition of landscape design.

Samuel Parsons Jr. was born in 1844 into a family acquiring a prominent reputation in American horticulture. Six years before Samuel's birth, his grandfather had established a nursery at Flushing, Long Island, an area known as a center of ornamental gardening. Samuel's father, Samuel Bowne Parsons, and his uncle, Robert Bowne Parsons, skillfully managed the business, which quickly grew to be one of the most famous nurseries in the country. Samuel Sr., who wrote a popular book on roses, even felt the authority to criticize Andrew Jackson Downing, America's foremost writer on horticultural matters, accusing him in print of promoting self-serving theories of fruit tree cultivation which favored Downing's Hudson Valley tree stock over the offerings of coastal nurseries.[2] Under Parsons Sr.'s direction, the firm began to specialize in importing ornamental trees and shrubs.

In the early 1840s, Parsons Sr. traveled to the Caribbean and to Europe on the first of many trips abroad in search of novel plants. From Belgium, he brought home the weeping beech, a tree whose gracious ground-sweeping branches captured the imagination of many Americans after he succeeded in transplanting a specimen on the grounds of the nursery. Thirty years later, when the sapling had grown to an organic "gazebo" some fifty feet high and fifty feet wide, Samuel Jr. would describe it as "a Gothic cathedral in similitude, equal in itself to a grove of choice trees."[3] Parsons Sr. also brought the Japanese maple to American gardeners and likewise pioneered commercial cultivation of Asiatic rhododendrons, a shrub that Olmsted and Vaux used abundantly in the Central Park Ramble and elsewhere.

Once the construction began in 1858 on Olmsted and Vaux's design for Central Park, the practitioners regularly turned to the Parsons firm for trees and shrubs and expert horticultural advice. Parsons Sr. was pleased to furnish Olmsted letters of introduction to European nurserymen and at least once accompanied him on a buying trip, traveling in 1859 to Brussels to find plant material for the New York park. This relationship continued for many years and was

The weeping beech that Samuel Parsons Sr. planted in the 1840s on the grounds of his nursery (the present Weeping Beech Park) became an American arboreal icon. It survived until the 1990s. Samuel Parsons Jr., *Landscape Gardening* (1891).

augmented after 1866 when Olmsted and Vaux were hired to design Prospect Park in Brooklyn and many other parks and grounds.

As a lad, Samuel Parsons Jr. took an avid interest in his family's horticultural world, eventually apprenticing himself to the nursery's chief propagator. Growing up in such an environment, Parsons acquired an understanding of ornamental flora that few in his day could match. He likely also absorbed much of his father's knowledge of and passion for the art of landscape gardening. The senior Parsons had read with enthusiasm those theorists of the Beautiful in nature, and undoubtedly, from time to time, talk between father and son turned to Repton, Knight, Downing, and other writers who had expounded on the aesthetics of landscape design. On his journeys in Europe and America to learn the lessons that famous gardens and estates could teach a sympathetic eye, Parsons cultivated a poetic appreciation of plants as living materials with which the gardener creates works of art. "In grouping and shaping forms, in contrasting and harmonizing of colors, and in all which the painter or sculptor means by art, horticulture . . . will ever remain dependent upon the genius of its votaries, aided only, as the painter is aided, by study of the past," he professed.[4] Indeed, the leafy grounds of the Parsons mansion themselves set a fine example of the art (despite the ostentation in the display, here and there, of specimen plantings). In Flushing, Samuel Jr. acquired that enduring love for nature and its beauties which was the motive force behind his work as a landscape architect and advocate for scenic preservation.

The carefully arranged grounds of the Parsons home in Flushing, Long Island, would have provided Samuel Parsons Jr. with his first lessons in horticulture. S. B. Parsons, "Possibilities of Horticulture," *Harper's New Monthly Magazine*, March 1881.

Discouraged by the intensifying materialism of the rich in the Gilded Age, Parsons Sr. believed that the future success of the gardening business lay with the rising middle class, who, properly guided, could be taught to appreciate the pleasures derived from tastefully appointed home grounds. "Among wealthy men there is a decadence of horticultural taste, and trees or plants fade into insignificance beside yachts or horses," he lamented in 1881; "yet among the masses of men of moderate means there is an increasing desire for the possession of plants."[5] Samuel Jr. absorbed his father's wisdom, later addressing himself to this increasingly enthusiastic audience. His first published article exhorted inexperienced suburban homeowners to take an active role in planting the lawn (by which he meant the grounds) around their dwellings. "To this end," he advised, "visit parks and nurseries and learn to love plants and recognize their individual characteristics, their likes and dislikes as well as their beauties. This will make you master of the situation."[6]

Another lesson learned at home was to be fearless in defense of what one believed was right and just, to mold one's life to one's principles. The Parsonses were descended from Quaker immigrants who had settled in Dutch Long Island in the seventeenth century.[7] Prohibited from openly practicing his religion by Peter Stuyvesant and the colonial authorities, Samuel Jr.'s ancestor John Bowne had courageously spoken out for religious tolerance. Parsons Sr. was apparently equally independent of mind. He actively promoted public education and a free library in his Flushing community when it lacked both institutions. In the years before the Civil War, when his son was a child, he had espoused the abolitionist cause and proudly boasted that he had helped more slaves reach a life of freedom in Canada than anyone else in all of Queens

County had done. Samuel must have admired his father's high-minded but illegal and dangerous activity. Later, steadfastness in the face of forceful opposition was a trait that he, too, displayed, especially in his recurrent battles over proposed unsympathetic changes to the original Central Park landscape. Devotion to principle was a characteristic that he likewise admired in Calvert Vaux.

Because education was such an important concern of his father's, Parsons likely received instruction at an early age in Flushing. He later attended Haverford, the respected Quaker liberal arts college near Philadelphia, on whose board of managers his father had served from 1830 to 1842. Entering in 1857, he left Haverford at the end of his junior year in 1860 to complete his education at the Sheffield Scientific School (then the science and engineering college of Yale). Parsons received his bachelor's degree from Sheffield in 1862. Undoubtedly because of his Quaker background, Parsons shunned the dogs of war and spent the next several years as a farmer, mostly on land he bought in southern New Jersey. In 1865, he married Martha Elizabeth Francis, and the following year their only child, Mabel, was born. By the end of the 1860s, Parsons had moved back to Flushing with his wife and child to work in the family nursery, which after 1871 belonged entirely to his father.

Possessed of a scientific education, knowledge of plants, and experience with agriculture, the young Parsons was in a good position to take up landscape gardening. Not later than the mid-1870s, he came to know Frederick Law Olmsted and Calvert Vaux, most likely through the family nursery business, which they patronized. (Also, Olmsted was friends with Parsons's comrades Clarence King and James T. Gardiner.)[8] Over the next few years, a rapport evolved between Parsons and the two pioneers of the nascent profession of landscape architecture. And as Olmsted began to spend increasing time in Boston (he eventually moved his home and office to Brookline in 1881), Parsons developed especially close ties to Vaux, who made New York his home until his death in 1895.[9]

By 1879, Vaux had asked Parsons to join him in Vaux & Company, Landscape Architects. Vaux also maintained an architectural practice with the British-born engineer George K. Radford. H. Van Buren Magonigle, who later had a successful architectural career of his own, labored as an apprentice to Vaux at the time and remembered the "funny old offices" that the two firms shared at 71 Broadway. The working methods employed by both partnerships were "very simple." Before the adoption of blueprints and the typewriter, all drawings, lettering, correspondence, and specifications had to be done by hand. Because Magonigle had splendid penmanship and an eye for detail, he spent much of his time doing these tasks for Vaux and Radford. He remembered that, to his dismay, "Mr. Parsons found me out . . . and flattered me into copying his plant lists by praising me for getting the Latin names right."[10] Radford would often cross over to the landscape side of things to make topographic surveys of property for which Vaux and Parsons had been hired to prepare a grounds plan. These detailed maps of the natural features of the site, Parsons learned, were fundamental to Vaux's process of conceiving a design that would preserve the best elements that nature had given the site. "The great merit of all the works you and I have done," Olmsted told Vaux toward the end of his career, "is that in them the larger opportunities of the topography have not been wasted. . . . We have 'let it alone' more than most gardeners can."[11] Under Vaux's

Of Calvert Vaux (1824–1895), Parsons said, "I rapidly came to look upon him as my guide, philosopher, and friend."
Mabel Parsons, ed., *Memories of Samuel Parsons* (1926).

kindly tutelage, Parsons, then in his mid-thirties, rounded out his education in the art of landscape architecture.

For his part, Vaux, it appears, developed greater professional confidence in Parsons than he had in his quixotic son, Downing Vaux, who was also active in both firms. In 1887, he made Parsons a partner in the landscape architecture practice. Perhaps Vaux, whom Parsons described as "constitutionally nervous and unsteady of speech," saw in his younger partner, whom others viewed as endowed with "a Quaker simplicity and directness of manner," a person who could more effectively represent in public the ideals for which he stood.[12] "On a question of principle," remarked Parsons, "Mr. Vaux never hesitated a moment and he was equally decided in enunciating clearly the laws of landscape architecture that applied to any case under discussion." Nonetheless, Parsons observed, Vaux "could with difficulty address a Park Board and carry his points effectively." Vaux's "temperamental peculiarities" aside, Parsons loved and revered his idealistic mentor, who remained ever true to the Romantic aesthetic and code of conduct. "I rapidly came to look upon him as my guide, philosopher, and friend," he warmly acknowledged. Moreover, when he compared Vaux with Olmsted, Parsons held the opinion that "Mr. Olmsted was a leader of men, a man of magnetism and charm, a literary genius, but hardly the creative artist that Mr. Vaux was."[13] (For his part, Olmsted thought that, as a designer, Parsons was too often prone in his landscapes to the "gardenesque" display of flowers and striking specimens of trees.) Vaux and Parsons's relationship lasted till the end of Vaux's life. At the home funeral in December 1895, which took place amid flowers and foliage sent from Central Park, Parsons was the only nonfamily member present.

Some fourteen years before, Vaux had been responsible for Parsons's employment at Central Park. It had come at a time of considerable turmoil in the park's affairs. Late in 1881, after nine years' absence from an official position with the park, Vaux, through the intervention of promoters and defenders of the Greensward plan, returned to public service as superintending architect of the Department of Public Parks.[14] As a condition of his acceptance, he asked that Parsons, his protégé, be made superintending gardener. In this capacity, the younger man would provide, noted an editorial in the *Tribune*, the "practical knowledge of all the materials to be used—of trees and shrubs, and of all the influences which are to control their growth under special circumstances."[15] From this statement in the press, it seems that Vaux nominated Parsons primarily because of his expert knowledge of trees and plants. Indeed, Jacob Weidenmann, a professional colleague of Olmsted and Vaux's, claimed at the time that Parsons had not "the slightest gift for the art" of landscape gardening.[16] Nevertheless, Vaux saw this as an opportunity to install in a permanent position someone who understood and would defend his and Olmsted's vision of the park as a place of passive recreation in a pastoral landscape of meadows, lakes, and woods. Vaux believed so strongly in Parsons's potential to assume these responsibilities that he volunteered half of his $2,500 salary to his otherwise unpaid deputy. Vaux's action had far-reaching consequences for Parsons: with the appointment, he began a nearly continuous official association with New York City's parks which endured, in one form or another, until 1911.

Throughout their years together, Vaux and Parsons worked on many city projects in addition to Central Park. By 1896, Manhattan and the Bronx together had increased by fivefold the amount

Parsons was especially fond of this spot in Central Park along the carriage drive near 110th Street and Seventh Avenue. *Landscape Gardening.*

of acreage devoted to parkland. Parsons, who in 1883 was made superintendent of Central Park and in 1886 elevated to superintendent of all city parks, helped Vaux to develop the designs for these spaces. First among them was Morningside Park in upper Manhattan. Olmsted and Vaux had made preliminary plans for the steep and rugged site before their partnership ended in 1872, but it was not until 1890–1895 that Vaux fully developed a design. "Everything that was done," recalled Parsons, "was conceived with the view of increasing the beauties already existing, or giving to them an attractive aspect from some unusual angle of vision. From Mr. Vaux's viewpoint and, I think, from that of all true landscape artists, this constitutes the very genius of the art." To

Parsons thought that the later plans (1890–1895) Vaux made for Morningside Park in New York were some of his best design work. Parsons, "The Parks and the People," *The Outlook*, May 7, 1898.

see the way Vaux developed the site's "remarkable nooks and corners" and to watch him "study all the unusual effects" that could be brought out "was a lesson of the utmost value for any landscape architect." Morningside Park, in Parsons's opinion, ranked as "the most consummate piece of art" that Vaux had created.[17]

Vaux and Parsons also undertook the design of several small parks that were created in the older and poorer sections of Manhattan after the passage of the Small Parks Act of 1887. These miniature green spaces—"vest-pocket parks" in later parlance—were often located on odd-shaped pieces of land that presented special challenges to the designers. Part of a larger social reform movement that included the construction of "model tenements" (Vaux was one of the few architects of the period who strove to improve working-class living conditions), these diminutive patches

Jeanette Park (1886; the present Vietnam Veterans Park) was one of several diminutive green spaces that Vaux, with Parsons's assistance, planned in densely built lower Manhattan. Parsons, "The Evolution of a City Square," *Scribner's Magazine*, July 1892.

William A. Stiles (1837–1897), editor of *Garden and Forest,* used his pen to help Vaux and Parsons defend Central Park from unsympathetic changes.
Memories of Samuel Parsons.

of nature, among them Canal Street, Jeanette, and Mulberry Bend parks, were instances of the naturalistic design aesthetic reduced to a near-bonsai scale. For many people confined to the crowded neighborhoods of lower Manhattan, they were the only respite from unhealthy and dismal surroundings.

Parsons's career was also affected by William A. Stiles, editor of the influential journal *Garden and Forest.* About the time Parsons first assumed superintendence of Central Park, tremendous pressures began to mount to introduce active recreation facilities and popular amusements into the park (the most infamous of which was a proposed speedway that would cut along the western boundary). Stiles used *Garden and Forest* and editorials for the *New-York Tribune* to promote the cause of keeping the park the way Olmsted and Vaux had planned it—a setting for the passive enjoyment of nature. Parsons, who had met Stiles at a dinner for

Yale alumni, prided himself for "turning Stiles' attention to matters connected with Central Park some time before I became an official of the Park Department." Apparently, it was also Parsons who introduced Stiles to Vaux, who firmly believed that the press had a primary role to play in educating the public about the true nature and purpose of the park landscape. Thus informed, the public could be trusted, Vaux believed, to preserve it from harmful alterations. Vaux and Stiles became close friends, and while Parsons and Vaux worked within the system to block the ill-informed proposals of ambitious commissioners and politicians, Stiles wielded his eloquent pen in support of their efforts.

A more problematic association, from the perspective of Vaux and Parsons's colleague Frederick Law Olmsted, was Parsons's friendship with Andrew Haswell Green. As the obdurate city comptroller, Green had been Olmsted's nemesis in the early days of Central Park's construction. Mistrustful of Olmsted as a talented artist but neophyte supervisor of men and budgets, Green had tried to micromanage park expenditures. His actions often hindered Olmsted in his role as superintendent—"my hands are often tied where it is the highest importance that I should act with an artist's freedom and spirit," he complained in 1861.[18] Green's constant interference became a source of difficulty for both partners, and Olmsted eventually resigned his post largely because of Green's meddling.

Vaux, on the other hand, learned to get along with the demanding comptroller, who truly respected the beauty and philosophy embodied in the Greensward plan. For his part, Vaux understood and respected Green, and over the years they often found themselves on the same side of issues affecting the parks and the city. After the downfall of William "Boss" Tweed and the so-called

Parsons maintained that Andrew Haswell Green (1820–1903) shared equally with Olmsted and Vaux in the creation of Central Park. *Memories of Samuel Parsons.*

Tweed Ring, which Green and his law partner Samuel Tilden had helped engineer, Green again assumed a role in the management of Central Park's affairs. It was likely at this time that Vaux introduced Green to Parsons, for whom the older man became another sort of mentor. "He was a Puritan from New England and with the virtues and faults of the race," Parsons remarked of him, "but he won his way and carried his points with great pertinacity and success. I doubt if Central Park, as we know it, would ever have been built, except for Mr. Green's ability to coax or force appropriations from Albany, and, above all, for his superb loyalty to the artists and scientists employed by the Park Department."[19] For Parsons, Green was just as critical to the realization of Central Park as Olmsted and Vaux. Moreover, during the last two decades of the century, Green staunchly supported Vaux and Parsons in their defense of the Greensward plan.[20]

At the time of Green's death in 1903, Parsons was serving as landscape architect of the expanded parks department. He was a pallbearer at the funeral, but paid an even more enduring tribute to the memory of Green by dedicating his magnum opus, *The Art of Landscape Architecture,* to him. He did so, Parsons said, "in recognition of the fact that he was Central Park's best friend from the time of its inception and because he was always and ever the loyal and powerful support of the author in his endeavors to protect the Park from ill-judged and injurious invasions."[21]

For three years after Vaux's death in 1895, Parsons continued to hold the position of New York's superintendent of parks. One of his duties was to serve with John Charles Olmsted, whose renowned father was unable to work after 1895, on a park board–appointed committee to review plans proposed by the directors of the New York Botanical Garden to construct buildings in the most bucolic area of the new Bronx Park. The committee (which also included Charles Sprague Sargent and the architect Thomas Hastings) soundly rejected the idea. In words that could have been penned by John Charles's father and Vaux (who had prepared plans for the park just before his death), the group affirmed that the "land in question was taken by the city for a public park, and its use and development, whatever subsequent arrangements may have been entered into concerning it, should always be limited by continuous regard for the beautiful natural features that are included within its borders. If the people are to appreciate and enjoy the unusually beautiful and broad, simple landscapes and secluded sylvan scenery of the main portion of Bronx Park, it is essential that the important buildings be kept as much as possible out of the characteristic scenery of the park."[22]

In addition to cooperating on the Bronx Park committee, Parsons and John Charles Olmsted acted in concert to form the American Society of Landscape Architects. The establishment of this organization in 1899 authenticated the professional status of the discipline, something Olmsted Sr. and Vaux had been at pains to promote. It was only fitting the John Charles, his father's successor, should become the society's first president, and Parsons, Vaux's disciple, should serve as its first vice president. (Downing Vaux assumed the role of secretary.)

In January 1898, the New York City parks commissioner, George B. Clausen, forced Parsons to resign his post as superintendent of parks, which Parsons had held since 1883. Parsons's place was filled, complained the *New York Times*, by "freaks of Mr. Clausen whose general qualification for public trust were not more conspicuous than his special disqualifications for this particular trust."[23] Parsons would not return to public service until March 1902, when a new park board appointed him the city's landscape architect. (Under the recently adopted Charter of Greater New York, the position had authority over all parks in the Five Boroughs.) "Mr. Parsons is not only a fit man for the place," proclaimed the *Times*, "he is distinctly the fittest man for it."[24] In 1898, Parsons had written an article for the *Outlook* summarizing for the readers of this popular New York weekly the charge of the new office. The landscape architect had the power, he said, to "veto the construction of anything in the parks, down to the smallest detail." Without his approval, "no planting, gardening, erecting of fences, buildings, roads, or walks can be done." It was true, however, that the park board could remove the landscape architect from office at any moment. Nevertheless, Parsons hopefully asserted, "while he retains the confidence of the public, abstains from politics and self-seeking schemes, few Boards will attempt to displace him."[25] Parsons would continue as the city's landscape architect, with only brief hiatuses, until 1911. In June of that year, a rancorous dispute with the commissioner of parks over soil management compelled him to resign. "The weak feature of the Landscape Architect's position," Parsons later reflected, "is that he is under the Park Commissioners, and they can, if they choose, discharge him and select some more subservient person for the place."[26]

In addition to overseeing existing parks, as the city's landscape architect Parsons had the opportunity to design several new ones. To create Coney Island Park (opened in 1902), Parsons called for great quantities of topsoil to be brought in to convert the barren site into a shady seaside retreat. The largest of these projects, however, was Van Cortlandt Park in the Bronx. Originally acquired by the city in 1888, the site contained the mid-eighteenth-century stone manor house of the Van Cortlandt family, who had farmed the land since the seventeenth century. The centerpiece of Parsons's work here was the Colonial Garden, a trim formal garden meant to recall the area's early Dutch heritage. Bordered on three sides by a twelve-foot-wide canal, the large, square parcel was set below grade and featured many fragrant roses, attractive varieties of evergreens, blossoming fruit trees, and colorful flower beds. These latter features, described one enthusiastic reporter at the time of the public opening in May 1903, were beautified "by a profusion of flowers most prized in the old-fashioned gardens of Colonial days, but likely to prove new to the eyes of the younger generation, familiar with the more pretentious blossoms of the modern garden."[27] Together with the venerable Georgian manse, the old-fashioned-style garden was an expression of the appreciation of early American history that was beginning to take hold in

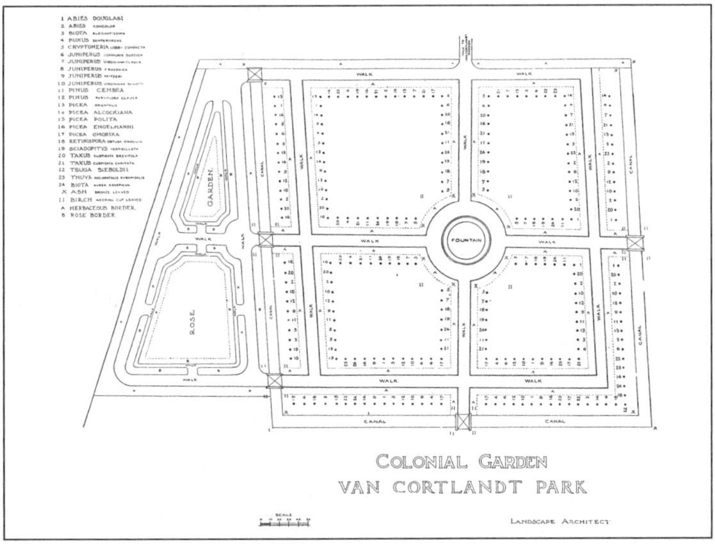

In his design for the Colonial Garden (1903) at Van Cortlandt Park in the Bronx, Parsons expressed growing appreciation of historic landscapes. Parsons, *Landscape Gardening Studies* (1910).

Parsons's Colonial Garden evoked the Renaissance tradition of Dutch garden design. *Landscape Gardening Studies*.

advanced circles of American society (and had motivated Parsons to join Green in 1895 in founding the Society for the Preservation of Scenic and Historic Places and Objects).

The Colonial Garden, which no longer exists, also reflected the resurgent popularity of the formal style of landscape design. Based on French and Italian Baroque precedents, the geometrically arranged landscape was generally seen as antithetical to the values of the "naturalistic" style that derived from England and was epitomized by Central and Prospect parks. Although Parsons himself remained loyal to the philosophy that had inspired Vaux and Olmsted—"to the standard of unchanged Nature her-

Parsons considered this passage in the Vale of Cashmere (1890s) in Prospect Park to be one of the most successful marriages of the formal and naturalistic styles of landscape architecture. Parsons, "Italian Villas," *The American Architect*, July 28, 1915.

self, and to those works of man which most reverently conform to the pattern of her teachings"[28]—he acknowledged that beauty existed in both styles. As an example of how the two traditions might even be happily combined, he pointed to a "charming little fountain and a bit of skillfully adjusted balustrade" that Stanford White had added in 1895 to the Vale of Cashmere, a lovely secluded area of Prospect Park. Vaux himself had performed a similar marriage of the formal and informal when he designed the Terrace in Central Park.

Another new design project that Parsons undertook as municipal landscape architect was St. Nicholas Park, located on St. Nicholas Avenue and 127th Street in the up-and-coming residential neighborhood of Harlem. Much smaller than Van Cortlandt Park, its narrow boundaries and steep rugged northern Manhattan topography presented special challenges. Returning to the naturalistic tradition and undoubtedly drawing on his earlier

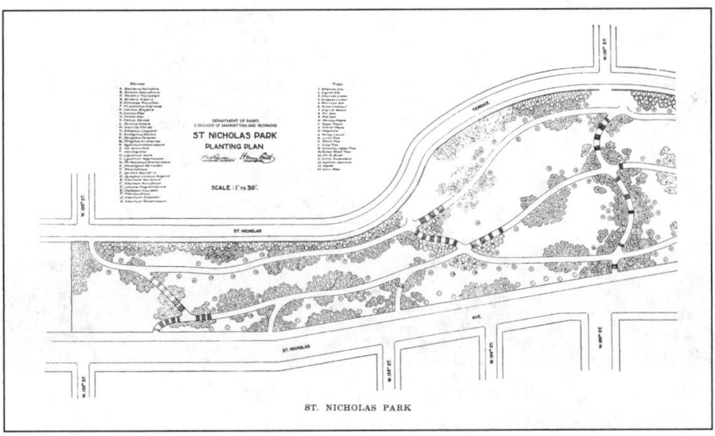

In his design for St. Nicholas Park (1906) in upper Manhattan, Parsons struggled with rugged terrain and narrow dimensions. *Landscape Gardening Studies.*

Parsons's plan for St. Nicholas Park embraced dramatic rock formations that characterize northern Manhattan's topography. Photograph by Carol Betsch, 2008.

Parsons created paths and stairs that allowed visitors to comfortably negotiate St. Nicholas Park's steep site. Photograph by Carol Betsch, 2008.

experience with Vaux at Morningside Park, Parsons created a plan in 1906 that both preserved and enhanced the picturesque landscape.[29] Parsons later wrote about this method, espoused by Olmsted and Vaux, that "all landscape gardeners of the right type . . . seek to exercise an art that has the power of 'selection, accentuation, grouping and the removal of defects or superfluities, to intensify and surpass the beauty of Nature, thus reaching the Ideal.'"[30]

A very different type of design program was demanded for the several smaller parks that Parsons created in the tenement neighborhoods of Manhattan. These spaces were more playgrounds than parks, he acknowledged, as constant vandalism made it difficult for any shrubs or trees to grow within their borders. The problem, he grumbled, was in varying degrees endemic to all the parks, even those frequented by "the best people of the city." Americans, he protested, held the view "that anything public belongs to them individually, and that they have a right to do with it as they choose; if they do damage in using it, that is all right, the city has got to stand it."[31]

De Witt Clinton Park on Eleventh Avenue at 52nd Street in the infamous Hell's Kitchen neighborhood was representative of the new diminutive parks.[32] Created on seven acres of land that the city had cleared of tenement buildings, it cost over one million dollars to construct. Within its symmetrically laid-out spaces were a running track, playgrounds for boys and girls, and a shelter house where a concessionaire sold refreshments and a band played light music. Yet, the pleasure of scenery was also to be had. "The Park, by reason of its sloping ground toward the North River, is one of the most beautiful in the city," proclaimed an early visitor. "From almost every nook of it," he observed, "the chil-

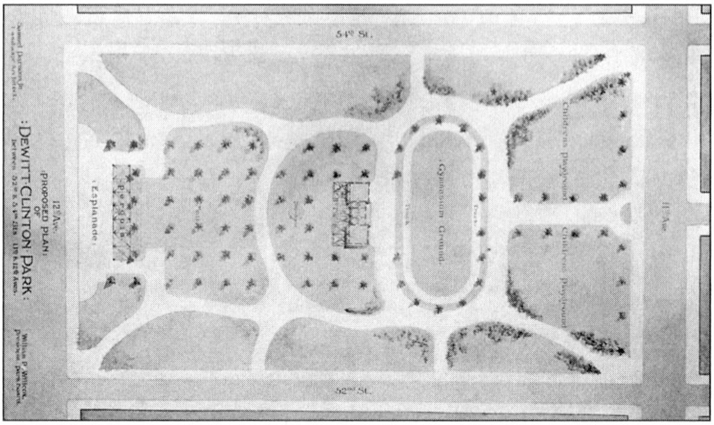

De Witt Clinton Park (1905) was one of several small recreational spaces that Parsons designed in Manhattan's tenement districts. *Landscape Gardening Studies.*

dren, while at play, can watch the shipping on the river and catch the breezes in Summer."[33] The park's most novel feature was a farm-garden, where children were taught how to raise vegetables, such as beets, cabbage, and turnips, on their own individual plots. Parsons took special pride in this innovation. He objected, though, to the presence of public baths in the basement of the shelter house. Baths were an attribute of smaller parks in poor neighborhoods, but in Parsons's view they caused unnecessary crowding in the limited grounds and should be located elsewhere in the city. Echoing an argument that he must have heard Vaux and Olmsted make many times, he declared: "A park should be essentially a park, and it should not be filled up with libraries, museums, schools, and all that sort of thing; the general public does not appreciate that, and it is a fight to prevent it."[34] Among the other small parks that Parsons designed were William Seward Park (1903), which provided recreation for residents of Little

Italy, and Thomas Jefferson Park (1905), an amenity given to the neighborhood of Italian Harlem.

As the city's landscape architect, Parsons was also charged in the early years of the century with beautifying urban spaces that were modernized as a result of the construction of the new subway system. These included parts of Union Square and City Hall Park where engineers located new stations. Parsons's most ambitious subway-related project, however, was the creation in 1908 of a strip of plantings to run along the center of Broadway from 59th to 122nd streets over the new underground line excavated beneath. To Parsons's disappointment, the soil in the planting beds proved too shallow to sustain trees of any size.[35] As a result, this ambitious sylvan ribbon (which was modified in the 1930s and 1980s) through the West Side failed, at first, to live up to its rather grand name, the Broadway Mall.

Through all of his years of public service, however, Parsons's foremost concern remained his beloved Central Park. Looking back on his three decades' association with it, Parsons had difficulty recalling "all the phases and varied ideas of the attacks on the Park," there had been so many. In addition to the speedway, he had successfully fended off a proposal to locate Grant's tomb on the Mall, to replace Vaux and Jacob Wrey Mould's stunning cast-iron Bow Bridge with a concrete replica, and to install sculpture throughout the landscape ("pseudo-ornaments," as he called them, that would spell the "desecration of the hills and valleys of Central Park, the best known country-seeming park in the world").[36] After his resignation in 1911, Parsons continued to openly express his concern for the welfare of the park. Ever "a gallant soldier who for a lifetime fought to a finish those who would destroy the Park, Mr. Parsons lowered his colors only

Parsons defeated an attempt to replace with a concrete replica Vaux and Jacob Wrey Mould's cast-iron Bow Bridge (1858) in Central Park. Photograph by Sara Cedar Miller, Central Park Conservancy.

when the hand that held them was lifeless," declared a close friend at his death.[37]

Of particular concern to Parsons after he had left public service was the condition of the Mall, that formal allée of American elms with their graceful wine-glass profiles which Olmsted and Vaux envisioned as a spacious gathering place. By the second decade of the twentieth century, the once grand tree-shaded promenade that had attracted thousands in its designers' lifetimes was in dismal shape. In 1919 the *New York Times* lamented, "It is a melancholy sight to ancient walkers along the Mall in Central Park to see the few poor, dilapidated, moribund survivors of its noble elms."[38] Parsons laid the blame for this sad state of affairs on inadequate park maintenance and deteriorated soil conditions. If something was not done soon, he warned, "Central Park is doomed."[39] In May 1922, as a private citizen working with an association created to establish a park memorial to Andrew H. Green, Parsons demonstrated how the Mall could regain its former glory. The tribute to Green took the form of a semicircle of mature American elms. Working under Parson's supervision, workmen transplanted from Westchester County several ten-ton, fifty- to sixty-year-old trees having diameters of fifteen to eighteen inches to the site of the former McGowan Pass tavern, near the East Drive at the level of 106th Street. The following month, Parsons called for a comparable public-private undertaking to place trees of similar dimensions on the Mall.[40] As chair of the Society for the Elms on the Mall, he sought to raise from citizens and organizations $1,000 for each of forty 50-foot trees. In this endeavor he was aided by a board of trustees that included artist William B. Van Ingen, journalist John Corbin of the *New York Times*, and Francis Gallatin, who as commissioner of parks pledged the city's full cooperation in the endeavor. The plan met with immediate success. Many donors stepped forward, including the newspaper publisher Adolph S. Ochs, banker Samuel P. Goldman, architects Delano & Aldrich, and the membership of the Knights of Pythias. Presumably, by the time of Parsons's death in February 1923, all the trees were in the ground or in hand and the Mall was on its way to becoming once again one of the most beautiful promenades in the world. It took time, however, for the adolescent transplants pictured in a photograph of 1927 to develop into the sylvan cathedral of today.[41] That magnificent stand of overarching trees along the Mall—one of the few groves of American elms to survive the Dutch elm disease—is Samuel Parsons's most conspicuous and enduring contribution to Central Park. Truly, the present-day Mall is a memorial to his decades-long struggle to preserve the great work of landscape art that Vaux and Olmsted had created.

Parsons's reputation as a landscape architect, enhanced by articles he published in *Scribner's Magazine*, *The Century*, and other periodicals, brought him public, institutional, and private commissions beyond the borders of New York. Among the cities that obtained his services were Birmingham, Alabama, where about 1898 he laid out the gracious residential square known as Glen Iris Park (now listed on the National Register of Historic Places), Philadelphia, and Washington, D.C., where in 1900 Parsons designed a naturalistic park extending from the Capitol to the Washington Monument. (He reproduced his unrealized plan for this area, which is known today as The Mall, in *The Art of Landscape Architecture*).

For the city of San Diego, Parsons designed one of his largest parks. At the urging of his friend Mary B. Coulston, a former editor of *Garden and Forest* who had recently moved to California from New York, the city hired Parsons in 1902 to make a plan for City Park (the present Balboa Park). Parsons's design for the 1,400-acre site, unfortunately, was only partially realized. It called for an array of landscape features within the wonderfully varied terrain that lay between ocean and mountains and was home to many species of wildflowers. "The keynote of the treatment . . . ," Parsons explained, "is to preserve the natural beauty that exists, by simple treatment, and to avoid marring grand and impressive scenery by introducing sensational and startling effects."[42] In its present form, Balboa Park, which is home to many cultural institutions, bears scant resemblance to Parsons's intentions. The city's decision in 1910 to locate the upcoming Panama-California

Exposition (1915) on the site ended Parsons's involvement there (John Charles Olmsted replaced him) and sealed the fate of his plan, which sought above all to conserve the landscape's inherent natural beauty.

Parsons took the same approach when designing the grounds of the New York State Normal School at Oswego, a commission that began about 1914. The new buildings of the school (now the State University of New York at Oswego) stood on meadowland that overlooked Lake Ontario some one hundred feet below. "It was necessary to study the lay of the land, to humor the natural topography," Parsons wrote about the project, "to make the surface roll and undulate sometimes in the gentlest manner and sometimes quite abruptly. It all depended on the trend or 'the genius of the place.'"[43] Clearly, he continued to apply the lessons he

The grounds of the New York State Normal School at Oswego (now SUNY Oswego) were among many commissions Parsons received from educational institutions. Parsons, "Landscape Surroundings for Academic Buildings," *The American Architect*, October 20, 1915.

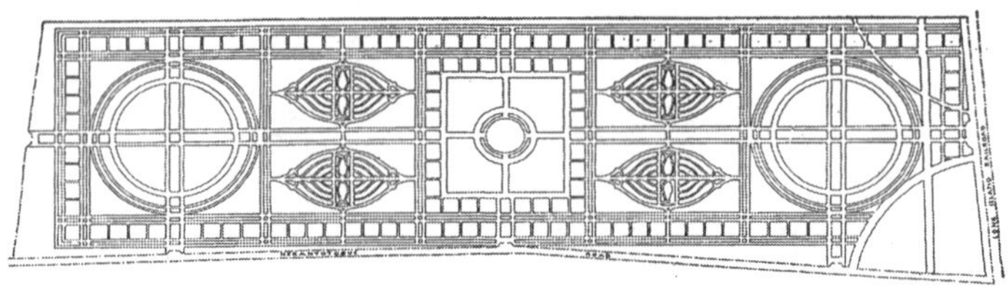

Parsons's layout of the roads in the Cemetery of the Resurrection (1916) in Suffolk County, Long Island, alluded to traditional Christian symbols. *New York Times*, July 30, 1916.

had learned from Vaux. Parsons had also visited Oxford to study how collegiate architecture might promote the scholarly environment, and his advice on campus design was sought by Pomona College, Princeton University, and the University of Pennsylvania, among other institutions.

Some individuals who had enjoyed the pleasures of the life of the mind in surroundings Parsons had created may also have come to rest in cemeteries of his design. In Suffolk County, Long Island, in an area that served as a veritable *camposanto* for the metropolis, Parsons laid out the 2,000-acre Pine Lawn Cemetery at Syosset in 1902, and in 1916 planned the 250-acre Cemetery of the Resurrection at Farmingdale. To maximize burial space and control costs, Parsons mapped the flat sites with systems of tree-lined roadways arranged in geometric patterns, rather than follow the older, more informal, and emotive rural cemetery style epitomized by Brooklyn's Greenwood Cemetery. Within his designs, Parsons provided another sort of imagery than picturesque natural scenery to console the living. At the Cemetery of the Resurrection, he incorporated traditional Christian symbols in the layout. "It will not be a park, but merely a garden in symbolized form," related a journalist who interviewed Parsons at the time he had undertaken the enterprise. The cemetery roadways would form "a cross with a circle, or glory, at each end," he reported. Furthermore, the plan provided that the "seven-branch candlesticks of the Revelation and the Holy Fish are represented in the emblematic scheme." Ample greenery would also bear witness to this figurative promise of heaven, continued the report, for "the main emblem will be marked out by large trees, which will also be planted along the border of the design."[44]

Together with his projects for parks, campuses, and cemeteries, Parsons cultivated a considerable practice advising individuals of wealth on laying out the grounds of their country seats. Many of these he discussed in his articles and books, including *The Art of Landscape Architecture*. James Ben Ali Haggin, a thoroughbred breeder, hired Parsons in 1897 to lay out Elmendorf Farm, the extensive bluegrass domain he had acquired near Lexington, Kentucky. In 1891, Francis Lynde Stetson, a well-connected New York corporate lawyer, called on Parsons for plans for his thousand-acre estate, Skylands, in the Ramapo Mountains of northern New Jersey. In the outreaches of Long Island, which in the late nineteenth and early twentieth centuries had become colonized by the privileged, Parsons counted among his clients Nicholas F. Brady, a public utility tycoon who sat on the boards of fifty corporations and devoted much of his wealth to the Catholic church. About 1916, Brady hired Parsons to lay out his estate Inisfada (Gaelic for "long island") at Manhasset. All these properties retain significant elements of the work Parsons did for their original owners.[45]

For a private work on a larger scale, Parsons drew plans in 1897 for Albemarle Park, a resort "residential park" at Asheville, North Carolina, which centered around an inn and comprised both

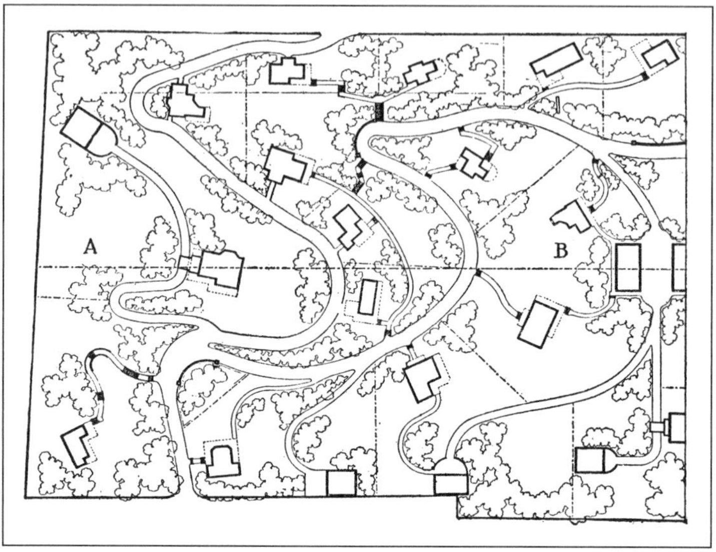

Parsons's residential community of Albemarle Park (1897) in Asheville, North Carolina, is listed on the National Register for its significance in the history of landscape architecture. Parsons, *How to Plan Home Grounds* (1899).

individually owned houses and rental cottages. Parsons planned curving roadways to conform to the natural lay of the land—rolling piedmont with views of the Blue Ridge Mountains—and installed plantings that afforded each house seclusion while allowing for pleasing prospects to the restful surroundings.[46]

Private practice was apparently a lucrative business for Parsons throughout much of his long career. After he left public service in 1911, he advertised that he was "now prepared to give my undivided attention to private estates and professional advice generally." For a fee of $100 per year, he would counsel individual homeowners "in relation to all the changes they may wish to make in their tree and shrub groups, lawns, rocky spaces intended for Alpine plants, and [to furnish] specific advice as to care and management."[47]

Whether the place was large or small, Parsons offered advice that conformed to a traditional naturalistic design approach. Thus, he admonished homeowners to mask the presence of outbuildings and minor drives and to relieve the baldness of open lawn with trees and groups of shrubs; to avoid the appearance of congestion near the house by leaving the area free of larger plantings; to capitalize on water features whenever possible; to wind the entrance drive through the property rather than have it approach the house directly; and to forgo formal flower beds on lawns—"they are apt to lend a garish and vulgar air to the place," he warned.[48] His design for the seven-acre grounds of a residence in Madison, New Jersey, fully embodied these principles. In an article for *Scribner's* titled "Small Country Places," he described how "standing on the road a little this side of the bridge, and looking

In his plan for the seven-acre grounds of this house at Madison, New Jersey, Parsons suggested solutions to problems "likely to confront" owners of similar properties. Parsons, "Small Country Places," *Scribner's Magazine*, March 1892.

on the still surface of the lake, one could see the whole green hillside with the house and trees charmingly mirrored."[49]

There was, then again, no example more evocative of Parsons's desire for harmony with the natural setting than the woodland cottage of John A. Staples at Balmville, near Newburgh, New York. Parsons chose a photograph of the sequestered property for the frontispiece of *The Art of Landscape Architecture*. The image depicts the snug little house opening amicably to its surroundings by way of a broad, old-fashioned porch from which one might see and hear a forest stream tumbling over cobbles and boulders. The tranquil retreat foreshadows Frank Lloyd Wright's Fallingwater,

Wright's Fallingwater (1936) is soul mate to the Staples estate, which Parsons features as the frontispiece to *The Art of Landscape Architecture*. *Historic American Buildings Survey.*

located in the woods near Bear Run, Pennsylvania, above a similar rock-strewn brook and cascade. Wright designed his masterpiece twenty years after Parsons's book appeared. Whether consciously or not, Fallingwater evokes the Romantic landscape tradition of which Parsons was proponent and publicist.

Samuel Parsons Jr. was not a protagonist in developing the art and profession of landscape architecture, but he probably did more through his publications than anyone since Andrew Jackson Downing to keep the subject before the public. His desire to use the pen in the service of his art was undoubtedly inspired by Parsons Sr.; at the time young Parsons was beginning his professional career, his father, citing the legacy of Downing, had exclaimed, "We need such writers still."[50]

Beginning in 1879 with essays on trees and suburban home grounds,[51] Parsons wrote many articles for the educated nonprofessional on plants, gardening, parks, and other aspects of landscape design. To this audience, he served as teacher and guide for a field of endeavor that was still new to most Americans. In 1891, Parsons published *Landscape Gardening*, the first of his several books. This generously illustrated volume contained advice drawn from his experience in New York's public parks, especially Central Park and Prospect Park. The book was fundamentally a primer on how to achieve the perfect lawn ensemble, how to successfully transform a rough, upgraded bank into a pleasing slope, and how to choose plants for beds and year-round interest in the garden.

The Art of Landscape Architecture, the last book that Parsons wrote, was quite different from his first. "This change is significant," commented a contemporary reviewer, "the landscape architect has pushed the landscape gardener . . . flatly to the wall."[52] *The Art of Landscape Architecture* can be read as an overview of

Together with the works of Calvert Vaux, Parsons considered Prince Pückler-Muskau's early nineteenth-century estate, Muskau, in Silesia, to be one of the finest examples of the naturalistic style of landscape architecture. Pückler-Muskau, *Hints on Landscape Gardening*, ed. Samuel Parsons Jr. (1917).

two centuries of literature that influenced the philosophy of the Romantic landscape tradition and inspired the early advocates of the American park movement. Although Parsons maintained the organizational structure—by constituent parts of designed landscapes—of his earlier book, he now gave precedence to theory over practice. In the pages of *The Art of Landscape Architecture*, one encounters extended quotes from many authors who had inspired Vaux, Olmsted, and Parsons, father and son. The author summoned for the reader earlier luminaries such as Rousseau, Walpole, Repton, and Pückler-Muskau, whom he particularly admired.[53] (Parsons even made a pilgrimage to the prince's remarkable park in Silesia and later wrote an adulatory introduction to the 1917 English translation of his 1834 book, *Hints on Landscape Gardening*.) *The Art of Landscape Architecture* was truly an all-inclusive synopsis of the ideas that had shaped Parsons's beliefs. Instruction, however, was its author's primary intent. "At present in landscape gardening as usually practiced," Parsons observed, "good ideas based on sound precedents are words almost without meaning to most people."[54] He hoped his book would fill the void.

Generally speaking, the waning of Samuel Parsons's renown as a writer followed the fading of his reputation as a landscape architect. The landscape historian Elizabeth Barlow Rogers has characterized Parsons as the man at Central Park who "presided over the end of what might be called the park's Greensward era."[55] With the rise of Robert Moses, who was appointed New York City parks commissioner in 1934, the governing philosophy of park management and use changed radically.

Heir to the Progressive Era belief in the superior value of active over passive forms of recreation, Moses undertook to modernize New York's parks in ways very different from what Olmsted, Vaux, and Parsons had envisioned. Moses's philosophy held sway over park administration until well after he left his post in 1960—the year death ended Mabel Parsons's long personal struggle to keep her father's park legacy intact.

After World War I and during the Moses era, Samuel Parsons and his writings were largely forgotten, especially by general readers. The one book that remained "above ground," however, was *The Art of Landscape Architecture*. When Henry Vincent Hubbard and Theodora Kimball published *An Introduction to the Study of Landscape Design* in 1917, the first textbook used by students of landscape architecture in colleges and universities, the authors included Parsons's volume in their reading lists. It appeared under several headings, including "General," where they described it as "a compilation from older writers, arranged by subjects, from the point of view of naturalistic design." Hubbard and Kimball recommended it to students together with works by Downing, Édouard André, Loudon, and other influential early theorists. Hubbard and Kimball's book, which they revised in 1929, continued to be used as a standard resource by American students of landscape architecture until the 1940s. After that time, even most professionals forgot *The Art of Landscape Architecture* and its author.

Nothing by Parsons was included by Mary Vance in her 1980 compendium *Landscapes: Landscape Architecture and Landscape Gardening, a Selective List of Books*. Nor did Parsons rate mention in William Tishler's *American Landscape Architects*, which appeared in 1989. This slim volume, published by the National Trust for Historic Preservation, nonetheless did mark the awakening of interest on the part of the preservation community in historic landscapes and in the earliest American practitioners of landscape design.

A year later, in this new intellectual environment, *The Art of Landscape Architecture* found a place in the National Park Service's *Preserving Historic Landscapes, an Annotated Bibliography* compiled by Lauren Meier.[56] Now, with this reprinting of *The Art of Landscape Architecture*, modern readers can enjoy Parsons's most important and influential text, one of the last pieces of literature from "the Greensward era."

The Mall, Central Park. Photograph by Sara Cedar Miller, Central Park Conservancy.

NOTES

The author would like to thank Sara Cedar Miller of the Central Park Conservancy and Joseph Disponzio of the New York City Department of Parks and Recreation for their assistance in the preparation of this essay.

1. W. B. Van Ingen, "A Lover of Nature," *New York Times*, February 8, 1923, 18.
2. See David Schuyler, *Apostle of Taste: Andrew Jackson Downing, 1815–1852* (Baltimore, 1996), 83.
3. Samuel Parsons Jr., "Rare Lawn-trees," *Scribner's Magazine* 28 (July 1879), 62. Today, Weeping Beech Park in Flushing preserves the site of the tree, which survived for one hundred and fifty years. Nearby, the present Kissena Park incorporates the grounds of another Parsons Sr. tree grove and perpetuates the Indian name he gave to the spot.
4. Samuel B. Parsons, "Possibilities of Horticulture," *Harper's New Monthly Magazine* 62 (March 1881), 515.
5. Ibid. His son shared his disappointment over the decline of taste among the moneyed class. In a letter Samuel Jr. addressed to the editor of the *Tribune*, he wrote: "During several recent visits to Newport I have been struck by the commonplace and even, I was going to say, vulgar taste displayed in the yearly plantings of most of the fine lawns on the [Bellevue] avenue." Samuel Parsons Jr., "The Cliff Walk at Newport," *New-York Daily Tribune,* April 16, 1881, 2.
6. Samuel Parsons Jr., "Village Lawn-Planting," *Scribner's Magazine* 28 (July 1879), 49.
7. Samuel Jr. must have known John Bowne's quaint old home well. The Bowne House Historical Society at 37-01 Bowne Street in Flushing now maintains the dwelling as a public museum. Samuel Parsons Jr.'s mother, Susan Howland, who died when her son was eleven years old, was descended from John Howland of the Mayflower Company.
8. Chums of Parsons's from Sheffield, Clarence King would become the first director of the U.S. Geological Survey; James T. Gardiner became director of the New York State Survey and would aid in the campaign to save Niagara Falls from industrial development.
9. Parsons's elder by twenty years, British-born Vaux had been the sainted Downing's partner and friend, and although brought up Anglican and inclined toward Unitarianism, he also had Quaker ancestors.
10. H. Van Buren Magonigle, "A Half Century of Architecture, 1: A Biographical Review," *Pencil Points* 14 (November 1933), 477–478.
11. Olmsted to Vaux, September 3, 1887, quoted in Robin Karson, *A Genius for Place: American Landscapes of the Country Place Era* (Amherst, Mass., 2007), 11.
12. Samuel Parsons Jr., *Memories of Samuel Parsons*, ed. Mabel Parsons (New York, 1926), 123; "Samuel Parsons," *National Cyclopedia of American Biography*, vol. 26 (New York, 1937), 308.

13. Parsons, *Memories*, 123.
14. Vaux would occupy the post from 1881 to 1883 and again from 1888 to 1895.
15. "The Park Board Still Trifling," *New-York Daily Tribune*, December 25, 1881, 6.
16. Weidenmann to Olmsted, January 13, 1882, quoted in *The Papers of Frederick Law Olmsted*, vol. 7: *Parks, Politics, and Patronage, 1874–1882*, ed. Charles E. Beveridge, Carolyn F. Hoffman, and Kenneth Hawkins (Baltimore: 2007), 595.
17. Parsons, *Memories*, 61. In 2008, the New York City Landmarks Preservation Commission designated Morningside Park a Scenic Landmark.
18. Olmsted to George Bellows, February 9, 1861, in the Papers of Frederick Law Olmsted, Manuscript Division, Library of Congress, Washington, D.C.
19. Parsons, *Memories*, 126
20. Green was also a prime mover in the consolidation of the Five Boroughs into a single metropolitan government, a role for which he earned the sobriquet "Father of Greater New York."
21. Parsons, *Art of Landscape Architecture*, iii. Green's beloved country home, Green Hill, in Worcester, Massachusetts, was made a public park after his death.
22. "Buildings in Bronx Park," *New York Times*, June 5, 1897, 4.
23. "Mr. Parsons and the Parks," *New York Times*, March 15, 1902, 8.
24. Ibid.
25. Samuel Parsons Jr., "The Parks and the People," *Outlook* 59 (May 7, 1898), 31.
26. Parsons, *Memories*, 57.
27. "Bronx's Parks Beautiful," *New York Times*, May 3, 1903, 20.
28. Samuel Parsons Jr., quoted in Van Ingen, "A Lover of Nature."
29. Recent restoration efforts have brought back some of Parsons's intentions for the park.
30. Samuel Parsons Jr., "Italian Villas, Their Place and Function in Landscape Architecture," *American Architect* 108 (July 1915), 55.
31. Samuel Parsons Jr., "Small City Parks," *Transactions of the American Society of Landscape Architects*, March 6, 1906, 79.
32. Others were Seward Park on Canal Street; Thomas Jefferson Park on 111th Street and First Avenue; St. Gabriel Park at 35th Street and Second Avenue; Hamilton Fish Park on Stanton Street east of the Bowery; John Jay Park on Cherokee Place between 76th and 78th streets; and Hudson Street Park.
33. "De Witt Clinton Park Opened to the Public," *New York Times*, November 5, 1905, 10.
34. Parsons, "Small City Parks," 79.
35. "Riverside Improvement," *New York Times*, February 6, 1916, 6.
36. Three years after his death, Mabel Parsons edited and published what was, in effect, her father's autobiography, *Memories of Samuel Parsons*, much of which was devoted to Parsons's accounts of how he had shielded Central Park from assaults from many quarters. Quotations from *Memories*, 49, 55.

    To be sure, much of what has been restored in recent years by the Central

Park Conservancy was there to be brought back because of the efforts of Samuel Parsons. According to Charles Birnbaum, Parsons shepherded the park during a crucial period in its history. "His intimate knowledge of the original design intent equipped Parsons to deal with an era of change: a time when automobiles replaced carriages, electric lights replaced gas lamps, health concerns ran rampant regarding the incubation of disease in the park's water features and priorities shifted from scenic enjoyment to active recreation" (*Samuel Parsons, Jr., and the Art of Landscape Architecture*, exhib. cat. [New York: Wave Hill, 1995], 25).

37. Van Ingen, "A Lover of Nature." The Parsons connection with Central Park did not end with Samuel's death in 1923. Armed with a degree in botany from Barnard College and inspired by a fierce devotion to her father's legacy, Mabel Parsons continued for many decades the fight to protect the park from invasive and destructive changes.
38. "A Treeless Park," *New York Times*, May 31, 1919, 12.
39. "Pleads for Trees to Beautify Parks," *New York Times*, August 21, 1921, 9.
40. "Trees for Central Park," *New York Times*, June 30, 1922, 11.
41. In an article headed "Appropriation of $1,000,000 . . . " the *New York Times* (August 14, 1927, XX3) compared views of the Mall in 1891 and 1927. The tradition of private organizations adding trees to the Mall continued at least until 1937, when the American Legion planted one to commemorate the tenth anniversary of Lindbergh's historic trans-Atlantic flight.
42. *San Diego Union*, January 1, 1903, quoted in Richard W. Amero, "Samuel Parsons Finds Xanadu in San Diego," *Journal of San Diego History* 44 (Winter 1998), 9. The Richard Amero Collection at the San Diego Historical Society is an extensive archive of articles and documents related to the history of the park.
43. Samuel Parsons, "Landscape Surroundings for Academic Buildings," *American Architect* 108 (October 20, 1915), 260.
44. "Church Symbols in Design for New Cemetery," *New York Times Magazine*, January 30, 1916, 15.
45. Skylands, which Parsons features in *The Art of Landscape Architecture*, is now the New Jersey Botanical Garden, included in Ringwood State Park; since 1937 Inisfada has been owned by the St. Ignatius Jesuit Retreat House.
46. Parsons had the assistance of George F. Pentecost Jr., a cofounder of the ASLA, with whom he formed a brief partnership in 1899.
47. Samuel Parsons, Landscape Architect, "Professional Advice and Reports on All Landscape Work," handbill, 3. Collection of the author.
48. Samuel Parsons Jr., "Small Country Places," *Scribner's Magazine* 11 (March 1892), 306.
49. Ibid., 310.
50. S. B. Parsons, "Possibilities of Horticulture," 516.
51. Cited above, notes 3, 6.

52. "Secret of the Garden Beautiful," *New York Times Magazine*, March 7, 1915, 18.
53. "It is not strange," Parsons remarked of Pückler-Muskau, "with his broad and prophetic outlook, he should impress us as almost a man of the present day." Quoted in Patrick Bowe, "Pückler-Muskau's Estate and Its Influence on American Landscape Architecture," *Garden History* 23 (Winter 1995), 199. Parsons's appreciation for the German nobleman's achievements had earlier led him to declare that "two of the greatest exponents of the art of Landscape Architecture were Calvert Vaux and Prince Pückler von Muskau" ("Italian Villas," 55).
54. Parsons, *Art of Landscape Architecture*, viii–ix.
55. Elizabeth Barlow Rogers, "The Landscapes of Robert Moses," *SiteLines* 3 (Fall 2007), 3.
56. Parsons's reinstatement to his rightful place of significance in the history of American landscape architecture was propelled by the work of Charles Birnbaum, who, as coordinator of the National Park Service Historic Landscape Initiative, curated a Parsons exhibition in 1994 at Wave Hill in the Bronx. The exhibition catalog was the first in-depth modern appraisal of Parsons's career. With his inclusion in the encyclopedia *Pioneers of American Landscape Design*, edited by Birnbaum and Robin Karson (New York, 2000), 287–290, Parsons's position was secured.

THE ART OF
LANDSCAPE ARCHITECTURE

The Art of Landscape Architecture

Its Development and its Application to Modern Landscape Gardening

By

Samuel Parsons

Fellow of the American Society of Landscape Architects
Author of "Landscape Gardening," etc.

With 48 Illustrations

G. P. Putnam's Sons
New York and London
The Knickerbocker Press
1915

The Knickerbocker Press, New York

To

ANDREW H. GREEN

the Father of Greater New York, this book is respectfully dedicated in recognition of the fact that he was Central Park's best friend from the time of its inception and because he was always and ever the loyal and powerful support of the author in his endeavours to protect the Park from ill-judged and injurious invasions.

PREFACE

THERE have been several authoritative books written entitled Observations or Hints on Modern Gardening or else the Theory and Practice of Landscape Gardening. In later times, however, it has been felt that a title of wider scope was needed than "landscape gardening," which seems to limit the subject in the minds of many to the treatment of a flower garden or an exhibition of brilliant colour in a parterre of bedding plants.

An architect, taken from the Greek, means master builder. He is one who designs and frames any complex structure; one who arranges elementary material on a comprehensive plan.

Plato made "the causes of things to be matter, ideas, and an efficient architect." Although the term architect has come to mean almost exclusively master builders in wood, stone, iron, etc., the term landscape architect is equally appropriate. A landscape artist, who creates scenery from trees and flowers and earth and rock and water, arranges elementary materials on a comprehensive plan. He has his standards of workmanship like the architect, and these standards are subtle and difficult to establish and explain, because they are dependent for their value on the growth of living things. Such artistic work is also dependent for value on the general consensus of opinion delivered by well recognized authorities. The work is done instinctively; criticism and rules may be deduced from the work afterwards, but good artistic design and craftsmanship are instinctive. Kant, in discussing æsthetic judgment, said, "judgments of taste are not susceptible of proof, but they may be evoked when an opportunity for immediate perception occurs. Their general validity is exemplary, *i.e.*, it is gained by means of examples, not rules." Investigating the production of the beautiful in art, the same writer says "that the production like the estimation is carried on without the guidance of abstract rules, and yet in such wise that that which is produced is the object of general recognition and may serve as a model," and Schopenhauer even goes so far as to say that "the fine arts do not advance beyond intention and hence give fragments, and examples, but no rule or totality."

Therefore, it will be conceded that the art of landscape architecture is not subject to the application of hard and fast rules as a science would be. The study of nature assisted by the best examples is the proper field for the art of landscape architecture. Models are based on approval by persons of recognized fitness for rendering judgment. One can no more indicate the rules that govern the development of the work of the landscape architect than he can explain how a Titian was painted. The result is evident, and ideas and suggestions are evoked, helpful to the artist, not only because he recognizes excellences himself, but because he is stimulated by the approval of respectable authorities and taught (if he has it in him) to do something of similar value transfused by the peculiar genius of his own mind and spirit.

In order to work out landscape designs properly some knowledge of good practice is necessary. Hints and suggestions point the way and lighten the labour of traversing it. The hints and suggestions of this book refer to both theory and practice and give as much information as the space will allow. The student should seek to dwell on the various features of landscape interest in gardens and parks or estates, a few of which are here considered and illustrated. Especially worthy of consideration are the features of small estates. They show less evidence of the academic influences which naturally make the large places hardly available as practical examples for general use.

It is rather remarkable that one of the oldest of the arts, landscape gardening, has had comparatively small attention given to the exposition of examples, and the ideas they evoke. In fact, among all the writers on this subject, scarcely half a dozen have attacked this particular phase of it; Whately, Repton, Prince Pückler, A. J. Downing, and Edouard André have shown in their writings that they have grasped the subject in a large and competent way. The difficulty of late years seems to have been that horticulture has developed so rapidly that in the desire to display novel and beautiful plants, the real essence of landscape gardening has been allowed to escape like a lost fragrance. If there are quantities of beautiful foliage and flowers available it has been thought only necessary to have what is called "good taste" to be able to arrange them on a lawn. The idea seems seldom to have been considered that models in the form of scenes on large and small estates should be studied in the light of the best literature on the subject before attempting to do landscape work.

Further proof of the ignorance of the general public of the essence of landscape gardening is shown by the lack of interest in the writings of the greatest of landscape gardeners, Whately, Repton, and Prince Pückler. The latter has not even been translated into English; Whately has been read in no new edition for more than one hundred years, and Repton, after almost an equal length of time, has been published by Houghton & Mifflin in an edition by John Nolen, a well-known landscape architect in Boston, Massachusetts, who has written an illuminating introduction of Repton's work, including his sketches and hints and his theory and practice of landscape gardening. The writings of Olmsted & Vaux, the designers of Central Park, New York City, whose pronouncements on the subject of landscape gardening are of the highest value, have never been collected from their reports, letters, and addresses. William A. Stiles, editor of the *Garden and Forest Magazine*, 1888–1898, where he frequently discusses with comprehension, and great literary skill, the fundamental principles of landscape gardening, is almost unknown to the public.

It will be found that the contents of some of the chapters deal with landscape gardening in ways that will be liable to give a slight shock to those who have the ordinary conception of the art. For example, the treatment of grading, of planting, of roads and paths, rocks, islands, water, the poetry of parks, the proper function of gardens may seem to go somewhat far in taking what might be termed novel views of the subject, in giving "a touch more than the maximum." It is for that reason, chiefly, that many quotations are used in order to prove that the ideas presented have the support of competent authorities both ancient and modern; and the reference to models of standard excellence in many periods and countries has a similar purpose in view.

My own contribution to the present work has been largely limited to the collection of these citations and references made in the text and footnotes, and such definition and explanation of ideas presented as will tend to simplify their proper understanding. I have endeavoured to show that landscape gardening has been and is the result of an evolution and growth of an important art, based on the deepest instincts of human nature.

Above most other arts, landscape architecture is based on nature, and my own particular function in this book I conceive to be to point out how and why the art should be practised on natural lines, and something of the degree to which this course, in spite of much seeming divergence, is supported by well-recognized authorities.

It has been, moreover, my object to show that the evolution of growing things, the development of distinct types of effect, although greatly varied, can be, and should be, made to bear the stamp alike of definite though perhaps instinctive ideas throughout the various kinds of landscape gardening, whether it be a park, an estate, a village garden, or a window box. It should make a fine picture no matter how small or how large.

The growth or evolution of landscape gardening has been more than a mere series of individual experiences, for "experience is extended and enriched by, we have to remember, not merely and primarily knowledge. We begin by trying and end by knowing. Practice is the parent of theory and realization the surest verification." Moreover, "evolution, strictly taken, presupposes a fundamental unity in which all that is eventually evolved or disclosed was involved or contained from the first. The whole is more than the sum of the parts, that is the character of evolution. A unity that is not more than its constituent elements is no real unity at all. Experience furnishes instances of this at every turn. The timbre of a musical note is more than the sum of its constituent tones: a melody, more than the sum of its separate notes"; again: "if the whole be a tree, it may be true that one fails to see the trunk because of the branches, and yet it is from the trunk that all these spring."[1]

It is for this reason that the past of landscape gardening is so fruitful of valuable suggestions for the present.

[1] *Realm of Ends*, Prof. James Ward, pp. 100, 101, 104.

The past is not only valuable as a lesson with which to correct and enrich present-day practice, but because it will help to develop, or release perhaps, germs of thought, which will eventually correct and enrich all we learn in the future.

My own experience has had considerable scope in the way of working out landscape gardening problems on parks and estates with Mr. Calvert Vaux, and by myself, not only in Central Park, New York, but in different estates and parks of America. I have naturally studied many examples both at home and abroad. Nevertheless, I have cited few examples of my own work and have taken the liberty of devoting the greater part of the book to extracts from writings of unquestioned authority in support of my ideas, hoping thereby to more firmly establish the art of landscape architecture in the dignified position it already occupies in the brotherhood of artistic professions.

It has been also recognized throughout the book that the object sought is the exposition of landscape-gardening doctrine and different methods of laying out grounds. The chapter at the end of the book is only intended to give practical suggestions in regard to the use of a certain number of choice groups of plants.

My endeavour has been to make my ideas clear, and this is one reason I have used so many and lengthy quotations, expecting that by the use of the phrases of masters of the language as well as of the art of landscape architecture I might attain a better degree of success. Master of the art of eloquent and lucid language I do not claim to be, but I feel that, as a landscape architect, in advocating important landscape-gardening principles and ideas I have a message to deliver and therefore propose to convey it to the best of my ability, hoping that I may be able to impart a reasonable portion of my meaning to the reader.

My thanks are due to Mr. August F. Jaccaci, Mr. William B. Van Ingen, and Dr. Fred Hovey Allen for the trouble they have taken to assist me by means of criticisms and valuable suggestions. Mr. W. W. Cook was the first to encourage me to undertake the work of writing this book and he has made many suggestions, the value of which I realize and appreciate. The compilation of authorities by Albert Forbes Sieveking has also afforded me assistance. As far as possible without unduly overloading the text I have endeavoured to give credit to the authorities from whom I have quoted. I wish to express my appreciation of the courtesy and kindness which I have received from the officials of the New York Public Library and from those of the Library of Columbia University. I cannot close without again referring to the inspiration of the late Calvert Vaux, the influence of whose ideas on landscape architecture has been and always will be for me a potent stimulus to seek to do only good work in the practice of my profession and to arrive at sound solutions of the various problems of the art.

S. P.

NEW YORK, January, 1915.

CONTENTS

ILLUSTRATIONS

The
Art of Landscape Architecture

I

INTRODUCTION

"HAVING studied carefully the works and the method of working of the Creator, the designer of a landscape can bring into successful play the great forces of nature, and, subordinating his own personality, can secure for his work an undying vitality, which can only follow from such a direct reliance on the resources of the Infinite. In every difficult work the key-note of success lies, of course, in the idea of thorough subordination; but it must be an intelligent penetrative subordination, an industrious, ardently artistic, and sleeplessly active ministry that is constantly seeking for an opportunity to do some little thing to help forward the great result on which nature is lavishing its powers of creation."[1]

[1] *Concerning Lawn Planting*, Calvert Vaux.

"All man's activity rests upon a given natural order; his work can only succeed when it strikes out in the direction prescribed by nature; it becomes empty and artificial if it tries to sever its connexions or to act in opposition to nature."[1]

"Let man turn where he will, undertake no matter what, he will ever come back again to that path that nature has mapped out for him."

When Goethe wrote the above words he doubtless knew Prince Pückler's great work on landscape gardening based upon his treatment of his estate at Muskau, for he has left on record a most appreciative estimate of Prince Pückler's ability and genius.

As he paced the garden walks with the Prince whose life had been devoted to landscape-gardening art, the recollection of these words he had penned would have seemed doubly true to him. Something also like the quotation, "Time is not able to bring forth new truths, but only an unfolding of a timeless truth," may well have been remarked by either of these two men, when the Prince told his companion his experience in travelling in many countries. How he had found the best in England, and yet perhaps quite as good here and there, elsewhere, and how everywhere he found the nearer he kept to nature the nearer he was to the true ideal of landscape art. We can imagine his relating how he revelled in an old rose garden of Damascus full of

[1]Rudolph Eucken's *Problem of Human Life.*

grace and charm and thus described in *Eöthen* by Kinglake:

"Wild as the highest woodland of a deserted home in England is the sumptuous Garden of Damascus. Forest trees tall and stately enough, if you could see their lofty crests, yet lead a bustling life of it below, with their branches struggling against strong numbers of bushes and wilful shrubs. The shade upon the earth is black as night. High, high above your head, and on every side down to the ground, the thicket is hemmed in and choked up by the interlacing boughs that droop with the weight of roses, and load the slow air with their damask breath. The rose trees which I saw were all of the kind we call *damask*—they grow to an immense height and size. There are no other flowers. Here and there are patches of ground made clear from the cover and these are either carelessly planted with some common and useful vegetable, or left free to the wayward ways of nature, and bear rank weeds moist looking and cool to your eyes, and refreshing the sense with their earthy and bitter fragrance. There is a lane opened through the thicket, so broad in some places that you can pass along side by side—in some so narrow (the shrubs are for ever encroaching) that you ought, if you can, to go on the first, and hold back the bough of the rose tree. And through this wilderness there tumbles a loud rushing stream, which is halted at last in the lowest corner of the garden and then tossed up in a fountain by the side of a simple alcove. This is all. Never for an instant will the people of Damascus attempt to separate the idea of bliss from these wild gardens and rushing waters."

At the same time Prince Pückler would probably remark on the trim artificiality and formalism of Versailles, and of even the Bois de Boulogne, which many years afterwards Napoleon III asked him to treat professionally.

Forget it if we will, and despise it as we may, in spite of our seeking after the striking and unusual, there is in the minds of most of us an instinctive love of the natural and simple. Often as we go about our duties and pleasures, there are bits of simple natural scenery which, if we think a moment, we will find most agreeable. These sensations are not necessarily the result of special knowledge. We like these scenes because the mind is constituted to like them. Doubtless, moreover, this appreciation of such scenes has always been consciously or unconsciously felt by intelligent beings whether they are wild or cultivated, provided they are not merely imitative, that is provided they are developed on natural lines.

"An imitation of nature, however successful," says Calvert Vaux, "is not art; and the purpose to imitate nature, or to produce an effect which shall seem to be natural, and therefore interesting, is not sufficient for success in the art of lawn planting, which depends on a happy combination of many circumstances that nature, unassisted, is not likely to bring about."

It is also time that we in these modern days learn that we have not been the first to develop a genuine and sound instinct in landscape gardening. The Chinese had it highly developed in their own peculiar style 2600 B.C., and of the Japanese the same may be said, although their ideas are different and not so old, and in a way not so original, having been derived from China and then transfused with the characteristic Japanese genius. They have that quality that persistently reminds one in a remote and miniature way of the best park designs of all countries.

The Hanging Gardens of Nebuchadnezzar are another instance of this ancient love of nature. They have been identified by explorers and found to be of such great size, as shown by their foundations, that they might readily support a replica of the natural hill or mountain which the monarch is said to have had fashioned at the whim of a homesick favourite who he had brought from Iran. Also in the garden at Damascus to-day we find a type of landscape gardening full of natural grace and charm built on good artistic lines of their kind, and which, in accordance with the unchangeable habit of the East, doubtless differs little from that of the Garden of Eden.

The primitive ideas of the savage also have a certain element of natural charm and evince fundamental conceptions of a sort of landscape gardening. John La

Farge, than whom no one had a keener instinct for good art, noted this during his visit to the Fiji Islands.

All through the Egyptian, Greek, and Roman times, however, an iron-bound, rigid theory of design seems to have dominated landscape gardening. Nero and Pliny could and did locate their villas in romantic spots, but the villas themselves were designed with grounds about them artificial and stiff, though there were in some instances trees and shrubs and lawns at a little distance so arranged as to be not entirely devoid of the charm of free nature.

> "Moreover Nero turned the ruins of his country to his private advantage and built a house the ornaments of which were not miracles of gems and gold, now used in vulgar luxuries, but lawns and lakes, and after the manner of a desert, here groves and there open spaces and prospects; the masters and centurions being Severus and Celer, whose genius and boldness could attempt by Art what Nature had denied and deceive with princely force. . . .
>
> "His Golden House, in a park stretching from the Palatine to the heights of the Esquiline, was on a scale of more than oriental magnificence. At last the master of the world was properly lodged. With colonnades three miles long, with its lakes and pastures and sylvan glades, it needed only a second Nero in Otho to dream of adding to its splendour." [1]

[1] Tacitus, *Ann.*, C. 31.

"My villa is so advantageously situated that it commands a full view of all the country round, yet you approach it by so insensible a rise that you find yourself upon an eminence without perceiving you ascended."[1]

Quoting from a letter of Apollinaris translated by Sir Henry Wotton the following words are used:

"First I must note a certain contrariety between building and gardening for as Fabrics should be regular so Gardens should be irregular, or at least cast in a very wild regularity. To exemplify my conceit I have seen a garden in a manner, perhaps, incomparable. The first access was by a walk like a Terrace from whence might be taken a general view of the whole plot below; but rather in a delightful confusion than with any plain distinction of the pieces. From this the beholder descending many steps was afterwards conveyed again by several mountings and valings to various entertainments of his *sent* and sight, which I shall not need to describe for that were poetical, let me note this, that everyone of these diversities was as if he had been magically transported into a new garden."

Down through the middle ages the classical or Roman spirit of formality dominates everything that can be possibly termed landscape gardening until the arrival of its late Renaissance in the seventeenth century.

[1] Pliny the Younger.

It is a strange fact that about this time (1690) the Jesuit Father Attiret, with his companion missionaries working in China, began writing home about the wonderful gardens in that country, where the imitation of nature seemed to be the dominating factor of their design. The Jesuit Father wrote about the end of the seventeenth century. Sir William Chambers, quoting him in 1777, says that in one of the Imperial Gardens near Pekin, was an imitation of the great city of Pekin, and thus describes their landscape gardening:

> "The Chinese Gardeners very seldom finish any of their walks en cul de Sac, carefully avoiding all unpleasant disappointments. In straight roads of smaller dimension the Chinese very artfully imitate the irregular workings of nature, for although the general direction be a straight line, yet they carefully avoid all appearance of stiffness or formality by planting some of the trees out of the common line; by inclining some of them out of the upright, or by employing different species of plants and placing them at irregular distances, with their borders sometimes bare, and at other times covered with honeysuckle and sweet briar, or surrounded with underwood."

Then, just as the same idea often comes to several people independently and without the knowledge of the other, this natural style of landscape gardening, the true art as now fully recognized, suddenly flowered.

At the same time Koempfer the Dutch botanist and traveller thus wrote home about Japanese gardens:

"A Japanese Garden must be at least 30 feet square and consist of the following essential parts.

"1st: The ground is partly covered with roundish stones—the large being laid in the middle as a path to walk on without injuring the gravel, the whole in a seeming but ingenious confusion.

"2nd: Some few flower bearing plants planted confusedly though not without some certain rules. Amidst the plants stands sometimes a Saguer as they call it, a strange outlandish tree, sometimes a dwarf tree or two.

"3rd: A small rock or hill in the corner of the garden made in imitation of nature curiously adorned with birds and insects cast in brass and placed between the stones, sometimes the model of a temple stands upon it, built, as for the sake of the prospect they generally are, on a remarkable eminence on the borders of a precipice. Often a small rivulet runs down the stones with an agreeable noise, the whole in due proportion and as nearly as possible resembling nature.

"4th: A small bush or wood on the side of the hill for which the gardeners choose such trees as will grow close to one another and plant and cut them according to their largeness, nature and the colour of their flowers and leaves, so as to make the whole very accurately imitate a natural wood or forest.

"5th: A cistern or pond as mentioned above, with alive fish kept in it and surrounded with proper plants, that is such as love the watery soil, and would lose their beauty and greenness if planted on dry ground. It is a particular profession to lay out these gardens and keep them so curiously and nicely as they ought to be. Nor doth it require less skill and ingenuity to contrive and fit out the rocks and hills above mentioned."

Milton a little earlier wrote a description of the Garden of Eden in *Paradise Lost*, which distinctly breathed the modern spirit of art, and was so graphic that Walter Bagehot asserts that "you could draw a map of the description."

Of Eden, where delicious Paradise,
Now nearer, crowns with her enclosure green,
As with a rural mound, the champain head
Of a steep wilderness, whose hairy sides
With thicket overgown, grotesque and wild,
Access denied; and overhead up grew
Impenetrable height of lofty shade,
Cedar, and Pine, and Fir, and branching palm,
A sylvan scene, and, as the ranks ascend
Shade above shade, a woody theatre
Of stateliest view. Yet higher than their tops
The verdurous wall of Paradise upsprung.

. . . .

In this pleasant soil
His far more pleasant garden God ordained.

. . . .

Flowers worthy of Paradise *which not nice* Art

A Japanese Garden.

From a Photograph by Underwood & Underwood. (Reproduced by Permission.)

In beds and curious knots, but Nature boon
Poured forth profuse on hill and dale and plain.

. . . .

A happy rural seat of various view:
Groves whose rich trees wept odorous gums and balm.

. . . .

Betwixt them lawns, or level downs, and flocks
Grazing the tender herb.

. . . .

Another side, umbrageous grots and caves
Of cool recess, o'er which the mantling vine
Lays forth her purpling grape, and gently creeps
Luxuriant; meanwhile murmuring waters fall
Down the slope hills dispersed, or in a lake,
That to the fringed bank with myrtle crowned
Her crystal mirror holds, unite their streams.[1]

By the middle of the eighteenth century the flower of this Renaissance of natural landscape gardening was in full bloom. Thomas Whately, who died in 1772, writes thus:

"The English in such a situation attempt to humour nature; the French in such a situation attempt to hide her."

And Abbé Delille about the same time taught as sound ideas of the art as could be found in the most modern books on the subject:

"Rapin has sung Gardens of the regular style, and the monotony attached to the great regularity has passed from the subject to the poem. The

[1] *Paradise Lost*, Book IV.

imagination naturally a friend to liberty here walks painfully in the involved design of the parterre, anon expires at the end of a long straight alley. Everywhere it regrets the slightly disordered beauty and the piquant irregularity of Nature. Finally he has only treated the mechanical part of the art of Gardening; he has entirely forgotten the most essential part, which seeks in our sensations, in our feeling, the source of the pleasures which country scenes and the beauties of nature perfected by art occasion. In a word his gardens are those of the architect; the others are those of the philosopher, the painter, the poet."

Horace Walpole declared that Mr. Pope undoubtedly contributed to form Kent's taste, and wrote as follows:

"At that moment appeared Kent; painter enough to taste the charms of landscape, bold and opinionative enough to dare and dictate, and born with a genius to strike out a great system from the twilight of imperfect essays. He leaped the fence and saw that all nature was a garden. He felt a delicious contrast of hill and valley changing imperceptibly into each other, tasted the beauty of the gentle swell and concave scoop, and remarks how loose groves crowned an easy eminence with happy ornament, and while they called in the distant view between their graceful stems, removed and extended the perspective by delusive comparison. Thus the pencil of his imagination bestowed all the arts of the landscape on the scenes he handled. The great principles on which he worked were perspective, and light and shade. Groups of trees broke too uniform or too extensive a lawn; evergreens and woods were opposed to the glare of the champaign, and where the view was less fortunate, or so much exposed as to be beheld at once, he blotted out some of the thick shades to divide it into variety, or to make the richest scene more enchanting by reserving it to a further advance of the spectator's step. Thus selecting favourite objects, and veiling deformities by screens of plantations, sometimes allowing the crudest waste to add its foil to the richest theatre, he realized the compositions of the greatest masters in painting. Where objects were wanting to animate his horizon, his taste as an architect would bestow immediate termination. His buildings, his seats, and his temple were more the work of his pencil than his compasses."

These landscape-gardening authorities in the eighteenth century had an influence which was more potent than that of any similar authority at the present time. Naturally there were fewer places in a smaller population, but comparatively speaking, people apparently took more interest in their country places then, than they do now, chiefly perhaps because they spent a far greater portion of their time in the country, and had fewer subjects of interest elsewhere and less facilities afforded them for travelling and living in other parts of the globe. It was moreover a great literary age, and writers and poets like Pope, Walpole, Shenstone, Gray, Cowper, and Addison all wrote enthusiastically and understandingly on landscape gardening. For instance take the following examples from Shenstone's *Essay on Landscape Gardening:*

> "Ground should be considered with a view to its original character whether it be the grand, the savage, etc."
>
> "The eye should follow down upon the water."
>
> "No straight lines."
>
> "Vistas should look natural, a kind of balance in nature."
>
> "Art should never be allowed to set a foot in the province of nature, otherwise than clandestinely and by night."
>
> "Hedges appearing as such are universally bad. They discover art in nature's province."
>
> "Art indeed is often requisite to collect and epitomize the beauties of nature, but should never be suffered to put her mark on them."
>
> "In gardening it is no small matter to enforce either grandeur or beauty by surprise,—for instance, by abrupt transition from their contraries,—but to lay stress on surprise only, for example on the surprise occasioned by a *ha-ha* (or ditch), without including any nobler purpose is a symptom of bad taste and a violent fondness for mere concetto."

Another authority writes that Shenstone allowed the

charms of the villa to overpower those of the furze and rock both in his grounds and in his poems, and remarks that one may smile at the following lines:

"But oh! the transport most allied to song
In some fair villa's peaceful bound
To catch soft hints from Nature's tongue
And bid Arcadia bloom around."

Alexander Pope says:

"Consult the Genius of the place in all."

Delille writes:

"Avant tout, connissez votre site et de lieu Adorez le génie et consultez le Dieu."

Joseph Addison in *The Tatler*, No. 218, speaks thus:

"Writers who have given us an account of China tell us the inhabitants of that country laugh at the plantations of our Europeans, which are laid out by the rule and line; because they say any one may place trees in equal rows and uniform figures. They choose rather to show a genius in works of this nature, and therefore always conceal the art by which they direct themselves. They have a word, it seems, in their language by which they express the particular beauty of a plantation that thus strikes the imagination at first sight without discovering what it is that has so agreeable an effect."

Montesquieu in his *Essay on Taste* has this to say:

"It is then the pleasure which an object gives

to us which carries us on to another; it is for this reason that the soul is always seeking new things and is never at rest. Thus you will always be able to please the soul, whenever you show it many things, or more than it hoped to see.

"In this way may be explained the reason why we take pleasure in seeing a perfectly regular garden, and yet are pleased to see a wild and rural spot; the same cause produces these effects.

"As we like to see a large number of objects, we would wish to extend our view, to be in several places, traverse greater space; in short our soul escapes from bounds, and wishes, so to speak, to widen the sphere of its presence; and derives great pleasure from a distant view. But how to effect this? In town our view is confused by houses, in the country by a thousand obstacles; we can scarcely see three or four trees. Art comes to our assistance and discovers to us nature which hides itself; we love art and we love it better than nature, that is nature concealed from our eyes; but when we find beautiful situations, when our unfettered view can see in the distance meadows, streams, hills, and these dispositions are, so to speak, expressly created, it is enchanted otherwise than when it sees the gardens of Le Notre; because nature does not copy itself, whereas art always bears its own likeness. That is why in painting we prefer a landscape to the plan of the most beautiful garden in the world, it is because painting only chooses nature where it is beautiful, where the sight can extend to a distance and to its full scope, where it is varied, where it can be viewed with pleasure."

Most of the prominent men of the day were profoundly and intelligently interested in landscape gardening. Even the monarch of the literary world, at that time, Doctor Samuel Johnson, although a purely city man, hating the country, was obliged to pay attention to landscape gardening and give it a whimsical and grudging criticism and approval.

France in a less degree, in the midst of the show and display of its decadent civilization doing most of its landscape gardening after the style of Le Notre, still gave this Renaissance of landscape gardening a prominent place in its life. Rousseau, the most profound literary influence of the century, made the spirit of the natural style the dominant note in his philosophy, and actually inspired the Marquis Girardon to create through the skill of M. Morel the great estate of Ermenouville, a well-known example of the modern development of the art.

Arthur Young, writing at the time, thus describes this place:

"You reach Ermenouvelle through another part of the Prince of Condé's forest which joins the ornamented grounds of the Marquis Girardon.

"We were first shown that which is so famous for the small Isle of Poplars, in which reposes all that was mortal of that extraordinary and inimitable writer. He was afterwards moved to the Pantheon. This scene is as well imagined and well executed as could be wished. The water is between forty and fifty acres; hills rise from it on both sides, and it is sufficiently closed in at both ends by a tall wood to render it sequestered. The remains of departed genius stamp a melancholy idea, from which decoration would depart too much, and accordingly there is little. We viewed the scene in a still evening. The declining sun threw a lengthened shade on the lake and silence seemed to repose on its unruffled bosom; as some poet says, I forget who.

"The other lake is larger; it fills the bottom of the vale, around which are some rough, rocky, wild, and barren sand hills; either broken or spread with heath; in some places wooded, and in others scattered thinly with junipers. The character of the scene is that of wild undecorated nature, in which the hand of art was meant to be concealed as much as was consistent with ease of access. The last scene is that of a river, which is made to wind through a lawn, receding from the house, and broken by wood: the ground is not fortunate; it is too dead a flat, and nowhere viewed to much advantage."

About the same time we find a part of the Versailles gardens taking on the new form under the name of Petit Trianon. Of this work Arthur Young writes:

"To Trianon to view the Queen's Jardin Anglais. I had a letter from Mons. Richard which procured admittance. It contains about 100 acres disposed in the taste of what we read of in books of Chinese Gardening whence it is supposed the English style was taken. There is more of Sir William Chambers here than of Mr. Brown, more effort than nature —and more expense than taste. It is not easy to conceive anything that art can introduce in a garden that is not here; woods, rocks, lawns, lakes, rivers, islands, grottoes, walks, temples, and even villages. There are parts of the design very pretty, and well executed. The only fault is too much crowding; which has led to another, that of cutting the lawn by too many gravel walks, an error to be seen in almost every garden I have met with in France."

Abbé Delille did his share in advancing the new ideas which had already been advocated by Père Huet and Dufresny in the middle of the seventeenth century before Addison or any of the English critics wrote on the subject.

In his *Huetiana* (1722) Pierre Daniel Huet, Bishop of Avranches, writes:

"Although natural beauties are preferable to artistic ones, that is not the taste of this century. Nothing pleases that is not costly. A fountain issuing in great cascades from the foot of a rock tumbling over a golden sand, the clearest and freshest water in the world will not please the people at court as much as a jet of fœtid and muddy water drawn at enormous cost from a frog marsh. A factitious parterre composed of earth brought together according to the plan of Monsieur Le Notre, having for its whole decoration but a few rows of box which never distinguish the seasons by change of colour, surrounded by vast sanded alleys, very compact and very bare; such a parterre forms the delight of polite society. It leaves to small cits and peasants this rustic lawn, this rural turf. It requires palisades erected with the line, and at the point of the shears. The green shades of those tufted birches and of those great oaks which were found at the birth of time are in bad taste and worthy of the grossness of our fathers. Is not to think thus to prefer a painted face to the natural colour of a beautiful countenance?

"Paint on one side a fashionable garden and on the other one of those beautiful landscapes in which nature spreads her riches undisguised; one will present a very tedious object, the other will charm you by its delight. You will be tired of one at first glance, you will never weary of looking at the other, such is the force of nature to make itself beloved in spite of the pilferings and deceits of art.

"I have no more approval of the gardens in fashion than for iron screens (Clairvoies)."

Of Charles Dufresny, 1648–1724, natural son of Henry IV and a gardener's daughter, soi-disant rival of Le Notre, creator of the gardens of Mignaux near Poissy and of the Abbé Pajot near Vincennes, a writer says:

"The first indications of the Jesuits of Chinese

gardens (1690) had struck his ardent and paradoxical imagination. He loved to work upon an unequal and irregular ground (Alphana). He wanted obstacles to overcome, if there were none. He raised a mountain on a plain. His style had something of the modern English manner, but his projects were rarely carried into execution. Gabriel Thouin asserts (*Plans raisonnée*) that the first example of modern landscape gardening was given by Dufresny in the Fauborg St. Antoine. Dufresny was a man of 'ideas,' one of which Montesquieu adopted in his *Lettres de Paysannes.*"

If Louis XIV had not thought the plans Dufresny made for Versailles too expensive we might have had something very different in spirit from that of Le Notre's final development.

In Germany about the middle of the eighteenth century we find Hirschfeld who exhibits a knowledge of the natural style and quotes predecessors who have the same feelings. It is wonderful how quickly a new and striking phase of art will all at once bud and come into full flower. The germ of the idea may be almost silently developing at a much earlier date as in the case of Milton and Père Huet, but the actual flower of modern landscape gardening appears only in its full beauty and perfection of artistic development in the middle of the eighteenth century in the works of Kent, Brown, and Humphrey Repton and soon afterward of Prince Pückler von Muskau.

Andrew Jackson Downing writes in 1844, in his work on landscape gardening:

"Brown seems to have been a mannerist with so little true sympathy with nature as to be the jest of every succeeding generation—great and fashionable as the fortune he amassed and the long list of royal and noble places which he remodelled sufficiently prove him to have been in his day. 'Capability Brown,' as he was nicknamed, saw in every new place great capabilities, but unfortunately his own mind seems to have furnished but one model—a round lake, a smooth bare lawn, a clump of trees, and a boundary belt—which he expanded with few variations, to suit the compass of an estate of a thousand acres, or a cottage with a few roods."

Loudon says:

"The places he altered are beyond all reckoning. Improvement was the fashion of the time, and there was scarcely a country gentleman who did not, on some occasion or other, consult the gardening idol of the day. Mason the poet praises this artist and Horace Walpole apologizes for not praising him."

Here are some wise and sensible remarks found in the writings of Humphrey Repton, about 1797:

"If it should appear that, instead of displaying new doctrines or furnishing novel ideas, this volume serves rather by a new method to elucidate old established principles, and to confirm long received opinions, I can only plead in my excuse that true taste, in every art, consists more in adapting tried expedients to peculiar circumstances than in that inordinate thirst after novelty, the characteristic of uncultivated minds, which from the facility of inventing wild theories, without experience, are apt to suppose that taste is displayed by novelty, genius by innovation, and that every change must necessarily tend to improvement."

There may have been less perfection and variety of finish in the use of trees and shrubs and flowers, and of other details of the garden and lawn, but the actual art work, the design, is hardly finer to-day than in the days of Repton and Prince Pückler. It might be well to note here that it is a mistake to think that a superior knowledge of plants gives a paramount advantage to the landscape gardener. His main strength should primarily lie in the exercise of the actual art, in the ability to design a park or country place on principles fundamental and long recognized; this is where the highest genius of landscape gardening should find scope.

Repton died in 1818, and in England he has had no successor who has conquered such a comparatively wide area of practice and such universal acceptance as an authority. J. C. Loudon and Wm. Robinson have each contributed in their own way much to the adoption of sound views in landscape gardening. The same statement applies to Andrew J. Downing, and to F. L. Olmsted and Calvert Vaux to whom America owes Central Park in New York, the finest example of park-making in the world. The French are great gardeners, and of landscape gardening principles and lore Edouard André is a worthy and competent exponent, but although the French generally make their parks nowadays in what is called the English style, which is really only what is recognized as good landscape gardening the world over, yet in spite of all, they sometimes allow themselves to instinctively recall Le Notre and Versailles in their designs of parks and estates.

Victor Hugo writes in *Odes and Ballads:*

> "Thought is a fruitful and virgin soil, whose products must insist on growing in freedom, and, so to speak, by chance, without arrangement, without being drilled into knots in one of Le Notre's classical gardens, or the flowers of language in a treatise on rhetoric. Let it not, however, be supposed that this freedom must beget disorder; quite the reverse. Let us expand our idea. Compare for an instant a royal garden of Versailles, well levelled, well kept, well swept, well raked, well gravelled, quite full of little cascades, little basins, little groves, bronze tritons in ceremonious dalliance with oceans pumped up at great cost from the Seine, marble fauns wooing dryads allegorically imprisoned in multitudes of conical yews, cylindrical laurels, spherical orange trees, elliptical myrtles, and other trees whose natural form, too trivial no doubt, has been gracefully cor-

rected by the gardener's shears; compare this garden, so extolled, with a primitive forest of the New World with its giant trees, its tall grasses, its deep vegetation, its thousand buds of a thousand hues, its broad avenues, where light and shadow play only upon the verdure, its wild harmonies, its great rivers which drift along islands of flowers, its stupendous waterfalls, over which hover rainbows. We will not say, Where is the magnificence? Where is the grandeur? Where is the beauty? But simply, Where is the order? Where is the disorder?

"In one, fountains, imprisoned, or diverted from their course, gush from petrified Gods, only to stagnate: trees are transplanted from their native soil, torn away from their climate and forced to submit to the grotesque caprices of the shears and line: in a word natural order everywhere contradicted, inverted, upset, destroyed. In the other on the contrary, all obeys an unchangeable law, in all a God seems to dwell. Drops of water follow their course and form rivers, which will form seas: seeds choose their soil and produce a forest. The very bramble is beautiful there. Again we ask, where is the order? Choose then between the masterpiece of gardening and the work of nature; between what is conventionally beautiful, and what is beautiful without rule; between an artificial literature and an original poesy."

There is much truth in these words as well as extravagance. Victor Hugo is thinking too much of the primitive forest, which should not be altogether the model as will be shown hereafter. Many of the French and Italian designs even at the present time strike a formal, artificial note in their most natural-looking conceptions. They make their curves so true and neat; there is too much artifice, and not enough suggestion or mystery, and mystery should form a part of nearly all landscape gardening in order to secure the highest kind of pleasure. The Germans and English and some other nations do excellent landscape gardening, but it is doubtful whether the present age is quite keeping up to the old standard of the art. Love of perfection in detail of tree and shrub and flowers has led many to forget or overlook fundamental principles as practised by the great masters of the profession. Certainly there is no landscape gardening of the present day that surpasses in fundamentals, if it equals, that done by Prince Ludwig Heinrich Herman Pückler on his estate of Muskau in southern Germany nearly a hundred years ago. In support of this statement I am sure I may be allowed to quote the authority of a landscape architect, the late Chas. Eliot, than whom there has been in modern times no better writer anywhere on the principles of landscape gardening if we perhaps except A. J. Downing and the distinguished artists Frederick Law Olmsted and Calvert Vaux, creators of Central Park, New York. Mr. Eliot writes that Prince Pückler undertook:

> "Nothing less than the transformation of the almost ugly valley of the Niesse into a vale of beauty

and delight; and the fact that he proposed to accomplish this transformation not by extending architectural works throughout the valley, not by constructing mighty terraces, mile-long avenues, or great formal water basins, such as he had seen in Italy, at Versailles, and at Wilhelmshohe—but by quietly inducing nature to transform herself. He would not force upon his native landscape any foreign type of beauty; on the contrary, his aim was the transfiguration, the idealization of such beauty as was indigenous. He was intent upon evolving from out of the confused natural situation a composition in which all that was fundamentally characteristic of the scenery, the history and industry of his estate should be harmoniously and beautifully united.

"One circumstance greatly favoured the happy accomplishment of his design—namely, the very fact that he had to do with a valley and not with a plain or plateau. The irregularly rising land skirting the river-levels supplied a frame for his picture: the considerable stream, flowing through the midst of the level, with here and there a sweep toward the enclosing hills, became the all-connecting and controlling element in his landscape. Well he knew that what artists call 'breadth' and 'unity of effect' was fully assured if only he abstained from inserting impertinent structures or other objects in the midst of this hill bounded intervale."

The river scenes of Muskau were changed with great effect by diverting an arm of the main line to another course leading a long distance around by the castle, enlarging the moat (see illustration), and so flowing on through several pools to the end of the artificial water far above where it again takes the main and original direction as shown in the illustration. To-day it all looks, not only natural, but as if it had never been otherwise.

Another plea for the natural style will be found in Olmsted and Vaux's Annual Report to the Prospect Park Commissioners, January, 1871:

> "As the park has come more in use, new habits and customs and with them new tastes have been developed. There is already many times as much pleasure driving as there was five years ago, and not a few persons are more attracted to the park by what is to be seen on the road, than by any conscious enjoyment of inanimate nature to be seen from it, consequently a new class of comment on the design is now sometimes heard: unfavourable comparisons are made between the park [Prospect Park] and certain foreign pleasure grounds, both for the lack of opportunity for enjoying the sight of a large gay assemblage, and its entire want of stateliness and artistic grandeur. In these comparisons and in the demands which they suggest there are important considerations which are generally overlooked.
>
> "In southern Europe where the ground is parched,

and turf and delicate low foliage wither unless carefully and laboriously watered and tended; where also, in most cases, rambling in the country or beyond the outskirts of towns is not only toilsome but dangerous; where ladies seldom go out-of-doors until after sunset and then closely veiled, and where the people look for amusement almost exclusively to social excitements, public pleasure grounds have usually been important chiefly as places of rendevous and general congregation. Their plans have been characterized by formal and stately plantations and much architectural and floral decoration. Where anything like landscape effects have been attempted to be added to these, it has generally been not as a temptation to exercise, but simply as a picture, usually of a romantic and often of a distinctly theatrical character. The primary and avowed object of such grounds is to supply people with accommodation for coming together to see one another, not merely as personal acquaintances, but as an assemblage.

"The style of laying out grounds adapted to this purpose has, till recently at least, prevailed, not only in Italy, Spain, and Portugal, but throughout France, and where French influence has been strong the woods and lawns of both public and private parks and chases are nearly always traversed by straight avenues, with well defined circular carrefours, often emphasized by architectural objects at their points of junction, as may be seen at the Bois de Boulogne. While, however, the custom of outdoor assemblage and of the promenade for recreation has even become far more important, a tendency to a different style in the preparation of pleasure grounds has been growing wherever the climate admits of its being adapted with success. The changes made in the plan of the Bois de Boulogne under the late Empire (partly under the advisement of Prince Pückler), those also in the Bois de Vincennes, the Parc Monceau, and other grounds in France, and the plan of the new park at Brussels, all show progress in this direction, though the liking for detached scenic effects which might be suitable for framing, or for the background of a ballet, still influences most landscape work.

"It is to be observed, too, that on the completion of the Avenue de l'Impératrice as an approach to the Bois de Boulogne, and of the narrow informal drive around the lake with its various landscape effects, that the part of this system of pleasure grounds which is laid out in the natural style was immediately adopted as the daylight promenade ground of Paris in preference to the much wider, more accessible, more stately, and in every way more convenient and magnificent avenue of the Champs Elysées.

"It will be thus seen that the grander and more splendid style of public pleasure grounds, while it is peculiarly adapted to display a great body of well dressed people and of equipages to advantage, and is most fitting for processions, pomps, and ceremonies, while also it seems admirably to extend and soften architectural perspectives and to echo and supplement architectural grandeur, is not preferred where there are moderate advantages for the adoption of a natural style, even for the purposes of a promenade. The reason may be that where carriages are used in the frequent passing over of long spaces of bare surface which they make necessary, formal arrangements and confined scenes become very tiresome. In passing along a curving road, its borders planted irregularly, the play of light and shade and the succession of objects more or less distinct which are disclosed and obscured in succession is never wholly without interest, while an agreeable open landscape is always refreshing in contrast to the habitual confinement of the city."

It is evident therefore that in entering on the consideration of the principles and practice of landscape gardening it is well to keep in mind that we are, if we are doing good work, not undertaking new artistic endeavour, but following lines literally as old as the hills. Practical everyday studies of nature are what are needed. All the references made confirm this view. Authorities are often indeed illuminating and have great value; not only to inform the student, but to stimulate to further study in the right direction, and to suggest where to find new material for study. Books of any kind, however, can be no more than helps in the right direction, for practical experience and the study of nature in park and garden and diversified woodland

and meadow and water should be considered of first importance, and good examples of such work continually sought. Turner and Claude found it of the greatest value for their painting to make thousands of sketches of trees and other natural objects; how much more should the student of landscape gardening find advantage in studying the appearance and habits of trees and shrubs and their best arrangement when composed in a park picture, and this picture or design should be when worked out idealized and transfused with genuine feeling for nature after the same fashion as the work of Claude. It is above all necessary to learn how nature treats her trees and shrubs, her hillsides and meadows, and her features of island and water. If one gives oneself to the study of examples of these effects in nature it will become fascinating, and the freshness of conceptions of endless combinations which continually meet the eye will lead one to be ever seeking to solve new problems and learning to study new lessons of a similar kind in landscape gardening.

Excellent, however, and all-important as this continual reference to nature is in landscape-gardening studies, it is quite as important to learn all about the habits of plants, the quality and treatment of soil, and, above all, how to fit the new into the old. On nearly every place there are some agreeable natural features that deserve preservation and the best effect should not be injured by any new elements that may be introduced. It is easy to see that this is the case, but it is a difficult proposition to manage to introduce the new arrangement without in some way destroying the fine quality of the old, natural beauty.

The success of the problem of the proper disposition and location of gardens and decorations adjoining the house or other buildings largely depends on the successful blending of the natural forms, whether old or new, with the strictly architectural conceptions. This is probably one of the most difficult undertakings in the whole province of the art of landscape gardening. There are many details which need to be studied in order to enable a student to solve landscape gardening problems, but this perhaps is the most difficult one.

Thomas Whately says:

> "These mischiefs, however, were occasioned, not by the use but the perversion of art; it excluded instead of improving upon nature, and thereby destroyed the very end it was called in to promote. So strange an abuse probably arose from an idea of some necessary correspondence between the mansion, and the scene it immediately commanded; the forms therefore of both were determined by the same rules; and terraces, canals, and avenues were but so many variations of the plan of the building. The regularity thus established spread afterwards to more distant quarters; there indeed the absurdity was acknowledged, as soon as a more natural disposition appeared, but a prejudice in favour of art, as it is called, *just about the house* still remains. If, by the term, regularity is intended the principle is equally

applicable to the vicinity of any other building; and every temple in the garden ought to have its concomitant formal slopes and plantations, or the conformity may be reversed, and we may reasonably contend that the building ought to be irregular, in order to be consistent with the scene it belongs to. The truth is that both propositions are erroneous, architecture requires symmetry; the objects of nature freedom; and the properties of the one cannot with justice be transferred to the other. But if by the term no more is meant than merely design the dispute is at an end; choice, arrangement, composition, improvement, and preservation are so many symptoms of art, which may occasionally appear in several parts of a garden, but ought to be displayed without reserve near the house; nothing there should be neglected; it is a scene of the most cultivated nature; it ought to be enriched; it ought to be adorned; and design may be avowed in the plan, and expense in the execution. Even irregularity is not excluded; so capital a structure may extend its influence beyond its walls, but its power should be exercised only over its immediate appendages; the flat form upon which the house stands is generally continued to a certain breadth from every side; and whether it be pavement or gravel may undoubtedly coincide with the shape of the building. The road which leads up to the door may go off from it in an equal angle, so that the two sides shall exactly correspond: and certain ornaments, though detached, are rather within the province of the architecture than of gardening: works of sculpture are not like buildings, objects familiar in scenes of cultivated nature; but vases, statues, and termini are usual appendages to a considerable edifice; as such they may attend the mansion, and trespass a little upon the garden, provided they are not carried so far in it as to lose their connection with the structure. The flat form and the road are also appurtenances to the house; all these may therefore be adapted to its form, and the environs will thereby acquire a degree of regularity; but to give it to the objects of nature, only on account of their proximity to others which are calculated to receive it, is, at best, a refinement."

Price thought the principles of Claude should be followed as a guide. Lord Windham, in a letter to Humphrey Repton, asks very pertinently:

> "Does the pleasure we receive from the view of parks and gardens result from their affording subjects that would appear to advantage in a picture?" and answers, "That places are not to be laid out with a view to their appearance in a picture, but to the use and enjoyment of them in real life."

This is true in the sense that the aims of the designs of the painter and the landscape gardener cannot be said to be identical nor that the position of a tree well placed on the lawn would necessarily be suited to the design of the painted picture. It should be enough to say, however, that the purposes of the designs of both painter and landscape gardener are analogous, they travel on similar and more or less parallel lines, and both should look reverently to nature as their sole mistress.

Loudon justly observes that:

> "The recognition of art is a first principle in landscape gardening, as in all other arts, and those of its professors have erred who supposed that the object of this art is merely to produce a facsimile of nature that could not be distinguished from a wild scene."

Mr. F. L. Olmsted recognized the justice of this when he wrote in the *Spoils of the Park:*

> "What artist so noble as he, who with far-reaching conception of beauty and designing power, sketches the outlines, writes the colours, and directs the shadows of a picture so great that nature shall be employed on it for generations, before the work he has arranged for her shall realize his intentions."

There has appeared a species of "natural" landscape gardening in the nineteenth century that is, to say the least, slightly specious and meretricious in its effect, and there is today even more than a suspicion of a tendency to yield to this desire to make the art of landscape gardening fine and exquisite rather than simple and natural.

M. Edouard André, who has been called the "most judicious and successful exponent of landscape gardening in France" by a high authority, writes thus:

> "Under the false pretext that lawns, waters, trees, and flowers are always pleasant, they have substituted for the old geometrical garden a still more artificial style. The former at least avowed its aim to show the hand of man and to master nature. The latter borrows the elements of nature, and under the pretence of imitating it, makes it play a ridiculous —I was going to say an effeminate—part. It is not —we say it emphatically—it is not this that constitutes landscape art. If art seeks means of action in nature, it is in order to turn them to account in a simple and noble way."

Mr. Olmsted in his *Spoils of the Park* further says:

> "In Paris this kind of 'natural' gardening received a great impetus in the days of Napoleon III because of the striking and spectacular effects it quickly produced by the profuse use of certain novel, exotic, and sickly forms of vegetation."

Unfortunately this style of landscape gardening persists more than it should down to the present day in Paris, and elsewhere in France, and for that matter in all the principal capitals of Europe.

In view of the great body of doctrine set forth in the following pages it will be evident that there should be more recognition of actual principles, more display of good artistic sense in the use of landscape gardening materials. A great deal of the writing on landscape gardening is not much more than a description of the virtues and vices of certain trees and shrubs and flowers, their beauties and their drawbacks. Some attention should be given naturally to the practical side of the subject, but only enough to make plainer the application of the fundamental ideas. There is undoubtedly a separation required—were it but temporary—between what may be called fundamental ideas and what is mere detail. At present in landscape gardening as usually practised, good ideas based on sound precedents are words almost without meaning to most people. A complete, all-comprehending system is of course impossible at present and doubtless always will be. Yet, if real effort of thought could be concentrated on cardinal issues and less padding of conventional and traditional details were foisted in, much might be done to make research into landscape-gardening lore more fruitful.

This at least should be always kept in mind, that the art of landscape gardening has been an evolution of ideas originated and developed down through the ages by the unfolding of the genius and the practical experience of skilled and cultured men.

No man is entirely original, indeed it was said by John La Farge that if an idea were an original one it would be safe to say it would not be a good one. Landscape gardening like everything else has its roots in the past, and the best art of this kind, or for that matter of any kind, is made up of the ideas obtained from many sources, both natural and historical. In *The Philosophy of the Practical* by Benedetto Croce are the following words:

> "He is a true poet (landscape architect) who feels himself at once bound to his predecessors and free, conservative and revolutionary, like Homer, Dante, and Shakespeare, who receive into themselves centuries of history, of thought and poetry and add to those centuries something that is the present and will be the future: chargés du passé, gros de l'avenir."

And this growth is ever moving on, not without setbacks, at what seems to be slow and irregular advance, but in the long future we can confidently believe there will be always a day of better things. There are periods of seeming deadness in the development of landscaping as of other things, but there need be no despondency for

> "there is never real regression in history (or in landscape gardening), but only contradictions that follow upon solutions given and prepare new ones."[1]

[1] B. Croce.

II

THE LAYING OUT OF A PARK OR ESTATE

"LAYING out grounds, as it is called, may be considered as a liberal art, in some sort, like poetry or painting; and its object like that of the liberal arts is, or ought to be, to move the affections under the control of good sense; that is those of the best and wisest; but speaking with more precision, it is to assist nature in moving the affections, and surely, as I have said, the affections of those who have the deepest perception of the beauty of nature; who have the most valuable feelings, that is the most permanent, and most independent, the most ennobling, connected with nature and human life. No liberal art aims merely at the gratification of an individual or a class: the painter or poet is degraded in proportion as he does so; the true servants of the arts pay homage to the human kind as impersonated in unwarped, enlightened minds. If this be so when we are merely putting together words or colours, how much more ought the feeling to prevail when we are in the midst of the realities of things; of the beauty and harmony, of the joys and happiness of living creatures; of men and children, of birds and beasts, of hills and streams, and trees and flowers; with the changes of night and day, evening and morning, summer and winter; and all their unwearied actions and energies, as benign in the spirit that animates them, as beautiful and grand in the form and clothing which is given to them for the delight of our senses."[1]

All parks and even the smallest ornamental ground should indicate at once the presence of a controlling scheme of design. It is not a question of size; there should be everywhere, no matter what the size, entire artistic unity.

A. J. Downing, in his work on landscape gardening, says:

"Unity or the production of the whole is a leading principle of the highest importance in every art of taste or design, without which no satisfactory result can be realized. This arises from the fact that the mind can only attend with pleasure and satisfaction to one object or one composite sensation at the same time. If two distinct objects or classes of objects present themselves at once to us, we can only attend satisfactorily to one, by withdrawing our attention for the time from the other. Hence, the necessity of a reference to this leading principle of unity."

Thomas Whately, in *Observations on Modern Gardening*, writes:

[1] William Wordsworth, letter to Sir G. Beaumont, 1805.

"In landscape gardening violations of unity are often to be met with, and they are always indicative of the absence of correct taste in art. Looking upon a landscape from the windows of a villa residence, we sometimes see a considerable portion of the view embraced by the eye laid out in natural groups of trees and shrubs, and upon one side, or, perhaps, in the middle of the same scene, a formal avenue leading directly up to the house. Such a view can never appear a satisfactory whole, because we experience a confusion of sensations in contemplating it. There is an evident incongruity in bringing two modes of arranging plantations, so totally different, under the eye at one moment, which distracts, rather than pleases the mind. In this example, the avenue, taken by itself, may be a beautiful object, and the groups and connected masses may, in themselves, be elegant, yet if the two portions are seen together, they will not form a whole, because they cannot make a composite idea. For the same reason, there is something unpleasing in the introduction of fruit trees among elegant ornamental trees on a lawn, or even in assembling together, in the same beds, flowering plants, and culinary vegetables—one class of vegetation suggesting the useful, and homely, alone to the mind, and the other, avowedly, only the ornamental.

"In the arrangement of a large extent of surface, where a great many objects are necessarily presented to the eye at once, the principle of unity will suggest that there should be some grand or leading features to which the others should be merely subordinate. Thus, in grouping trees, there should be some large and striking masses to which the others appear to belong, however distant, instead of scattered groups, all of the same size. Even in arranging walks, a whole will more readily be recognized, if there are one or two, of large size, with which the others appear connected as branches, than if all are equal in breadth, and present the same appearance to the eye in passing."

The difficulty with many landscape designs, whether the result of caprice, or of too strict adherence to the canons of a school, is that the plan selected is not really intelligent.

In the words of an acute and able writer, Harald Höffding:

"Gradually man learns to substitute methods for systems and to ask *how* and *how much* in place of *why*. Instead of constructing the world according to the caprice of his imagination, he learns to discern the interconnection which actually obtains from it, and when in this way he gradually arrives at finding one great unity running through all things his imagination will regain in a more secure form all that it has lost when its daring pictures were crowded out by critical investigations."

It becomes a question, once the general plan is made,

of establishing unity of details, of eliminating obtrusive, discordant, or redundant elements, of changing existing conditions by planting, grading, and otherwise establishing harmonious relations between the old parts and new parts of the place, for it is quite as important to carefully retain the valuable old part as to add new effects however charming. There is a superior quality peculiar to an old tree or the old and natural swell of the ground that should have the most careful attention, often to the extent of leaving it entirely alone and doing new work elsewhere where there is less to harm. It is one of the most difficult problems of landscape gardening to manage this combination of the old with the new in accordance with a good general plan so that you can feel yourself in the presence of genuine nature. The result we should seek to avoid is a gathering together in woodland masses trees and shrubs incongruous with their surroundings and therefore unnatural in appearance, and altogether unfitted to the general artistic scheme.

To lay out a park or garden properly it should be studied on the ground and the peculiarities of the place carefully estimated and recorded so as to give due regard to comfort and convenience as well as artistic possibilities. The idiosyncrasies and even the less peculiar likings of the owner should also be considered and constant effort put forth to make a home that is a realization of his taste and requirements.

"How is it possible that any persons can make a good design for any garden whose situation they never saw. To draw a beautiful regular draught is not to the purpose, for although it makes a handsome figure on the paper, yet it has quite a different effect when executed on the ground."[1]

There should be also full realization of the fact that the work of laying out a park or estate, large or small, should always be considered more or less experimental. Plans of ornamental grounds have much less value than plans of architectural structures because changes are more likely to be necessary with live trees and shrubs than with wood and iron and stone. No landscape work is likely to be well done unless it has been changed from time to time. The study of the place should be continuous and kept up long after the initial work is finished. Sometimes a radical mistake is discovered when the landscape gardening is well advanced, but none the less should the mistake be remedied at the time, because the remedy is often difficult and expensive to apply and therefore likely to be left unapplied in after years.

"The building of a place should be begun and carried out with consistency throughout; it is therefore necessary to have it thoroughly thought out from the first, and guided along all the way through by one controlling mind, a mind that should make use of the thoughts of many others, welding them into an organic whole so that the stamp of indi-

[1] Battey Langley.

viduality and unity be never lost. But let me not be misunderstood; a general plan should govern the whole, there must be no room for random work; in every detail the guiding creating brain must be recognized, and it is essential that the scheme should originate from the special circumstances of the artist, from the experience and conditions of his life or the former history of his family, limited by the locality with which he has to deal; but I do not counsel that the whole exact plan should be worked out in detail at first and doggedly maintained to the end. I would, to a large extent, recommend just the opposite, for even if the main scheme comprehends many features which may be considered from the start, in working it out the artist must continually follow the inspiration of his imagination. From time to time, the painter will alter his picture (which, after all, is much less complicated than the picture the landscape gardener has to create), here and there making a part more true to the general effect or to nature, here improving a tone, there giving more accent, more power to a line. Why should the landscape gardener who works in such refractory, changeable, and often impossible-to-estimate material, and who, moreover, has to unite many different pictures in one, succeed in hitting the mark at the first attempt infallibly? Much will be discovered as he goes on studying, observing, both within and without the confines of the place, the light effects on his raw material (for light is one of his chief assets), establishing cause and effect, and thereby finding new ways of working out in detail his early motives, or giving them up altogether if other notions for the treatment of parts strike him as being better.

To see, remaining undisturbed, some particular feature which has proved a failure, is pitiable. The reason the blemish is left is because it has cost so much time, so much money, and because a change would add to the expense, costing as much again or even more. Constant discipline is indispensable in the proper exercise of any art, and when means are not sufficient to treat every part of a park as it should be treated, what money there is had better be devoted towards the improvement of the old established features than to the making of new ones. The postponing of alterations which are recognized as advisable is a dangerous proceeding, also, because existing faults easily lead to the wrong treatment of new features.

"It has been truly said that 'Artistic production is a matter of conscience,' hence a person with an artistic conscience cannot remain content with parts that have been recognized as not up to the standard, or failures. Following the example of nature, which starts and completes her humblest work with the same assiduous care she bestows upon her most sublime creations, one would rather make any sacrifice than leave the blemish one has become aware of, even if in itself it is but a subordinate matter.

"Although in my work at Muskau I never departed a moment from the main idea which I shall have occasion later to describe, yet I confess that many portions have not only been retouched, but that they have been entirely changed, often once, sometimes thrice and four times even. It would be a great error to suppose that confusion results from repeated alterations undertaken with intelligence, for sound reasons and not from caprice. Rather than that they should be undertaken from pure caprice it would certainly be best to never have alterations for improvement. In general the dictum *novum prematur in annum* holds good. One must never rest with correcting and refining until the best possible results have been attained; a principle never to be relinquished and of which often time alone proves to be the great teacher."[1]

In addition to the study of the possibilities of the place for use and beauty, in order to secure good results, it is necessary to equip oneself with the data required. A map of the contours or *lay* of the land is important, not perhaps so much for the landscape gardener, who must make up his mind by a study of the actual land, but for the purpose of giving some idea to the client of how his grounds will look and for estimating the probable cost of constructing them. It is hardly possible however to estimate what the exact cost of such work will be. It is so much the result of a due

[1] *Hints on Landscape Gardening*, Prince Pückler.

exercise of taste and artistic skill that its cost cannot be foreseen any more than that of a painting. Experiments can hardly be avoided, and experiments cost money.

The initial trouble met by anyone proposing to lay out a place is the difficulty of foreseeing how his ideas will look in the future. Experience in the behaviour of different soils and plants in different situations and a natural genius can alone enable one to form a picture in the mind of how a piece of landscape gardening will look ten or twenty years hence. One tree will grow more rapidly in this place than in that one, and in many places unforeseen results will necessarily occur, but something of the real nature of these trees should be realized beforehand, so as to be able to see the picture somewhat in the way it will look years hence.

> "One can see from this how unwise it is to invite a strange artist for some days or weeks or even months with the view of making a plan in which every road and every plantation, the commanding features and all the details, are exactly fixed. And worse still to send such a person merely a survey of the place so that he may proceed at once with a plan, when he has no feeling of the character of the region, no knowledge of the localities, of the effects of hill and dale, of high or low trees in the immediate foreground or in the distance, for him to draw on submissive paper his lines, which no doubt may look very pretty and good there, but which realized into

facts are bound to achieve at best an inappropriate and unsatisfactory design. Who so intends to build up a landscape must do so out of the actual materials from which that particular landscape is to be created, and he must be familiar with them in every particular. Both in plan and execution he works quite otherwise than the painter on his canvas; he deals with realities. The beauty of a bit of real nature, which rendered by the art of the painter can only be partly hinted at, cannot on a plan be given at all; I am inclined to believe, on the contrary that except in a very flat region where no views are possible and little can be achieved anyhow, a plan which is agreeable to look at with lines pleasing to the eye cannot truly stand for beauty in nature. My experience is that in order to achieve fine results in landscape gardening one is often obliged to select lines which have no charm on a plan drawn on paper." [1]

In order to approach properly the consideration of the laying out of any place it is well to go farther than the contour map and secure photographs of features that are characteristic of its scenery, and that may be memoranda to be used in forming a mental picture of what the final scheme should be. This picture will be at first vague, but after considerable study of the existing landscape, dreaming over it if you choose, looking at it from every angle, measuring the contour

[1] *Hints on Landscape Gardening*, Prince Pückler.

map, and comparing photographs, there will gradually dawn on the mind some idea of what the whole design when completed should look like, how the various parts should develop individually and grow into a unified whole. This is the vital part of the work, the part that involves concentrated thought more than any other. It may reveal itself quickly or take a longer time and come only after continued study of the place itself as well as various models, for such a picture should be made to realize a decided and carefully thought-out clear conception such as would satisfy any one as a real artistic creation, and not a vague phantasm or a hodge-podge.

Yet it should be remembered that, though the art faculty exists in some degree in all men, in its creative degree it is the privilege of comparatively few. The process of creation has been thus described: "Reflection and voluntary adaptation intervenes in a moment of inspiration, and inspiration supervenes on afterthought and remembrance. 'And as I mused the fire kindled.'"

The order in which a scheme of laying out should be studied is: First: The necessary limitations, roads, and spaces intended for buildings of different sorts. Second: Views to be revealed or kept open by cutting out existing woods or arranging planting so as to lead the eye to pleasant prospects. Third: The shutting out of disagreeable objects by planting trees and shrubs and leading roads and paths as far as possible away from them, and then a definite picture controlled by these limitations.

"The perfection in landscape gardening consists in the four following requisites: First it must display the natural beauties and hide the natural defects of every situation. Secondly: it should give the appearance of extent and freedom, by carefully disguising or hiding the boundary. Thirdly: it must studiously conceal every interference of art, however expensive, by which the scenery is improved, making the whole appear the production of nature only; and fourthly, all objects of mere convenience or comfort, if incapable of being made ornamental, or of becoming proper parts of the general scenery, must be removed or concealed." [1]

Another principle that needs emphasis in laying out places is the general plan of bordering plantations around the entire boundaries with walks and roads running in and out through the trees and shrubbery, leaving great open spaces of greensward with only here and there an isolated tree or small group of shrubs set near the main mass. The value of these open spaces of greensward from a strictly artistic standpoint cannot be overestimated. It is a helpful idea to recognize that the lawns of a place have frequently a shore line, as it were, like that of most lakes, with promontories and bays, thus making the grass space really the eye of the landscape. Catullus says in addressing his own lake in the country:

[1] Humphry Repton, *The Art of Landscape Gardening.*

> "Dear Sirio that art the very eye of islands and peninsulas that lie deeply embossed in calm inland lakes!"

The example I have in mind, a painting of Menand, shows how a picture of a lake of this kind among wooded hills should be constructed. The artist evidently knew and loved his type. Moreover, this picture forms an excellent example of how the presence of water of a certain sort may make with most charming effect the very eye of the landscape.

Writers on landscape gardening in the eighteenth century dwell much on the value of the sensations produced by various kinds of landscape gardening.

> "Gardening besides the emotions of beauty by means of regularity, order, proportion, colour, and utility, can raise emotions of grandeur, of sweetness, of gaiety, melancholy, wildness, and even of surprise or wonder. In gardening as well as in architecture, simplicity ought to be the governing taste. Profuse ornament hath no better effect than to confuse the eye and to prevent the object from making an impression as one entire whole. A third idea of a garden approaching perfection is of objects assembled together in order to produce not only an emotion of beauty essential to gardens of every kind, but also some other particular emotion, grandeur, for example, gaiety, or any other of those above mentioned."[1]

[1] Henry Home, Lord Kames.

This idea has its value doubtless, but it can be easily overworked. Truly, a special scene may suggest such feelings in the beginning, and help from the landscape gardener may readily increase their strength, and it should be the aim of the designer or artist to recognize this quality of a place, and to encourage in various ways the feelings it naturally produces. But such a note cannot be forced and may even come to make the effect absurd. Imagination may add much to the pleasure of a piece of landscape gardening, but too much in a more or less vague way may easily be attempted, producing unsatisfactory results.

The condition of the mind at the time of experiencing the effects of the scene counts largely, and the effect produced by the environment is not always simple melancholy, gaiety, or awe. It has a larger compass and may take the form indicated by the following beautiful quotation from Maine de Biran:

> "I have experienced this evening in a solitary walk taken during the finest weather, some instantaneous flashes of that ineffable enjoyment, which I have tasted at other times and at such a season of that pure pleasure that seems to snatch us away from all that is of earth, to give us a foretaste of heaven. The verdure had a new freshness and took beauty from the last ray of the sinking sun, all things were instinct with a soft splendour, the trees waved tenderly their majestic crests, the air was full of balm, and the nightingales inter-

changed sighs of love, which yielded to accents of pleasure and joy.

"I walked gently in an alley of young plane trees which I planted a few years since. Above all the vague incomplete impressions and images which were born of the presence of the objects and my moods, hovered this feeling of the infinite which bears us onward sometimes towards a world superior to phenomena, towards this world of realities which links itself to God, as the first and only reality. It seems in this condition when all sensations without and within are calm and happy, as if there were a peculiar sense appropriate to heavenly things, which, wrapped up in the actual fashion of our existence, is destined perhaps to develop itself one day when the soul shall have quitted its mortal husk."

It was men of a similar type, in this respect, to Maine de Biran who earlier, back in the seventeenth century, felt the impulse of a rising desire for free landscape gardening, and developed an instinct for the enjoyment in nature of something higher than melancholy or terror or gaiety or what is understood ordinarily as *feeling*. There were men even in those days who like Fénelon, the spiritual ancestor and acknowledged master of de Biran, would write in flat Versailles what is said to be the first ode of praise of distant mountain tops; who like Racine would murmur in the alleys of the park:

Quand elle est en liberté,
La Nature est inimitable.

Fénelon loved a "beau désert" and in his *Dialogues des Morts* appears the following: "La Nature a ici je ne sais quoi de brut qui plait et qui fait rêver agréablement." Fénelon also says: "On aime d'autant plus purement alors qu'on aime sans sentir comme on croit avec plus de mérite lorsqu'on croit sans voir." This state is not essentially different from that intellectual love of God which Spinoza declares to be beyond *emotion.*

It may be thought that impressive effects can be developed by making combinations of colour of the foliage of trees and shrubs. But this leads to disappointment because all such colours vary from year to year according to the atmospheric and soil conditions, fertility, heat, cold, etc. Prince Pückler has this to say in his *Hints on Landscape Gardening:*

> "How far one may plant with the deliberate intention of attaining artistic light and shade and colour contrast, I will not venture to state. The matter has great difficulties, and in my experience these attempts if I went too far into detail have seldom succeeded very well, and on the other hand, plantations mixed quite recklessly often unfolded the most unexpected charms; nay, they earned me many compliments for my art wherein I was as innocent as many a physician who has effected a

great cure without knowing how. I do not lay much stress on any instructions in this matter as I have always taken an easy middle course. It must also be remembered that the foliage of trees will often assume an entirely different and unexpected shade when transplanted to a different soil and this cannot always be regulated in a large plot. It may happen that a dark coloured maple intended for shading grows a very light foliage. It is quite obvious, however, that one should avoid too variegated a mixture of leaves, too frequent alternations of dark and light green foliage, but here also where it would be hard to lay down good, sharp rules in detail, the taste of the owner must be the best guide.

Colour effects of a reasonably exact and foreseen character can be obtained during the summer with bedding plants such as coleuses and geraniums.

Finally it is important for the designer of landscape work to keep his mind free from fads, and from the tendency to place undue weight on some special part of the place, for the garden is just as important as the shrubbery, trees, and grass spaces, and equal in value in their own ways are the roads and paths, and walls and water pools, or lakes or streams.

"Everything has its own perfection, be it higher or lower in the scale of things, and the perfection of one is not the perfection of another. Things animate, inanimate, visible or invisible, all are good in their kind, and have a best of themselves, which is an object of pursuit. Why do you take such pains with your garden or your park? You see to your walks, and turf, and shrubberies, to your trees and drives, not as if you meant to make an orchard of one, or corn or pasture land of the other, but because there is a special beauty in all that is goodly in wood, water, plain, and slope, brought all together by art into one shape, and grouped into one whole."[1]

Another important illustration of laying out parks and estates is the world-famed Windsor Castle. The broad plateau on which it stands dominates the entire surrounding country and yet it rests easily, and its great size preserves its dignity in the midst of noble scenery extended in all directions. Prince Pückler von Muskau visited England about 1826, and preserved the records of his visit in letters to his wife, from which the following extracts are made:

"The grandeur and magnificence of the castle are truly worthy of the King of England. Situated on a hill above the town, while it presents a noble object from every side, its position gives it an immense advantage. Its historic interest, its high antiquity, and its astonishing vastness and extent unite to render it single in the world. . . . As to your opinion about parks I must remark that the extent of them, especially when properly rounded, can never

[1] John Henry Newman.

Mount Vernon, the Home of George Washington.
Reproduced by Permission of Doubleday, Page & Co.
From a Photograph by Arthur G. Eldredge.

Bosca, or Grove, on a Place near Elmsford, N. Y.
Photograph by William J. Wilson.

be great enough. Windsor park is the only one which has fully satisfied me as a whole and the reason for that is its enormous size. It realizes all I would have:—a pleasant tract of country within the bounds of which you can live and do what you like without privation or constraint; hunt, fish, ride, drive without ever feeling cramped; in which you never see a point except just at the entrance gates, at which you remark, Here is the boundary; and to which all the beauties of the surrounding country to the remotest distance have been rendered tributary by a cultivated taste. In other respects you are right; one must not throw away good and bad together; and it is better to conceal many defects and limitations of the ground by skilfully planned paths and plantations, than to make disproportionate sacrifices to them."

Almost next in importance to Windsor Castle, although not to be mentioned in connexion with it for size and magnificence, is Mt. Vernon, the home of George Washington. Its fame is world-wide, but its value as an example of how to lay out an estate has received little attention. It is really an excellent model for landscape gardeners. Here will be found qualities such as simplicity, breadth, good proportion in the various features, and the dignity which all such places should possess. On one side of the house, a broad lawn slopes down to the banks of the Potomac with not a tree or shrub to disturb the surface. On the borders of the lawn large shade trees frame the picture. Approaching from the other and less interesting side you are led to the house by well-balanced winding drives which are screened by trees and shrubs. Back of the trees and shrubs are large vegetable and flower gardens, very properly shut out from view. It is a good example of what an estate of a cultivated country gentleman should be, and is a place which reflects a character which any man, though ever so rich, should wish to have presented to the world as his own.

Germany, the home of landscaping in its fully developed form, presents the estate of Prince Pückler and the Park of Babelsberg near Potsdam, as well as other parks in the empire, as good examples of the art and its proper practice. The illustration of the park at Muskau affords a view of a size and extent that is a fine example of the best landscape gardening, and the plans of the front lawn of the castle as it originally appeared before Prince Pückler's alterations are, as it now appears, illuminating as to the possibilities of skilful rearrangement.

But while we dwell with admiration on the great landscape architecture of the world at Windsor Park, England, and Central Park, New York, we should not forget the small places, the nooks and corners where the houses stand on a quarter of an acre, one acre, or five or ten acres. There are myriads of such places which need study of an intelligent sort, where the grounds have laid themselves out in accidental fashion, and where any ideas of design are difficult to discover. It should

The Lawn in Front of the Castle in the Park of Muskau as Originally Laid Out.
Taken from Old Print.

The Same Lawn in Front of the Castle, in the Park of Muskau, as redesigned by Prince Pückler.
Redrawn from an Old Print.

always be remembered that nearly every idea concerning the composition of landscape put forth in this book applies equally to a small as to a large place, in one country as in another, even in one age as well as another, and in all future chapters it will be found that this recognition of the universality of fundamental ideas will continue to be emphasized. However, as example is always more impressive than precept, it may be well to give two or three sketches to explain and to illustrate this comprehensive idea. In this way, the subject may be made clearer.

Newburgh is a considerable town on the Hudson about sixty miles from New York. It is an old town and has had for a hundred years a reputation for the beauty of its homes standing in full view of some of the finest scenes of the Hudson. The father of landscape gardening in America, A. J. Downing, lived seventy years ago at Newburgh, where his home still exists. To his influence may be attributed some of the landscape-gardening excellence visible in different parts of the city and in its immediate neighbourhood. While it is hardly at the present time what one would call a smart place where the estates are like those on some parts of Long Island, or at Newport, or in the regions where fashion draws the very rich, Newburgh is a dignified and fine place. The art shown in its estates would be recognized anywhere as that of people who knew how to appreciate and care for fine specimens of old shade trees, pools of water, and vistas across the lawns and through the foliage. It is not surprising therefore that one is able to discover in such a region small places that fulfil the requirements of a high type of landscape art.

Mr. John Staples a few years ago bought an estate in Newburgh where he had lived as a boy. It is strange how people, when they come to prosper a little, instinctively seek abiding places in the region where they lived when they were children, or even in the houses where they were born. Mr. Staples found on the place at Newburgh, which he bought, everything that should dignify an estate and render it worthy of admiration, undulating lawns, fine shade trees, and a house beautifully draped with vines. The estate is not pretentious; it is simply fine in a highly satisfactory way.

But Mr. Staples loves the woods and everything connected with the woods, and consequently sought the wooded territory that formed a considerable part of his domain. He liked to wander through this little wilderness and watch all sorts of wild effects and animated things, and to study what he could do with them. A born woodsman, there were few objects of interest his eyes missed. It was delightful to be out in the woods and contrive things. Mr. Staples, though a man of few words, liked to say that a man, a dog, and a brook belonged together. So year by year, he played with his brook which was at first hidden in a ravine where spring freshets destroyed it. First he tapped it and used its water, and made a pool; then, after preparing a small lawn for it with shrubs and trees where lately a rubbish heap existed, he led it along the hillside bordering the open space, and finally thinking the brook did not look altogether happy, he brought it over alongside the wood road and took it by a circuitous route to the waterfall and so down into the pool. He also built a bungalow, or a tea house, or a picnic house, whichever you may choose to call it, which had in its simple rustic way the comforts of a home. This bungalow stands on the banks of the brook just above the falls on the edge of a charming spot where several trees appear in a group, and a small footbridge spans the stream and leads to the building. The scene is entirely American; just such a scene would hardly appear anywhere but on the Hudson. There is nothing whatever alien about it. The picture has been composed by Mr. Staples for the purpose of making what may be termed a little home in the woods to be occupied a longer or shorter time as his fancy may lead him. The curious part of the design of the picture is that somehow it is Japanese in effect. It may be said that the Japanese lantern and little arched wooden bridge have a distinctly Japanese quality, but that alone would not account for the suggestion of Japanese scenery. You might set these accessories in a landscape on other lawns and they would not create a Japanese effect. The fact is that Mr. Staples, whether consciously or not, has worked out his little picture on right artistic and natural lines, that would make good art in the landscape gardening of any part of the world. The Japanese, true artists as they are, work out their landscape schemes on entirely natural lines, although we, who as a rule fail to understand their peculiar highly symbolized garden theories, and know little of the scenery of Japan, may not at first see it. Here is a proof of the truth of what has been said, a proof that is based on fact. A Japanese artist of high standing in his own country visits an artist in America who has been his guest in Japan. Together they go to Central Park, New York, and the Japanese looks around and remarks, "How like this is to scenes in Japan." This seems at first thought a little absurd, as gardens in Japan are so different from those of other countries.

The idea, however, to be enforced is that landscape gardening in any country will, if it is good art, be inspired by certain fundamental ideas, which whether they have an American air, or a Japanese air, are recognized by all nations as having a universal or world-wide kinship. Curious is it not? But notice how the Japanese butler who made the photograph of Mr. Staples's little home in the woods has recognized and caught this Japanese spirit, and limited his picture to the exact scope that would make it Japanese, and yet distinctively American. Note how American the grove of trees is, and how happily, from the American standpoint, the building is located, and yet very likely the Japanese thought of home when he took the photograph. The perspective of the picture is excellent and you wonder what is beyond, which always adds charm to a landscape. There is a universal quality pertaining to such landscape work that any man, if he expresses his real feelings, prefers to distinctively English, French, or Italian gardening. The mistake should not be made of thinking Mr. Staples is not well informed in the art of making landscape scenery, and that he does things in any haphazard fashion. He is really highly informed in the secrets of his art. An intelligent eye must realize that he knows how to manage the scenery along the shores and banks of the brook, knows how and where to set his trees and shrubs and flowers, where to make his pools, and where to locate a building and give it a proper background. It takes study and a special gift to do such work. Mr. Staples, doubtless, would say that he did not claim to be a landscape gardener or a horticulturist, but nevertheless he knows good landscape art when he sees it, and he has seen it, you may depend upon it. There can be no question that his skill has been "aided and disciplined by frequent reference to and companionship with finely suggestive artistic precedents and examples."[1] It is interesting to note how entirely sympathetic two artists may be, and how they may work with entirely different motives, and yet the skill of both show equal evidences of frequent "references to and companionship with finely suggestive artistic precedents and examples." This is shown by the illustration where Mr. Beale, a distinguished artist, and an intimate and most appreciative friend of Mr. Staples, has made a formal garden on just as good lines of its kind as those of the little woodside cottage just

[1] Gino C. Speranza.

5

described. Mr. Beale has travelled and seen the best examples of landscape art in different countries. Yet, on his quaint old country place on the Hudson, with its great shadowing trees, small lakes, and open lawns and fine distant vistas, he has seen that the conventional Italian garden would look entirely out of place. Consequently what does he do? He simply attaches to the verandah a platform of gravel and a balustrade and steps where the same character of architecture is used. Thus his garden becomes actually a part of the house. The architecture of the house is simple and plain, but excellently suited to the grounds; and in the same spirit Mr. Beale has kept his flowers on a low key of colour and made all the main part of the garden a broad carpet of greensward with a fountain in the centre. Along the walk that outlines the greensward and borders the walls are massed the flowers. The rough stone walls are completely covered with vines and the background of trees and house and a considerable lawn space visible beyond, completes the picture. It is, moreover, a sunken garden because the shape of the ground in the original valley suggested it. If the ground had been on a level with the house, a sunken garden would have been entirely out of place. The point that needs making emphatic is the simple, broad design with its fitness to the house and characteristic quality of the place.

How strange and interesting it is to note the kinship and universality of certain ideas of landscape art latent, not only in the present but in the past, as expressed by written documents and examples of various kinds.

In Newburgh a garden is made by a distinguished artist which fits the house and the landscape, and yet sends the roots of its art down into the past through Italian, Roman, Greek, and Persian until it reaches the garden of Eden itself. In another place in Newburgh one finds a bit of woodland scenery which is so managed as to suggest a Japanese garden and at the same time an American home, and which is also in a way akin to the Chinese garden, parent of the Japanese type.

Furthermore, one remembers Marco Polo, who on his return from a twenty-four years' sojourn in Northern China (Cathay) gave his friend Rusticien de Pise his notes and much oral information, thus enabling him to write an account of his travels. An English chronicler, Purchas, wrote some account of Marco Polo's travels, taken doubtless from this book, and one day Coleridge, the poet, fell asleep after reading as follows: "Here the Khan Kubla commanded a palace to be built and stately gardens thereto, and thus ten miles of fertile ground were enclosed with a wall." During his nap Coleridge had a dream and on awakening wrote down these lines:

In Xanadu did Kubla Khan
A stately pleasure dome decree
Where Alph the sacred river ran
Through caverns measureless to man
Down to a sunless sea,
So twice five miles of fertile ground
With walls and towers were girded round:

And here were gardens bright and sinuous rills
Where blossomed many an incense-bearing tree,
And here were forests ancient as the hills
Unfolding sunny spots of greenery.

Evidently the poet, under the untrammelled inspiration of his imagination, dreamed something much nearer the best type of gardens and lawns than the lines of the old chronicler would indicate. This is easy to understand: Coleridge was an Englishman of the nineteenth century, and was doubtless more or less familiar with the modern schools of landscape gardening. The strangest part is that it seems that Oderic of Pordenone, a Venetian and a Franciscan friar, went to Cathay in the fourteenth century, many years after Marco Polo, and in his account of his travels verified the truth of the narrative about the fountains and gardens of the Xanadu of Marco Polo, and also related how the Chinese architects built these wonders of the age in accordance with instructions of the Great Khan Kabula, who had dreamed a picture of how they should be designed. Doubtless his dream was based on a knowledge of the landscape gardening of his day, just as Coleridge was unconsciously influenced by his recollections of the parks of England. This comparative identity of ideas becomes more evident when we read in Marco Polo's narrative how the Khan built in one part of his park a mount, a hundred paces across the top and a mile in circuit at the base. This hill he had covered with large evergreen trees moved from a distance with the assistance of elephants, hence the name

Green Mount. The earth required to make this mount, when excavated, left a place for a small lake which was supplied by a running stream. Thus we have all the necessary elements of a landscape picture such as we find not only to-day, but also in the pictures of the gardens around Pekin made long before the Christian era. Travellers state that this artificial hill can be seen to-day bearing the original name King-Khan, meaning Green Mountain.

These studies of two or three places at Newburgh lead to the further consideration of the value of simplicity and characteristic art in developing homes. The ambition to make a showy place that indicates the possession of wealth, and the ability to have what most people cannot hope to obtain, or by going to great expense to secure some feature in its highest development because it has come to be the fashion, may not always be desirable. In visiting the show places in America, England, and on the continent, much as one may be impressed, the feeling that finally gains the upper hand is often not unlike that of Sydney Smith in the following quotation:

> "I went for the first time in my life some years ago to stay at a very grand and beautiful place in the country where the grounds are laid out with consummate taste. For the first three or four days I was perfectly enchanted; it seemed something so much better than nature that I really began to wish the earth had been laid out according to the latest

principles of improvement and the whole face of nature were a little more the appearance of a park. In three days' time I was tired to death; a thistle, a nettle, a heap of dead bushes, anything that wore the appearance of accident and want of intention, was quite a relief. I used to escape from the made grounds and walk upon an adjacent goose common where the cart ruts, gravel pits, bumps, irregularities, coarse ungentlemanlike grass, and all the varieties produced by neglect, were a thousand times more gratifying than the monotony of beauties the result of design and crowding with a luxuriance and abundance utterly unknown to nature."

Although there is no question that many grand estates have their place and serve a good purpose, yet the best taste will often suggest something quite different, as may be seen in Central Park, New York, and the great park at Muskau, Germany. As much beauty and display as belong to an intelligently designed park is of course admissible, but it does not therefore necessarily place it in the highest rank of artistic endeavour. In these days of rapid accumulation of great wealth the tendency is to develop wonderful plant effects rather than beautiful, finely modulated landscape studies. Nor can it be said that landscape gardening designs are generally nowadays inferior to those of fifty or a hundred years ago such as the creations made by the designers of Central Park, New York, and Park Muskau, and certain English estates; but the display

A View of the Residence and the Drive at Skylands—a Country Estate in New Jersey.

From a Photograph by William J. Wilson.

of wealth on the modern estate has seemingly drawn much of our attention from the better work like that of the instances just cited. There has been, however, a gradual evolution of the best ideas of landscape gardening,—and the work of fifty years ago is better in some places than it was fifty years before that time; and some of our work is still better to-day than ever. While it may be true, as Leibnitz says, that nature never makes leaps, it must nevertheless be conceded that at the present time, when we are more highly instructed than ever before, we do not seem to be able to advance as rapidly and as persistently as we should, and have not yet attained to the high standards which have been so commonly professed. Perhaps we are too academic, too bound down by precedent, not always of the best and simplest sort. Our work of this kind is not always worthy of our traditions. It may be indeed a period of slack water, but it is nevertheless sure that there is good work being done, the value of which will be evident as time goes on. "To an even greater extent, the present assimilates the past, and can no longer remain subject to the changing wishes and caprices of to-day; the past is taking on a new meaning for us and we are finding that amid all that was peculiar to their own age, there was some element in them that transcended time and could be transmitted to all times." Surely we could not so link the landscape gardening of to-day with that of former ages, if there were not "the same eternal order operating there and here, an order in which all that is deepest in human nature has its root."

The trouble is, that the designers of our country places are oppressed, perhaps unconsciously, at the present day by a false kind of erudition and their work too often lacks personality. "All art speedily declines so soon as it ceases to be continuously re-created, so the present must in the last resort shape its own life. Its relation to the past is not something fixed and given; it has always to be ascertained anew. The present will always mould its conception and judgment of the nature of the past by its own conviction of the value of the work it is doing." Thus speaking from the point of view of a landscape architect, the past is by no means a finished story. It is always open to the present to discover, to stir up something new in it. "Even the past is still in the making."

In order to realize what has been given to the landscape architecture of the present day to enable it to reach a higher plane of development than ever before, let us survey the present condition of the art. We will find that we have a broader basis for its practice, more vigour of movement, an exhaustless profusion of constructions and examples for our consideration; in addition we are securing a clearer insight and a more balanced judgment; finally we are gaining an incentive to follow up for ourselves the clue that has been transmitted to us, a call to co-operate actively in the great undertaking of creating landscape-gardening work of high character.

Nobody can deny that in the modern renaissance of landscape gardening and its evolution and adapta-

Strathfield Saye, the Estate of the Duke of Wellington, England.

From a Photograph by Brown Bros. (Reproduced by Permission.)

tion to new conditions of life, there has come a growing and hopeful tendency towards individual development, to the bestowal of a definite personality to work of this character. By the small owner as well as the prosperous man of affairs, or of elegant leisure, there is an increasing effort to carry out his own ideas on his own place. The emphasis of personality has come in spite of all to be a deep note of the landscape gardening of the present day. Whatever we have of it is a hopeful sign, although it also has its drawbacks.

So wide has been the interest in horticulture, so great has been the development of trees and shrubs and flowers, that the value of the basic ideas that should always be kept in view in the practice of the art has been partially left in abeyance or lost sight of. Some sacrifice doubtless is needed. Those who are interested in landscape must forgo somewhat of their regard for extraordinary floral and arboreal effects, and return to the study of the ideas that lie at the foundation of the art. "No one can advance without surrender, no one can gain without losses, no one can reach great goals without giving up many things in themselves desirable." An extraordinary horticultural effect may be in itself desirable, yet it may be positively unsuited to the landscape scheme adopted. There is a rivalry of the horticultural and the strictly landscape gardening effects which no one making an estate can escape, for in order to achieve success in one typical line another possible line may have to be sacrificed. Moreover, the landscape architect has to employ his weapons on the side of truth and nature, and these very weapons, sharpened by intelligence and experience, have to be continually rediscovered and refashioned to fit the facts and ideas the present stage of the development of the art has found and verified. Not only is there less pure imitation but there is a better realization of the truth of the words of Nicholas de Cusa written more than four hundred years ago: "There is nothing in the universe that does not enjoy a certain singularity which is to be found in no other thing." But there is more to be done than to impress one's own personality on a place. That alone will not suffice. "The more experience advances the more there is of adaptation *of* environment as well as adaptation *to* environment." An estate should have due attention paid to the retention as far as possible of any essential charm it may possess, but the owner should, at the same time, feel entire liberty to impress his or her personality on the place to any degree that will not destroy that supreme quality, "the genius of the place." A natural scene may be beautiful in itself, without change, but change, if it be personal and human in its origin, increases the charm of the place for most people, tenfold. What would Wordsworth's descriptions of nature be without the human note?

The following reference to an actual place in the country will perhaps give a better illustration of what I mean. A little cottage in the hills, it is about five miles back of the Hudson and ten or twelve miles from the northern border of New York City. It occupies

A Country Home near Elmsford, N. Y.

From a Photograph by William J. Wilson.

only a nook of three quarters of an acre, high enough to dominate a fine view to the north, and entirely secluded on a steep narrow back road embowered with many trees. The region is an inhabited one, but except for a house here and there, it might be in the Adirondacks. There are hundreds of similar places within fifty miles of New York City, only most people do not look for them. The dwelling itself is a small farmhouse of a quaint, yet familiar, and commonplace character. The purchaser of the place really left the house almost alone. A simple wing and a stoop were added, also closets, cupboards, and some changes of partitions. The exterior was little changed, except for a coat of paint. Even plumbing was left out, and yet the owner and her friends and relatives often spend considerable periods of time in this little nook. The place has a wonderful charm for its owner, who has lived much abroad, especially in Italy. Her respect, however, for the thoroughly American quality of the place, its simplicity and quaint natural beauty is great, and no foreign fashion is allowed to mar its inherent, native charm; just a plain old-fashioned house near the road, of no special style at all, not even Colonial. On the steep sidehill from where the house stands a narrow path wanders about in somewhat uncertain fashion, just to suit itself and the flower garden of roses and old-fashioned perennials with some of the herbs in a bed by themselves that one sees so often in Italy. The path winds down to a deep hollow where a cool spring reposes in the shadow of many trees. Passing through this woods the path leads to a small knoll crowned by a little group of forest trees, oaks, and sassafras. This is called the Bosca of the place where in Italian fashion the family gather to meals in pleasant weather. The homely vegetables and on the house the Virginia creepers and grape vines keep the spirit of the place unfalteringly American. No Italian gardens and pergolas mar the essentially American beauty of the scene. Just the little grove, the Bosca, with its rude table and benches and quaint oven in the open made of a few stones, and the herb garden, scarcely anything else Italian, and yet you feel that the owner loves Italy, and remembers Italy, but yet loves America still more with its brave simplicity and its absolutely natural charm.

This makes only one more instance of the supreme value of the application of good landscape-gardening ideas to "the genius of the place" in all countries and times, provided the personality of the owner and his other idiosyncrasies receive due consideration. In this way, one may achieve, at lesser or greater expense, a home the result of many aspirations born of diverse experiences. One may have an English or American or French home bearing evidence of the effects of a strong personality, and yet it may have a touch, by no means overpowering, of a more alien, and possibly more desirable style, whether it be Italian, or Japanese, or clearly semi-tropical in effect. The landscape gardening thus becomes basic and universal in its essential quality, and is at the same time full of personality and human feeling.

III

SIZE AND EXTENT OF AN ESTATE

IT should appear from what has been already said that a beautiful piece of landscape gardening may be of many sizes from the village yard to the estate of thousands of acres.

Many considerations, however, need weighing in each case, although the general laws of arrangement hold true throughout. These laws consist in the establishment of certain types of treatment, each a unit, all varied continually, lapping over, contrasting with and contradicting each other; built on the lines of nature yet really not nature, but nevertheless faithful to her spirit. The treatment of these various large or small country places and village lawns is chiefly, therefore, a question of relations between different parts.

Therefore there should be a proper rhythm in these relations, a spacing, a notation that naturally applies to all kinds of design whether it be music, poetry, painting, architecture, or landscape gardening. The true spirit of design lies in the balance and poise of the parts, their variation, whether rapid or slow, tense and violent, or suave and tranquil.

In the village yard the sense of cosiness, the having something of one's own seems desirable, and enclosure is therefore needed on all sides, and the same with equal force applies to the country place. How much finer would the village yards be if this idea were put in practice, a bit of grass, bordering shrubbery, and such trees as the space will allow, and, instead of a straight path through the centre, one passing along half concealed through the foliage, with, at the feet of the bushes, flowers of all kinds, iris, etc.

Then again there may be a little square or green in the quadrangle of a group of cottages: this place does not need shrubs, only trees; its charm lies in its open greensward and trees. Prince Pückler mentions an instance in England:

> "Not far from the parks is an interesting establishment called 'The Cottages.' The proprietor, Mr. Harford, has endeavoured to realize the beau ideal of a village. A beautiful green space in the midst of a wood is surrounded by a winding road; on it are built nine cottages all of different forms and materials, stone, brick, wood, and roofed with thatch, tiles, and slate; each surrounded with different trees, and enwreathed with various sorts of clematis, rose, honeysuckle, and vine. The dwellings, which are perfectly detached though they form a whole, have separate gardens, and a common fountain which stands in the centre of the green, overshadowed by old trees. The gardens, divided by neat hedges, form

a pretty garland of flowers and herbs round the whole village. What crowns the whole is, that the inhabitants are all poor families, whom the generous proprietor allows to live in the houses rent free. No more delightful or well chosen spot could be found as a refuge for misfortune: its perfect seclusion and snugness breathe only peace and forgetfulness of the world."

On the other hand, when we turn to larger places, twenty acres or many thousands of acres, the same principles apply to the architectural and the natural features, to the high and low, and broad and narrow masses, related and contrasted in a hundred ways. The house, the barns and stables, vegetable gardens, are all given due attention on their practical side, for use as well as for beauty,—nothing forced, nothing seemingly meant for display, dignified, noble, grand if you will, but never a sense of strain, although full of nuances, full of delicate elusive beauties. One great picture, or a series of attractive small lawns and glades, now various, now contradictory, and now contrasting.

Here are two not altogether imaginary instances. One is a charming villa with beautiful outlooks in various directions over Florence and the Arno. The setting is formal, rightly, and highly decorative, for it is a part of the Boboli Gardens. Fountains, beautiful trees, everything choice and charming. But it is chiefly as a foreground to many views that we value it. One sits and feasts the eyes and mind on the lovely distant scenes and their many associations, and yet one remains in a resting place, a circumscribed area.

In another place we find the location of a house and its tributary buildings made in a dense woods where the forest has been cut away to gain the necessary room. Here again the basic law of design applies, but how differently? The open space is made large enough for the buildings, gardens, and lawns with their enclosing plantations. Around these open spaces, however, along the border of the woods are found plantations of more trees and shrubs, running in and out of the forest, contrasting, contradicting, and yet harmonizing the new with the old, a fringe that straggles, blends, and loses itself, dies away so that the natural scene may still triumph and live; boundary lines that evidently exist but hardly appear. Such work needs artistic training and real knowledge of plants, and quite as great is the ability to open paths properly to beautiful glades and fine groups of trees, or perhaps to a pool or brook or some picturesque mass of rock. The roads through such regions should lead in devious ways, never straight, but on revealing lines that would inspire the imagination to wonder what will be next slipping around the corner. Doubtless, most persons have seen a straight vista cut through woods, to allow some statue or building to appear at the end of it. Read what Richard Jeffries says about this in his chapter on "An English Deer Park":

> "Wide straight roads—you can call them nothing else—were cut through the finest woods so that on

A Distant Vista in the Park of Prince Pückler von Muskau, Silesia, Germany.
From a Photograph by Thomas W. Sears, Providence, R. I.

looking from a certain window or standing at a certain spot in the grounds you might see a church tower at the end of the cutting. In some parks there are half a dozen such horrors shown to you as a great curiosity; some have a monument or pillar at the end. These hideous disfigurements of beautiful scenery should be wiped out in our day. The stiff straight cutting could soon be filled up by planting and after a time the woods would resume their natural condition. Many common highway roads are really delightful, winding through trees and hedgerows with glimpses of hills and distant villages. But these planned straight vistas, radiating from a central spot as if done by ruler and pen, at once destroy the pleasant illusion of primeval forest. You may be dreaming under the oaks of the chase of Rosalind: the moment you enter such a vista all becomes commonplace."

The object of these two examples is to show how extent and space in landscape of all sizes, especially the largest, can constitute many diverse and individual problems and yet how they should be unified into one scheme of landscape design. It should be all simple and yet almost infinite in its contrasts and harmonies. Prince Pückler speaks in *Hints on Landscape Gardening* about "frozen music" thus:

"Even so one might compare the higher garden art with music, and at least as fitly as architecture

6

has been called *frozen music*, call garden art *growing music*. It too has its symphonies, adagios, and allegros, which stir the senses with vague and powerful emotions. Further, as Nature offers her features to the landscape gardener for use and choice, so does she offer to music her fundamental tones, beautiful like the human voice, the song of birds, the thunder of the tempest, the roaring of the hurricane, the bodeful wailing of branches—ugly sounds like howling, bellowing, clattering, and squeaking, yet the instruments bring all these out and work according to circumstances, ear splitting in the hands of the incompetent, entrancing when arranged by the artist in an orderly whole. The genial nature painter (landscape architect) does the same. He studies the manifold material given him by nature, and works the scattered parts by his art into a beautiful whole whose melody flatters the senses, but only unfolds its highest powers and yields the greatest enjoyment when harmony has breathed true soul into the work."

This is not altogether sentiment. If you do not cut out your woods in this way, a way born of much study and a good sense of harmony and trained skill, you will simply get the effects against which Jeffries rails, and Pückler exclaims.

Every one of the lawns with great outlooks, or only village street scenes, should have the same application of contradiction and contrast breaking into each other and finally producing the harmony of a unified scheme, a design which has rhythm and flow. The important thing is to keep the mind fixed on the broad outlines, the articulation of any place, even the smallest, its bones and sinews, and not allow oneself to be diverted to producing more or less petty effects where a large one should be accomplished, setting out some rare or curious tree or shrub where it does not belong, just because you have a whim to set it there. The improper use of rocks, water, and paths and roads creates a strain and an incongruity that is not the contradiction and contrast that makes for harmony within the scheme of the landscape design. The artistic effect sought should be just as refined and rare and delicate as that of a Constable landscape.

Perhaps the ordinary man, the man of the street, may believe he cannot achieve the desired result. Perhaps he cannot. The longer he works at it, however, the more beauties he will discover he can bring into being, and the more he tries the more he will want to try, for it all becomes more and more fascinating as he brings out more beauty of tree and shrub and flower. Many a man has been astonished at what he can accomplish in landscape making. The trouble is that few think of doing such work on artistic lines. They simply set out plants and grade grounds with what they consider good taste. This artistic work they think belongs to the landscape architect, and doubtless it does, but no man will ever inspire or even assist the designer in his work, unless he follows and sustains him intelligently with an appreciation of his effort that can only come from actual love of the work and a certain knowledge possessed by himself. Landscape gardening means, therefore, much more than hiring a gardener to grade and plant the lawn, or a consultation with the tree agent about trees and shrubs to be bought, and it means much more than the preparation of plans of location of buildings, roads, and plantations by some celebrated expert; it should really mean an unceasing struggle for years to attain results the accomplishment of which, with the help of men, of nature in field and forest, and of books, will prove an unceasing delight. Prince Pückler worked at it for half a century, on his estates at Moskau and elsewhere, and never ceased to enjoy it and to acquire fresh ideas. Read what he says about the extent and size of a park and it will be evident at once that he found on artistic lines inspiration for the most elevated conceptions wrought out in a duly ordered scheme.

Prince Pückler says:

"In order that the landscape gardener should achieve a great effect, it is not necessary that a park should be large. An extended estate is often so bungled, so belittled by incompetent treatment, that, lacking in unity, it appears quite small. I may here remark, by the way, that I think Michael Angelo totally wrong when he said about the Pantheon, 'Ye marvel at it on the earth, I will set it in the heavens.' He meant thereby to achieve a more imposing effect, and as he said, so he did. He gave the dome of

St. Peter's the same size as the Pantheon, but how unfortunate is the result! Looming up in the air above the enormous masses of the building, St. Peter's Dome appears in proportion small and insignificant, whilst the dome of the old Pantheon, placed on the right base, appears after centuries as sublime as the arch of the firmament.

"Poised on the summit of Mont Blanc the Pyramids would hardly appear as large as sentry boxes, and Mont Blanc itself, seen from the distant plains, looks like a little snow hill. Large and small are, therefore, relative terms. It is not from the thing itself we judge, but from its appearance in given surroundings, and it is here that landscape architecture has the widest of fields. For instance, trees a hundred feet high, which in the middle distance hardly rise above the horizon, will at a short distance tower above it, hence, with intelligent management, with due appreciation of the value the foreground has to distance, it is possible to give character and expression to the landscape and secure an effect of grandeur and extent.

"I cannot help remarking here that if I have always held up as a model the general appearance of English parks, which testify to a universally diffused taste for park culture and embellishment, I still believe that in given ways England might have done much better. It seems to me that with much beauty most English parks have one blemish which makes them rather tedious and monotonous on long acquaintance. I have in mind neither their pleasure grounds, nor their gardens, which are full of variety, but their parks. For instance, in regard to the deliberate treatment of these parks as features laid out on a diminutive scale, the effect seems to be altogether inadequate when compared to the grandeur and magnificence of the open country round them. Indeed, in my opinion, the outside country not infrequently resembles far more a region ennobled by art in variety than the parks.

"I have previously stated the proposition that size is not an absolutely necessary element in the making of a park, yet where it is possible, I think it very desirable, in order that a greater variety of parts be gained, a quality which will always present the supreme charm of novelty. Laid out with equal intelligence I should always prefer the more extensive to the smaller park, even if the latter should be more favoured by nature. In Prussia, where land has so much less value than in other countries, such large estates are easily obtainable, and I advise every one of my countrymen to strive for large places. It is certain that, considered as a little world sufficient unto itself, a park where one cannot ride or drive for an hour at least without going over the same roads, and which does not comprise many more walks, very soon tires one, if confined to it alone. But where a rich picturesque nature has already idealized the region around and has made it, as it were, into a great work of art, as in the case of many parts of

Switzerland, Italy, South Germany, or Silesia, then I am, on the whole, of the opinion that projects of parks are *hors d'œuvre.* It would be like a little landscape in the corner of a magnificent Claude Lorrain. There one's work should be confined to the laying out of good roads so that the enjoyment of such rare scenery be made easier, while here and there taking down some isolated trees in order to open views which are hidden by nature, always indifferent to the display of her beauties.

"Near the house, however, one should seek for the charm of a garden of modest proportions, which, whenever possible, would contrast with nature around. In such a garden one should have in view not so much the variety of a landscape, but comfort and charm, safety and elegance. The garden art of the Romans, which through the study of the classical writers, and especially through the description which Pliny gives of his villa, again came into practice in the fifteenth century in Italy, and was later altered into the so-called French gardens, into colder, less comfortable forms, deserves particular consideration on this very point. This rich and sumptuous art, which may be called an extension of the art of architecture from the house into the garden, or, as the English might say, the approach of the landscape to the very doors of the house, may be most suitably applied to this purpose. Imagine, for instance, among the precipices and waterfalls, the dark pine woods, and blue glaciers of mountainous Switzerland, a classical, antique building, a palace from the Strada Balbi, sumptuous in its decorative flourishes, surrounded with high terraces, rich multi-coloured parterres of flowers, studded with marble statues and alive with the movement of waters; what a contrast would this be to the tremendous naked grandeur of the setting of mountains? A few steps aside in the woods, and palace and gardens would have vanished from view, as by a magic wand, to make room again for the undisturbed loneliness and majestic wilderness of nature. Farther on, perhaps, a bend in the road would open up an unexpected vista, where, in the distance, the work of art like a realized fairy dream would show through the dark firs, glowing in the light of the setting sun, or rising up over the mysterious darkness of the valley in a mass where, here and there, the tiny sparkles of lighted candles would glow. Would not such a picture be wonderful, and owe its chief beauty largely to contrast? When nature offers her material, the scheme must be different; then the park, an oasis in a broad, flat space, must first create its own environment. Although the same laws are everywhere the foundation of beauty, they have to be interpreted and expressed in various ways. In such a case, where no impression by great contrasts can be achieved, one must carefully seek to create a pleasant and gentle, general harmony, bringing into view large elements, such as the distant views which may be secured, into correspondence with the character given to the park. In such a problem the size of the domain becomes a chief consideration. In the former example it is only necessary to embellish a single spot to make all surrounding nature serve one's own purpose. Here, the treatment should extend to the whole region. Examples which lie between these two schemes will require modifications of both propositions and be tastefully treated according to the respective localities. In all these cases the principles I have laid down are basic ones."

Finally, careful consideration should be given to the dimensions of an estate or park with regard to the limitations that the topography, the hills and woodland and water naturally impose on the purchaser. It is easy for a person of means to add field unto field, but the question is, does he secure thereby an estate or park that naturally fits into a well-considered landscape scheme?

If this cannot be done, it would be wise to abandon the scheme altogether and go elsewhere, or else accept the limitations of the smaller place.

Nothing is more important than the establishing in the beginning the proper boundaries to a place. Time and study and the best advice are well employed in securing this end.

The illustration of a view from West Point, New York, called the Gates of the Highlands, is given to show to what extent the eye can reach and feel that it contains within its domain a definite landscape picture.

The advantage of studying such a scene is that you have before you a perfectly good model for landscape-gardening work designed to any scale even the smallest. It is simply a grand example of the way nature, in her best mood, designs her scenery. The view also illustrates how by replacing the water of the river by grass you could obtain the meadow effect, with trees and shrubs jutting out into the sea of green, and thus create the pastoral scene which as well as the water effect may prove to be the eye of the landscape.

The Gates of the Highlands of the Hudson River from West Point, N. Y.

From a Photograph by William Hale Kirk.

IV

ENCLOSURES

THE question of fences is not altogether one of landscape art, for protection of this kind becomes a necessity in most countries; however, it has its advantages from the artistic standpoint; outside of and beyond all the practical advantages of an enclosure its landscape effect has value. It individualizes a place, it sets a boundary, it marks the confines of a home or a possession, if it does nothing more. It indicates that the frame of the picture is here, and the enclosure warns one and all that here they must stop, and go no farther except as the proprietor may allow them the freedom of his domain for picnics, cross-cut paths, and various other privileges. Landscape art should seek to plant out and shut out in great part the boundary walls or fences and allow only occasional glimpses to prove that they exist and are performing their proper function.

There is a tendency at the present time to favour the open lawn scheme where a dozen houses or more show no boundary line between them except the surveyor's monuments. These places are generally comparatively small, and throwing them all together into one lawn is thought to make a better display of whatever beauty they may possess, or that may be added to them by planting trees and shrubs and flowers. But it will be found on studying the situation in the light of the laws of landscape design that a number of these buildings, included together and owned by persons of diverse interests and tastes, will not lend themselves successfully to one landscape scheme. The variety of human interests create contrasts and contradictions that will not come into harmony with each other on account of the "personal equation," the difference of make-up of the owners. Theoretically it is a beautiful idea and seems practicable, but to obtain a really artistic effect in this way, no, it is not likely to be done. People may fancy they have lawns with many houses and owners, in one great enclosure, that is satisfactory, but the probability is that they do not know a well-designed lawn when they see it, and think they have something which they have not.

The intimate way of treating the small home will really commend itself to everyone who is not led away by the influence of a caprice or fashion. It gives the surest way of securing the most comfort and pleasure for the dweller under his own vine and fig tree. With wire fence covered with vines entirely, or a rough wall of stone, quarry stone, uncut, with the interstices devoid of cement and filled with rich earth and rock plants, stonecrop, prickly pear, and other rock plants, the home becomes one's very own. Flowers cluster around the base of the wall, or honeysuckle fence, and shrubs partially screen it, and the lawn within becomes a park in miniature, its design obedient to park laws. Everything would naturally be in proportion, trees and shrubs of moderate and even dwarf growth finding place on the smallest lawn. There is likely on the small place to be danger of overcrowding, for there should be a breadth of grass plot or lawn sufficient to make the place look larger rather than smaller than it really is. The sense of comparative breadth can always be maintained in the smallest place.

It should hardly need repeating that a boundary enclosure of this kind should have along its borders shrubs and trees so arranged as to not only carry out the general law of design, but to reveal at intervals brief glimpses over the boundary to pleasing objects beyond.

A fence is generally an unattractive part of the landscape. It is artificial, no matter how it is designed, whether of iron, wood, or stone. Wire fastened to iron posts makes a cheap fence that will last at least twenty years in many cases, but it is ugly. Cover it with honeysuckles and it is beautiful. There can be little objection to any fence, if covered with vines or other vegetation, especially if trees and shrubs lend the support of their protecting and screening foliage. The fence then becomes quite as attractive as any other part of the place, especially as it need not shut out, and indeed never should entirely shut out, important views of spaces exterior and beyond.

A small place especially if enclosed as it should be ought to have nothing spectacular about it, no showy plants, trees or shrubs or flowers, set out solely for display. If there is a proper place for them in the landscape scheme, use them, but not otherwise. No grottoes, no rock work unless rocks crop out of the soil, no pergolas unless an arbour is wanted for a grape vine, and then it only finds a proper place in the general scheme provided it is perfectly simple. All more or less theatrical arrangements only make the enclosure seem more confined and unnatural.

In the case of the large place there may be a series of lawns unenclosed, groups of buildings, mansion region, farm region, woodland of vast extent; then the boundary lines disappear except where openings are made to disclose far-distant scenery and then the enclosures count little in the scheme. Perhaps it may be a territory like Central Park where the city needs to be shut out altogether because there is nothing beyond to tempt the eye. On the other hand, on a place like Muskau, Germany, Prince Pückler would naturally seek to retain many of his distant views because they were as important to him as those near his house. In so large a place (thousands of acres) the enclosures would hardly mean much except when one went near them.

> "I have often heard the opinion expressed that nothing is more contrary to the way of nature—which is, after all, what landscape gardening seeks

to conform itself to—than the enclosures of a park, but I think otherwise, and quite approve of the English fashion of having every park enclosed with great care, but this enclosure should be varied and in large part it should not be felt inside the park. At bottom this question of enclosure is rather a matter of expediency than of æsthetics, and yet as an element of beauty I do not condemn it. Are not such beautiful uncultivated spots marked off as it were by distinct boundaries, and does not such a division often increase their charm? For example, a valley shut in by a dense forest or impassable rocks, an island surrounded by running water, give the feeling of home, of entire possession, of security against intrusion or disturbance, allowing us to enjoy all the more comfortably the beauty of the surroundings. And, therefore, in a park the presence of a protecting wall or fence should be welcomed as a highly desirable element, necessary for the peace and security of our enjoyment in excluding the unwelcome intruder, but which should be so contrived as to permit us to go out from the park into the surrounding country. Hence the sight of an enclosure can only be obnoxious to those who hold so exaggerated a notion of freedom that, hating everything that bears the name of barrier, they would wish to overturn even imaginary barriers! In England, as I have said before, not only every park, but on account of the precious cattle, every section of it, every coppice and every exposed young tree is surrounded with a fence, and although this disturbs the general effect by being carried to excess, I have frequently found that here and there a fence is very picturesque, especially where the character of the landscape changes, the fence in this case preparing the mind for new impressions and affording an easy transition to new scenes.

"So for security's sake let our parks have an enclosure high and strong, assuming that this is possible—for to be sure, just as French cookery books very wisely begin their receipts with '*Ayez une carpe, ayez un perdreau*,' etc., I preface my advice with the proviso that, locality being favourable and means at hand, the park should be enclosed. But inasmuch as the heavier and bigger the wall, the worse, as a rule, is its appearance, and bearing in mind also that it is a great mistake to limit the field of fancy by too familiar a view of its limits, a close and broad plantation should hide the greater part of it. If such a barrier is made by a wooden fence it should never be seen, but supplied with interesting points at intervals, and a deep ha-ha, or ditch, alongside, while all the abruptness of the hollow thus made can be avoided by covering it with varied plantations. The paths should only approach this ha-ha or ditch when, for instance, by means of a small bridge, one wishes to sally forth through an opening into the surrounding country. The manner of screening the bridge and the boundaries should be as varied as possible. In one place the foliage should run two or three hundred paces along the boundaries, showing a high plantation of trees: in other places again it should be made up of narrower and lower groups of trees so that over and beyond one can catch glimpses of the outside country. In other places, these far-distant views should be visible above coppices and under isolated trees, standing from among but high above the shrubbery. If a wall surrounds the park this can, at intervals, be allowed freely to emerge, broken only by scattering bushes and trees, and will look best in a ruined or unkempt state, covered with ivy and Virginia creeper, or let the foliage be merged into a building, a gallery, etc. Under such conditions the wall will never be a disturbing influence, but an improvement.

"Along this plantation on the boundary, sometimes broad, sometimes narrow, but hardly ever more than 3 *rüthen* (48 feet), should run irregularly a grass road 24 feet wide. On the side towards the interior of the park begins the mixed plantation for forming a screen for the general view. Here deciduous-leaved trees predominate and in summer hide the too monotonous evergreen foliage which should be left conspicuous only where it is desirable. It is surprising how such an arrangement enlivens a park even in melancholy winters, and how the lawn or grass path even amid snow and ice, where everything else is bare, makes the most charming walk. The evergreen foreground which covers the boundaries both winter and summer and borders the grass path gives colour to the whole region, and supplies a want greatly sought after in winter days, although a well grouped and designed park should, even without colour, during all seasons of the year, satisfy our sense of beauty, especially in winter when all ordinary decoration is absent, making an interesting picture by the harmony of its masses of trees, lawns, water, its pleasant lines of paths and banks. That the border plantation of pines and other evergreen trees should be planted so as to appear a natural growth is obvious, and in the chapter on Plantations examples will be given in detail. Meanwhile the sketch in Plate I. will make my views clearer. At *a* the green path from the park is practically hidden, at *b* it appears only as a cutting which loses itself in the shrubbery.

"Along the boundary wall of many English parks, where was carried out in old times the work of Brown and his followers, there runs a path between an almost regular band of foliage planted with shrubs and trees, so that the wall is often conspicuous between the tree trunks.

"My reader must not confound my plan with this English plan, as the green path I advocate is a part of the lawn, and has no definite distinction from the lawn, but simply melts into it. The English idea originated in the infancy of landscape gardening, when parks of such size were first laid out, and it was a matter of vanity to make them appear as large as possible; but the means defeated the end, since they ostentatiously pointed out what they should have

Goethe's Cottage at Weimar.
Redrawn from an Old Print.

A Honeysuckle Hedge Growing on Wire Mesh and Iron Posts.

artistically concealed. Apart from this enclosure, which is necessary for protection, it is obvious that every interesting feature of the distant landscape should be included in the park, all outer rays concentrating into this focus. Distant views of great extent lying way beyond the actual grounds give an appearance of measureless extent. When such opportunities are skilfully utilized they greatly surpass the reality. They must, however, be so managed that one should never become aware of the intervening park boundaries. Moreover such special features should never be seen twice in the same way. For instance: many partial glimpses may be given of a distant hill, but only once should the hill be revealed in its entirety. The same applies to the town or city. Such effective planning, affording glimpses which tempt one's imagination and excite the pleasure of anticipation, and compositions in which each part is interdependent, are far more difficult to achieve than full revelations. When people stumble on a remarkably beautiful view and, after lingering long, remark, 'What a pity that great tree stands in the foreground, how much more grand the view would be if it were absent'—they would be much astonished if one did them the service to hew away the condemned tree. They would have a stretch of country before them, but no more picture—for a garden in the great style is really a picture gallery and pictures demand a frame."[1]

The appearance of a fence made of picturesque-

[1] Prince Pückler, *Hints on Landscape Gardening*.

looking stones or a vine-covered iron wire has real value as a landscape feature in itself. The use of the vines and the stone, or the wire, are however chiefly a means of making known the existence of a boundary line. Consequently the blending of boundary plantations, trees and shrubs and vines, should be so complete as to largely confine itself to the suggestion of the presence of a limit to the place. There would naturally be views here and there, out and beyond, except on occasions when discordant elements need shutting out. The "hedge" sensation should be eliminated, and the border plantation made after the type which in the case of trees and shrubs and flowers is intended to apply to the composition of every part of the place. The illustration showing a boundary fence on the estate of Muskau is intended to explain how the trees and shrubs should be massed along the boundaries. The fence is made of wood and on that account is not altogether to be commended. Otherwise, the irregularity of the height of the pickets gives it an attractive appearance. Carrying out the same idea, the base, outside of the fence bordering the sidewalk, should be planted with flowers, irises, the larger sedums, saxifrage, anemones, phlox, and goldenrod, with here and there one shrub or three;—groups of shrubs planted in odd numbers always compose better. The sidewalk, in a sense, belongs to the public and therefore it would be unwise to leave shrubs to be injured on the curb line; otherwise the planting of shrub groups among the shade trees that border the road would be desirable, because even here it is well to follow out consistently the typical scheme of planting that pertains to the landscape of the entire place. At least we can go far towards retaining a natural effect by planting trees on the curb at unequal distances—35 feet—40 feet—45 feet and even 50 feet or 60 feet apart. The kinds of shade trees used can also be made to vary the effect, not by changing the species continually, but by planting a dozen or more of one sort together. If the road winds, it is a good idea to plant one kind from one turn to the next as far as the eye can see. The beauty of this system of irregular planting, especially in the case of shrubs and flowers, is that any damage done by the public does not produce such defacing effects as would occur in a symmetrically formed group, or in a hedge.

It is a fact, however, that a carefully worked out group, an evidently foreordained design would be more likely to survive unscathed than carelessly made plantations, the composition of which is characterized, to use a homely phrase, by neither rhyme nor reason. Thoughtless and uninstructed persons are apt to think that whenever they see a plantation along a fence that looks as if it had sprung up there naturally, it must be evident that the arrangement can never have been the result of a carefully studied design.

This concealment of intention is truly what ought to be instinctively practised if the design is good. But in attempting to do such work it should be remembered that every plant counts in the scheme and that not one plant can be safely planted in any haphazard fashion.

V

LOCATION OF BUILDINGS

IN several ways the spot where buildings are located should be controlling. They occupy the key to the situation. Here most of the time the human beings live, the men, women, and children, and their physical needs and comforts should be satisfied and their mental and spiritual desires, for here man abides and finds his home, and if he wanders he returns here, and wants in this spot especially the very best that life can give him. Consequently, the house must have the chief part of his attention, and therefore too much care cannot be given to the choice of the site. This is the way Humphry Repton expresses the same idea: "However various opinions may be on the choice of a situation for a house, yet there appear to be certain principles on which such choice ought to be founded; and these may be deduced from the following considerations: First: The natural character of the surrounding country. Secondly: The style, character, and size of the house. Thirdly: The aspects of exposure, both with regard to the sun and the prevalent winds of the country. Fourthly: The shape of the ground near

A Gardener's Cottage at Skylands—A Country Estate in New Jersey.
From a Photograph by William J. Wilson.

Windsor Castle, England.
From an Old Print.

the house. Fifthly: The views from the several apartments; and Sixthly: The numerous objects of comfort—such as a dry soil, a supply of good water, proper space for offices, with various other conveniences essential to a mansion in the country, and which in a town may sometimes be dispensed with, or at least very differently disposed."

Architects' advice is not sufficient, landscape architects should be called in to study the shape of the ground and to select the place where the lawns and shrubbery will make the surroundings of the house most convenient and comfortable and secure the best landscape effect. The engineer should also advise as to the drainage and the chemist as to the character of the soil with a view to its fertilization and also as to the quality of the drinking water. It seems a great deal of trouble to take to locate a house, but the wise man decides on all these things beforehand and saves himself a great deal of trouble in the end.

The architect naturally looks to the many questions of comfort and beauty that the landscape architect is not necessarily called on to discuss, such as the way the sun comes in at the windows and from what quarter the cold winds blow. The modelling of the land however is the landscape architect's special province, and every pound of soil that comes from the cellar, and such other soil as has to be taken from elsewhere, should be under the control of the landscape architect and his assistants. To them exclusively should be delegated this work, for only in this way can an artistic result be accomplished satisfactorily on the most important part of the grounds. On the other hand, the architect should be consulted by the landscape architect concerning the kind of vines that should be grown on the house. Again we find the contrasting and overlapping of contradictory elements in the use of plants of various kinds that are needed over and in the verandas and porticoes to produce harmony between the house and the adjacent landscape, a sort of interlocking of horticultural and architectural features which can be made to produce charming combinations.

As an illustration of the importance of this way of treating the site, read the account of Tintern Abbey given by Prince Pückler in his *Tour of England:*

> "It would be difficult to imagine a more favourable situation or a more sublime ruin. The entrance to it seems as if contrived by the hand of some skilful scene painter to produce the most striking effect. The church, which is large, is still almost perfect, the roof alone and a few of the pillars are wanting. The ruins have received just that degree of care which is consistent with the full preservation of their character; all unpicturesque rubbish which could obstruct the view is removed, without any attempt at repair and embellishment. A beautiful smooth turf covers the ground, and luxuriant creeping plants grow amid the stones. The fallen ornaments are laid in picturesque confusion, a perfect avenue of thick ivy stems climbing up

the pillars and forming a roof overhead. The better to secure the ruin, a new gate of antique workmanship with iron ornaments is put up. When this is suddenly opened, the effect is most striking and surprising. You suddenly look down the avenue of ivy-clad pillars, and see their grand perspective lines closed at a distance of three hundred feet by a magnificent window eighty feet high and thirty broad; through the intricate tracery you see a wooded mountain from whose side project abrupt masses of rock. Overhead the wind plays in the garlands of ivy, and the clouds pass swiftly across the deep blue sky. When you reach the centre of the church, whence you look to the four extremities of the cross, you see the two transept windows nearby as large and as beautiful as the principal one; through each you command a picture entirely different, but each in the wild and sublime style which harmonizes so perfectly with the building. Immediately around the ruin is a luxuriant orchard. In spring how exquisite must be the effect of these grey venerable walls rising out of that sea of fragrance and beauty. A Vandal Lord and Lord Lieutenant of the country conceived the pious design of restoring the church. Happily Heaven took him to itself before he had time to execute it."

Everything that has been here said about the location of buildings applies equally to other buildings on any place; the interlocking of vines and other plants with the buildings can nearly always be made to accomplish beautiful results.

If the estate be comparatively small the house and the outbuildings should be segregated, grouped together and planted with trees and shrubs, so as to seclude them from the general landscape. In the case of some fine view it may be wise to leave an outlook from the house into the distance. On the other hand, the trees and shrubs always help the house where they partially screen its entire mass from view, only affording glimpses of the roofs through the foliage. This does not mean that the trees and shrubs should be allowed to smother the house, for there should be open space, lawns and formal gardens, near the house, and outbuildings, but only that as you approach it from certain directions the roofs should emerge from a mass of foliage.

One of the most difficult problems to be settled is the height of the first floors of the principal living rooms above the surrounding lawn. This is always a question that requires careful consideration both by architect and landscape architect. An open level space is generally desirable for the site of a house unless it is designed in a special manner on two or more levels, and in any case it should not be set on a pinnacle or peak of ground.

> "All natural shapes of ground must necessarily fall under one of these descriptions, viz., convex, concave, plane, or inclined plane. I will suppose

it granted that, except in very romantic situations, all the rooms on the principal floor ought to range on the same level, and that there must be a platform, or certain space of ground, with a gentle descent from the house every way. If the ground be naturally convex, or what is generally called a knoll, the size of the house must be adapted to the size of the knoll: thus a small building only one hundred feet in front may be placed upon such a hillock, with a sufficient platform around it; but if a building three hundred feet long should be required it is evident that the crown of the hill must be taken off, and then the shape of the ground becomes very different from its original form: for although the small house would have a sufficient platform, the large one will sometimes be on the brink of a very steep bank; and this difficulty would be increased by raising the ground to set the large house on the same level with the smaller one. It therefore follows that if the house must stand on a natural hillock, the building should not be larger than its situation will admit; and where such hillocks do not exist in places proper for a house in every other respect, it is sometimes possible for art to supply what nature seems to have denied. But it is not possible in all cases; a circumstance which proves the absurdity of those architects who design and plan a house, without any previous knowledge of the situation or shape of the ground on which it is to be built."[1]

[1] Humphry Repton, *Art of Landscape Gardening*, chap. iii., p. 28.

Too great stress cannot be laid on the advisability of securing directly about the house the highest degree of horticultural finish. Here should be found the most perfect turf (a difficult problem), the richest flower garden, the choicest and rarest evergreens and shade trees;—these represent in a way and for the lawn statuesque beauty better than statues themselves, which indeed have no place there. Richard Payne Knight wrote sensibly on this subject of landscape gardening around the house at the end of the eighteenth century. He was a trustee of the British Museum and a noted Greek scholar, and united with Sir Uvedale Price in reacting against the extremes and exaggerations of the landscape school of Brown and Repton. He speaks thus of the house and its immediate surroundings:

> "For this reason we require immediately adjoining the buildings of opulence and luxury that everything should assume its character; and not only be, but appear to be dressed and cultivated. In such places neat gravel walks, mown turf, and flowering plants and shrubs trained and distributed by art are perfectly in character.
>
> "In the decoration of grounds adjoining a house, much should depend on the character of the house itself; if it be neat and regular, neatness and regularity should accompany it; but if it be rugged and picturesque and situated amid scenery of the same character, art should approach it with more caution: for though

it be in itself an avowed work of art, yet the influence of time, with the accompaniments of trees and creepers, may have given it a character of nature which ought to be as little disturbed as is consistent with comfort: for after all the character of nature is more pleasing than anything that can be given by art. At all events, the character of dress and artificial neatness ought never to be suffered to encroach upon the park or the forest; where it is contrary to propriety as it is to beauty, and where its introduction by our modern landscape gardeners affords one of the most memorable instances of any recorded in the history of fashions of the extravagant absurdity with which an insensate passion for novelty may infect a whole nation."

The problem of how to plant around buildings should be solved by considering the house or stable as distinct and yet related, each one to be treated individually and collectively, especially with due regard to the general effect. The more the outbuildings are screened from the house the better, but there may be a like graduated treatment adopted as was shown in the case of the passage of the pleasure ground to the garden. The landscape treatment of the territory of the outbuildings and vegetable gardens needs as careful study as any other part of the estate in order to make a harmonious general effect.

Prince Pückler writes thus in *Hints on Landscape Gardening:*

> "Buildings should never stand freely exposed, lest they appear as spots, unconnected with the nature surrounding them. Concealment enhances beauty, and here something should always be left to the imagination. The eye frequently finds more pleasure in a single chimney in the distance, with its spiral of grey smoke curling upward against a background of trees, than in a bare palace exposed to view on all sides, which nature has not yet lovingly approached and embraced. It is highly important that buildings should always take on the character of the landscape in which they figure. A contrast may also occasionally fit in with the character of the whole, but it must always harmonize, as I have pointed out in the example in the last section: the sublimity of wild nature and magnificent art. A pretty villa would not be a fitting contrast, while an imposing ruin would present an analogy but no contrast. Many of our German architects regard this too little. Buildings in a city for instance must be different from buildings in a park. In the one case they are complete in themselves; but in the other they are only a component part of the whole and are dependent on it for picturesque effect, which they in turn are also called upon to produce; hence their effect in the landscape must be carefully studied."

In other words, there should be conformity to the character of the landscape in the design of the buildings. The landscape architect and architect need to study this problem in the utmost sympathy. It is not only the character of the buildings but the selection of the site, as before pointed out, that demands their co-operation in the interests of their client.

Here again in *Hints on Landscape Gardening*, chapter iv., Prince Pückler's words of advice are pertinent as illustrating one side of the question:

> "In general, a certain irregularity is preferable in buildings in a park, as being more in conformity with nature and more picturesque. A temple devoted to a cult, a theatre, a museum devoted to art, doubtless demand symmetry and a more severe style, but the mansion or villa gain by greater irregularity, in comfort as well as picturesqueness. This same principle appears in the designs of the ancient villas and country houses, as we may gather from the ruins. The most noteworthy example is perhaps the villa of Hadrian near Tivoli. Traces of this principle are also found in the Italy of the Renaissance, in the fifteenth and sixteenth centuries. Buildings half hidden by others, large and small windows on the same face of the building, side doors, projecting and receding corners, occasionally a high bare wall with a richly ornamented cornice, roofs jutting out and balconies unsymmetrically placed, in short, everywhere a great but by no means unharmonious irregularity, which pleases the fancy because the reason for every departure from regularity is evident or may be surmised."

In the same chapter there are some remarks on the selection of a site that are worth studying:

"The site of a building must also be carefully considered. For instance, a feudal castle in the midst of a level field of grain, as we find at Machern near Leipzig, appears somewhat comical. And so is the Egyptian pyramid which is to be found there in the idyllic surroundings of a gay birch wood. As well imagine a straw thatched hut surrounded by a French *parterre*. All these are undesirable contrasts that destroy the harmony. For example, pointed Gothic buildings would make an unfavourable impression if set among spruces and Lombardy poplars, while amongst oaks, beeches, and pines they would be quite in place. On the other hand, spruces and poplars harmonize with the horizontal lines of an oriental villa.

"The importance of harmonious beauty has for its corollary that the purpose of a building must be evident in its style. A Gothic house, for instance, which is nothing else, and has no other significance, being built just for the sake of having something Gothic on the grounds, produces a feeling of dissatisfaction. It is a *hors d'œuvre*, uncomfortable as a dwelling, and as a decoration unrelated to its surroundings; but if we see on a distant hill the spires of a chapel rising above the ancient trees, and we are told that this is the burial place of the family, or a temple actually used for worship, then we feel satisfied, because we find utility combined with fitting beauty.

"The same effect of dissatisfaction is produced by an immense palace set on a small estate, which is surrounded by the huts of poverty, or a vast park with an insignificant cottage in the centre.

"Buildings then must stand in appropriate relation to their surroundings and always have a positive purpose. Hence one should be very careful in the matter of temples, which in ancient times had a quite different, popular religious significance, and also with meaningless monuments, if they are to leave a deeply moving and not a trivial impression. The trite, incoherent manner in which in these days Mythology is taken up, makes it desirable to abandon it entirely, and similarly to refrain from the rule of inscriptions which are intended in certain localities to arouse certain sentiments.

"The most important building in the estate or park is naturally the dwelling house. It should be suited not only to the surroundings, but also to the position, the means, and even to the calling of the owner. The roomy castle and its battlements and towers are perhaps unsuitable to the merchant, but quite becoming to the noble aristocrat, the fame of whose family has been handed down for centuries, and whose forefathers really needed them, to enclose their abode in strongholds. The elder Repton (Amenity Repton so named) went so far as to hide entirely with trees the fine view of the city of Bristol, in order that the owner of a certain villa, a merchant who had retired from business, should not be unpleasantly reminded of his past cares and worries by beholding the city where he had spent his laborious days. This is thoroughly English, as well as the endeavour of many egotists there to hide from view everything that belongs to their place, no matter how picturesque it is. Without going so far, I will say here that the view from the dwelling house should harmonize as much as possible with the individual taste of the owner, since the eye always rests on it, and hence the view of the house should be secondary to the view from the house, while the reverse might hold good for most of the other buildings of the park."

Here evidently the author thinks the architect and landscape architect should work together. It might be well to add his remarks on the retention of old houses, which even in America have pertinence.

"Where there are genuine old castles (or manor houses) which have been in the possession of the family for a long time (not new buildings in imitation of an old style) I am of the opinion that their ancient character should be preserved when they are enlarged or made more comfortable, even if a much finer building might be erected on the spot. The memory of a bygone time, the majesty of years, also count for something, and it is a real misfortune that our pasteboard age has destroyed so many of these relics.

"The English have not yet been guilty of this folly, and nowhere else are family possessions more religiously and more proudly preserved. We also find there many estates of mere bourgeois families which for more than six centuries have passed from father to son, and with so little change in general that, for instance, in Malahide in Ireland, the family seat of the Talbots, even the woodwork and the furniture of entire apartments date back to those early years. And who can behold the splendours of majestic Warwick Castle, with its colossal tower a thousand years old, or the royal seat of the Duke of Northumberland, without feeling penetrated with romantic awe, and without delighting in the matchless beauty of these grand piles?"

An extract from Prince Pückler's *Tour of England* gives a wonderful idea of Warwick Castle from the landscape critic's point of view:

"It was an enchanted palace decked in the most charming garb of poetry, and surrounded by all the majesty of history, the sight of which still fills me with delighted astonishment." Again he writes: "Going on, you lose sight of the castle for a while, and soon find yourself before a high embattled wall, built of large blocks of stone, covered by Time with moss and creeping plants. Lofty iron gates slowly unfold to admit you in a deep hollow way blasted in the rock, the stone walls of which are tapestried with the most luxuriant vegetation. The carriage rolls with a dull heavy sound along the smooth rock, which old oaks darkly overshadow. Suddenly at a turn of the way, the castle starts from the wood into broad daylight, resting on a soft grassy slope; and the large arch of the entrance dwindles to the size of an insignificant doorway between the two enormous towers, at the foot of which you stand."

"Let your fancy conjure up a space about twice the size of the Coliseum at Rome, and let it transport you into a forest of romantic luxuriance. You now overlook the large court surrounded by mossy trees and majestic buildings, which, though of every variety of form, combine to create one sublime and connected whole, whose lines, now shooting upwards, now falling off into the blue air, with the continually changing beauty of the green earth beneath, produce, not symmetry indeed, but that higher harmony elsewhere proper to nature's own works alone."

And describing the scene more fully he writes in the same letter:

"The first glance at your feet falls on a broad simple carpet of turf, around which a softly winding gravel path leads to the entrance and exit of the gigantic edifice. Looking backwards, your eye rests on the two black towers of which the oldest, called Guy's Tower, rears its head aloft in solitary threatening majesty high above all the surrounding foliage as if cast in one mass of solid iron; the other, built by Beauchamp, is half hidden by a pine and a chestnut, the noble growth of centuries. Broad-leaved ivy vines climb along the walls, here twining around the tower, there shooting up to its very summit. On your left lies the inhabited part of the castle, and the chapel, ornamented with many lofty windows of various size and form, while the opposite side of the vast quadrangle, almost entirely without windows, presents only a mighty mass of embattled stone, broken by a few larches of colossal height and huge arbutuses which have grown to a surprising size in the shelter they have so long enjoyed. But the sublimest spectacle yet awaits you, when you raise your eyes straight before you. This fourth side, which has sunk into a low, bushy basin forming the court, and with which the buildings also descend for a considerable space, rises again in the form of a steep conical hill, along the sides of which climb the rugged walls of the castle. This hill and the keep which surrounds it are thickly overgrown at the top with underwood, which only creeps round the foot of the towers and walls. Behind, however, rise gigantic, venerable trees, towering above all the rock-like structure. Their bare stems seem to float in upper air; while at the very summit of the building rises a daring bridge, set, as it were, on either side within trees; and as the clouds drift across the blue sky, the broadest and most brilliant masses of light break magically from under the towering arch and the dark coronet of trees. . . . You must imagine the river at a great depth below the castle plain, and not visible from the point I have been describing. The first sight of it you catch is from the castle windows, together with the noble park, whose lines of wood blend on every side with the horizon. You ascend from the court to the dwelling rooms by only a few steps, first through a passage, and thence into a hall, on each side of which extend the entertaining rooms in an unbroken line of three hundred and forty feet. Although almost 'de plein pied' with the court, these rooms are more than fifty feet above the Avon, which flows on the other side. From eight to fourteen feet of thickness of wall forms, in each window recess, a complete closet, with the most beautiful varied view over the river, wildly foaming below, and farther on flowing through the park in soft windings till lost in the dim distance."

Note how the location of this castle fits in, adapts itself to the surrounding scenery and dominates and seems to own it all. It also shows how important the site of the building and how the most careful study should be given to its placing.

It may be truly said that the landscape can be just as well fitted to the building by a proper display of landscape-gardening ability as the building fitted to the landscape by the architect. Each one is needed to help the other; for in actual experience it is often found that a change of fifty feet will greatly improve the appearance of the house as well as that of the landscape as seen from the house.

In order to further realize the significance of what has been said in this chapter on the important subject of the location of buildings one instinctively remembers Haddon Hall. Take it altogether, Haddon Hall has come to be recognized by many of the best judges as the finest, although by no means the largest or most expensive, country seat in England. Most people instinctively prefer it to Versailles or the Italian villas, but it may be said that is a matter of taste, though good taste should naturally have a basis on acknowledged precedents of good art. In this respect Haddon has a great advantage in its setting. This all will concede is most admirable. It rests pleasantly on the gentle slope of a sidehill. On one side is a simple and broad terrace backed by the most wonderful beeches, which, standing in just the position they occupy, enhance the beauty and dignity of the house tenfold. Passing down the steps of the terrace one sees wide simple stretches of soft pastoral English landscape which is certainly the most beautiful in the world. The trees and grass spaces seem to love each other and the house rests quietly in the midst of them like a rare jewel.

VI

GRASS SPACES

"WHAT the gold backgrounds of the old masters, which set out the sweet, lovable faces of madonnas and saints in so ideal a manner, are to religious pictures, green luxuriant grass spaces are to a landscape. They are, as it were, the canvas of nature painting, the playground where the sun disports an element of brightness which sets out the whole landscape."[1]

By grass spaces, something more is meant than is usually understood by the term *lawn*. All the little corners and nooks of greensward are included, the glades edged with flowers and planted with trees and shrubs, the grass walks in the gardens and along the boundaries of plantations, the rides through woodland ways where saddle horse and carriage may find pleasant passage. These grass spaces are the choice spots of the place. It is there that the clouds play with their lights and shadows and the showers make diamond and silver nettings. No building that can be avoided,

[1] *Hints on Landscape Gardening*, Prince Pückler.

The Open Lawn near the Obelisk and the East Drive, near the Art Museum, Central Park, New York City.

From a Photograph by William Hale Kirk.

or that can be placed elsewhere, should usurp any part of this stretch of green. If the ancients worshipped trees and groves, surely, in the landscape scheme, it should be considered desecration, a treading on holy ground, to unnecessarily destroy greensward that flourishes in a favoured and fitting spot.

The illustration is taken from Central Park and its value lies in its open character. The eye revels in the rich green turf, passes with pleasure over the hill into the unknown with few trees, some of them just peering over the hill and thus disclosing a considerable declivity on the other side. To make these grass spaces illustrations of excellence the art of the skilful gardener needs employment for grading, and the principles of this art will be considered later. But for the benefit of those who may wish some general instructions concerning the establishment of a lawn it should be said that high culture is as necessary for grass space as for any other kind of vegetation natural to this climate. It is the fine pulverizing of the first two or three inches of the soil intended for a lawn that counts most. Deep ploughing or trenching and drainage are indispensable, but the aim should be to treat the cultivation of the top surface of the lawn very much as an onion patch.

Next comes the establishment of the proper mechanical condition and the fertility of the soil, possibly the most important of all in the attainment of final success. It is not necessary in a book of this character to indicate in detail peculiarities of soil, but only to point out that grass spaces need for their most perfect development nitrogenous fertilizers from natural sources, organic products like humus, stable or cow or sheep manure, as distinguished from superphosphates of lime, potash, and bone meal: these latter fertilizers are best suited to orchards, and for vegetables that grow quickly in one season. There is a valuable quality peculiar to stable manure of the right kind in its full strength that exactly suits the lawn, but the difficulty is to get such manure. It is either burned (fire-fanged) from neglect to turn it over and stir it up at the proper time, or it is mixed with poisonous disinfectants or sawdust or a superabundant amount of straw. So much for manure secured in the city. In the country no one wants to sell manure, especially the farmer who has use for all he can make. Consequently it is a good idea to make a storage place for all kinds of organic matter as well as ordinary manure and treat it with water and stir it and turn it over and drain it into a vat and thus develop and preserve its strength for future use. If stable manure is not available a good substitute for it is decomposed muck dried and pulverized and aërated.

As nature is apt to accomplish such work better and cheaper than man, it is a good idea to use a top dressing of muck soil taken from fields that have been used for trucking vegetables. This material when dried should contain about 80 per cent. humus with at least 3½ per cent. ammonia. The ash or remainder should be mainly silica and lime and a minimum of .35 per cent.

phosphoric acid and .40 per cent. potash. This, of course, may vary somewhat and still make a good top dressing.

Sandy ground as well as worn out ground is also greatly benefited by the application of a clay loam taken from good grass land or where crops have already thriven. The clay content of such loam should vary from 25 to 50 per cent., of the whole. This treatment may be said to be indispensable, in a way more so than manuring, to get the best results. Moreover, it should always be kept in mind that the problem is continually varying according to the nature of the special spot of land under consideration.

The use of clay, sand, lime, and stable manure or humus may seem to involve considerable expense. But their value for the establishment of a good lawn is great. If the foundations of a lawn are not well established by drainage and by cultivation and by enriching with a top dressing of clay soil or sand or manure, it will be comparatively useless to sow grass seed. These underlying principles of treatment of the soil need application first to give value to the skill displayed afterwards in carrying out such work.

"The ingredients in the soil may be divided into two classes: 1st, the purely mineral matters; 2d, the organic ingredients constituting the humus.

"There is a vast difference in the fertility of a sandy and a garden soil. Sandy soil may contain all the necessary mineral matters, but it lacks the something needed for plant growth which the garden soil contains. This something is called humus, an element rather difficult to define and still more difficult to describe in chemical terms. It is abundant in fertile soil, but scarce or wanting in barren soil. Though its chemical value is too complex to be stated or even known, its origin is easy to understand.

"Humus is the remains of life of previous generations. When plants die, their roots, together with their leaves, branches, and fruits, inevitably become incorporated into the soil. Animals, too, leave upon the ground a quantity of excrement and other discharges; and plants likewise probably discharge excretions into the soil. When animals die their bodies, also, may become mixed with the earth. Thus practically all kinds of organic matter from animals and plants are being mixed continually with mineral ingredients in the surface layers of the soil. The micro-organisms in the soil feed upon these dead materials, causing an extensive series of decompositions and recombinations. To this mass of complex organic bodies undergoing decomposition in the soil has been given the name humus. It will be evident from this explanation of its origin that humus cannot have a definite composition, and that it will hardly be alike in any two soils. It will be composed of different materials to start with, and there will be a variety of different stages of decomposition. We cannot hope to find any definite composition of humus, but we can study the kinds of decompositions and recombinations that are going on in it and that result in making it a suitable food for plants. In this study we must ever keep in mind the fact that dead bodies of animals and plants are not in condition to serve another generation of plants as food. We cannot feed plants upon eggs, or urine, or starches, or sugars. Though containing carbon and nitrogen in abundance, these elements are locked up in them out of the reach of the green plants, and before they can be utilized again they must be freed from their combinations and brought into simpler forms. This is accomplished by the micro-organisms (bacteria) in the soil. Our study of these changes may best be centred around the two chemical elements, *carbon* and nitrogen.

. . . .

"Farming without the aid of bacteria would be an impossibility, for the soil would yield no crops."[1]

Concerning the value of humus as a fertilizer many authorities may be quoted besides those in the footnote.[2]

[1] See *Agricultural Bacteriology*, H. W. Conn, Prof. Biology in Wesleyan University, Connecticut, U. S., 2d edition, p. 39.

[2] *Peat, Its Uses as Fertilizer and Fuel*, S. W. Johnson, p. 90, ed. 1859. Also *Soil*, etc., by Dr. E. W. Hilgard, Professor of Agriculture in the University of California and Director of the California Agricultural Experiment Station, ed. 1907, chapter v., pp., 72, 73, 74; chapter viii., chapter ix. Also in *Peat and Muck*, etc., by Saml. W. Johnson, Professor of Agricultural Chemistry, Yale College, U. S., edition 1859, pp. 67, 80, 81, 82; p. 107, Ans. 14; p. 109, Ans. 14; p. 113, Ans. 14; p- 121, Ans. 14; p. 145, Ans. 13; Remarks, 147, Ans. 13; Remarks, 149. Ans. 13. Also *Soils*, etc., S. W. Fletcher, Professor of Horticulture, Michigan Agricultural College, chapter iii., pp. 60, 61, 62; chapter xiii.

It makes really no difference whether the clay loam and humus or stable manure are mixed first and then applied or whether the two soils are applied separately; only for grass spaces they should not be mixed too deeply with the native soil, simply raked or harrowed two or three inches deep.

Virgin soil of high quality has always been the standard of fertility for almost any culture. The fact that virgin soil of high quality is rare and difficult to secure in most places will explain why this mixture of stable manure or humus and clay loam, the nearest approximation to virgin soil to be obtained, is recommended for top dressing on sandy soils. With heavy clay soils naturally the clay loam should be left out and possibly sand substituted.

Cultivation, that is aeration, is necessary for soils in order not only to remove acidity but to give activity to the fertilizing agents present. It is also wise to use lime to correct this same acidity and add a valuable element to the soil. An application of lime should be made about once in six or seven years. The application should not be greater than a ton to the acre, ordi-

---

chapter xii., pp. 323, 324, 327, 328, ed. 1908. Also, *Soils*, etc., Harry Snyder, pp. 113–114, 3d ed., 1908. Also Correspondence between Professor E. W. Hilgard and Samuel Parsons, Landscape Architect, of New York City, August, 1908. Also letter in 1914 to Professor Hilgard from S. Parsons, stating that the fertile soil treated with humus referred to in their correspondence of August, 1908, and applied at that time to a tract of land in Central Park on the west side of the Ramble and east side of the West Drive near 79th Street, Transverse Road, and the Swedish school house has accomplished and exhibits excellent results at the present time.

narily not more than 600 to 1000 pounds. To a certain degree the acidity present should control the amount used. The acidity is easy to test by means of litmus paper and there is no great difficulty in getting humus or dried muck, for there are cultivated patches of such land in the neighbourhood of most large cities.

Probably the most economical and best method of establishing the conditions most favourable for a lawn is the use of green crops. By spreading sufficient manure to make a green crop in case the soil is not rich enough for the purpose, a growth of legumes, like red clover, cow peas, vetches, and soy beans, can be readily secured. When this crop has grown, just before it reaches maturity, it should be turned under with a plough or spade. In this way the legumes will be enabled in the process of decay to add to the soil a larger amount of organic matter than would the non-legumes like rye, etc., as the legumes gather much of their nitrogen from the air through the agency of bacteria contained in their roots. This process will naturally cause a delay of a year or two but will eventually produce a superior lawn at the minimum expense.

The appearance of the grass spaces depends naturally on the character of the seed used. The general practice of the trade in grass seed is to use a considerable variety of kinds on the theory that in that way the exigencies of cold and drought and wet weather will be met more successfully, and that the turf will grow thicker and the roots be closer set. On the other hand, some prefer only three or four vigorous kinds—Kentucky or

Canadian Blue Grass (*Poa pratensis*), red top (*Agrostis vulgaris*), and brown Creeping Bent Grass (*Agrostis canina*). To this it is generally thought best to add white clover, which thrives on poor soil and in dry weather better than the other grasses named. It should be said, however, that a grass sod without a mixture of white clover is considered by many, and with good reason, likely to make a more attractive lawn. Some go so far as to recommend the use of one grass only and that the strongest growing kind of a permanent nature like the Kentucky or Canadian Blue Grass, the Canadian to be preferred for sandy soil and comparatively northern regions. It may be said, truly, that no matter how many kinds of grass seed are planted, the Blue Grass is likely sooner or later to almost entirely usurp the place of the others.

The use of the short-lived grasses like timothy, rye grass, and red clover, although well suited to go with and succeed for a few years a grain crop, is not suitable for a permanent lawn.

When the grass seed has been sown and properly rolled, it helps the young recently germinated seed to go safely through the winter to sow some grain (rye in autumn and oats in spring) to make what is called a cover crop.

It is interesting to note how much the treatment of lawns nearly one hundred years ago resembles that in vogue at present and especially how much even in those days properly prepared muck, or humus, and clay loam as a top dressing was valued.

"For the construction of lawns I can recommend the following rules, which the experience of several years in my neighbourhood has confirmed:

"(1) Whether in a meadow or for a park or pleasure ground it is of no avail to sow only one kind of grass seed. With only one kind of grass, perennial or not, it is not possible to secure a close grass texture.

"(2) For the first two, namely meadows and park, I consider the richest mixture to be the best, but with this proviso, that the particular kind of grass which experience has found to be the most suitable to the special soil should dominate, to the extent of a third to a half of the mixture. In wet ground the greater part timothy; for heavy soil, rye grass; for loam, yellow clover and French rye grass; for light soil, honey or velvet grass (*Holcus lanatus*); for high ground, white clover, etc.

"(3) If the plot that is to be sown is dry, it is advisable to trench it twelve to eighteen inches first, whatever the soil may be, but the top soil must be spread over the surface again if the soil below is inferior, and a sandy soil must of course be improved *by muck* (humus), *compost*, or *field* soil.

"If the expense of digging trenches is too costly. then one must plough to at least the usual depth, and in most cases still deeper with a subsoil plough. The field so prepared should be sown (here from the middle of August to the middle of September) in rather moist weather and very thickly, and the seed at once well rolled in. On heavy soil it is best to wait for a dry day. By the end of October the most beautiful green will already cover the new meadows. The next year they should be mown quite early, in order to obtain an even growth, but the seed should be allowed to ripen and fall to the ground, thus securing a greater density of turf for the following year. Nothing more is now necessary but to roll it well every year after each mowing, and every three or four years, as may be required, to fertilize it plentifully with a compost of field soil and muck, or with the manure from the place from which it can be easiest secured. In this manner on light rye soil, and to the surprise of many landowners, I have produced the most luxurious meadow, which, instead of giving out in ten years as was prophesied, steadily improved, and from a pecuniary point of view has proved quite a good investment, as in four years the capital spent on it has been repaid."[1]

One important feature of the grass spaces of the estate or park that should be carefully looked after is the degree to which it is mown or cut. Like the twigs or ends of the branches of trees and shrubs the charm of the blades of grass lies in their growing tips. They lend grace and life to the surface of grassy spaces. By skilful use of the scythe or the proper adjustment of the mowing-machine this object can be to a certain degree obtained, and it is a good idea to allow the grass in secluded nooks, especially on estates where there is

[1] *Hints on Landscape Gardening*, Prince Pückler, chapter vi.

no public to intrude, to grow at will, flower and seed, and then be cut down. In most places this would not be advisable, but a happy medium may be contrived, and the grass saved from looking shaven and shorn. The people who use lawns often fail to gain a sufficient realization of the need of care in their development. They would not think of walking over flowers or beautiful dwarf foliage plants used in bedding. Just as much in their own way do the blades of grass need to be cultivated and preserved. The limitations of the use of the mowing-machine should be strictly maintained during abnormally wet or dry weather, hot or cold weather, or during certain stages of growth. There is a colour and shade and actual grace peculiar to a lawn thus maintained that is of the highest importance in landscape gardening. The use of sheep on lawns has its advantages, and certainly the grass will do well under the effects of such pasturing, and gain a more natural appearance, and give a more pastoral effect.

VII

ROADS AND PATHS

"FOR what is the good of a park that presents the same recurring picture from a few points of view, a park where I am never led, as by an invisible hand, to the most beautiful spots, seeing and comprehending the picture in its entirety and at my ease? This is the purpose of roads and paths, and while they should not be unnecessarily multiplied, too many are better than too few. Roads and paths are the dumb conductors of the visitor and should serve in themselves to guide him easily towards every spot which could afford enjoyment. Roads and paths, therefore, should not be too conspicuous but should be carefully laid out and concealed by plantations. I mean too conspicuous in the English sense where a property of a thousand acres has only one or two main roads or paths, yet the opposite system of our imitation English gardens, where often two or three adjacent paths all show the same points of view and lead to the same spot, is also very objectionable.

"It follows from what I have said elsewhere that

the roads and paths should not run in continual curves like a serpent wound round a stick but should rather make such bends as serve a definite purpose easily and effectively, following as far as possible the natural contours of the ground. Certain æsthetic rules dictate these bends in themselves and hence in places obstacles must be set up where they do not naturally occur in order to make the graceful line appear natural. For instance, two curves close together in the same road or path seen at the same time do not look well. If this cannot be entirely avoided then a sharp turn should be relieved by a larger, more rounded turn and the former should seem justified by trees or plantations on the inner side, or by elevations where the road or path is apparently more easily led around than over them.

"See Plate V., *a*, *b*, *c*, and *d*. If there is no obstacle the road should be allowed to run straight or only slightly curved, no matter what the distance. Wherever an obstacle appears it is better to make a short turn close to it than a long gradual turn for the sake of the so-called curve of beauty. The sharp turns are by far the most picturesque, especially if the road disappears with such a turn in the depth of a forest. Nor should a road running parallel with another be visible from it unless there is a distinct division of hill and valley between or a dip in the ground, for without this natural division two adjacent paths leading in the same direction appear superfluous, especially when they are on the same level, for the mind must recognize the fitness of the details before the eye will be satisfied by the entire picture.

"In a landscape of wide sweep, the form given to the grass plots especially by the enclosing roads must be carefully considered. One may entirely spoil an extensive territory by a short piece of road badly arranged. I call to mind one example which first attracted my attention to this point. There is a hill in my park which extends out conspicuously in a wide stretch of meadow, thereby apparently dividing it into two equal parts. The river flows along this entire stretch of country and a road follows its course. See ground plan, *e*. Observe particularly the line of the ridge indicated by the shading in the plan, being the most conspicuous object in the neighbourhood, as well as the two markedly divided portions of the meadows which are overlooked by a certain building on the height. Another road leads to this building along the upper side and for the sake of convenience I required a footpath connecting the two roads which had to be at the left side leading to the castle. I first laid it down as in Plate V., *e*, where the ascent is easiest, this being the line it would follow in accordance with ordinary rules, yet I was never satisfied with it and although I changed the line ten times, the path persisted in spoiling the harmony of the view until it finally occurred to me that since the hill once for all conspicuously divided the prospect in two almost symmetrical portions, the path interrupting the stretch of

A Diagram Showing the Planting Scheme for Trees and Shrubs.

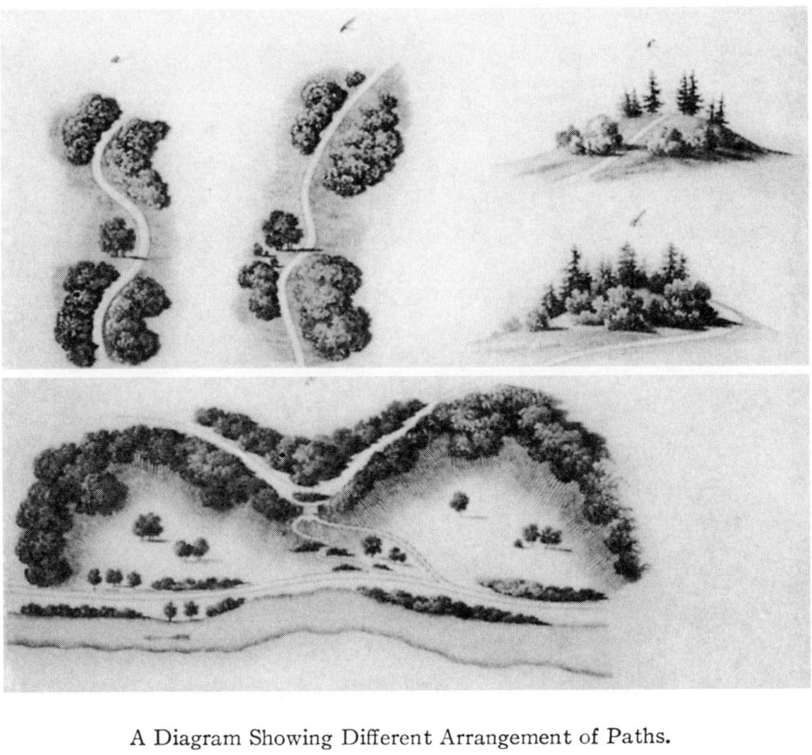

A Diagram Showing Different Arrangement of Paths.

From Pückler's Atlas, 1834.

meadow would have to follow the same direction so as not to destroy the harmony, or, if I may say so, the balance of the picture; for there is a certain kind of undefined, hidden symmetry in which there is no contradiction whatever, but which must be evident in every expanded arrangement of this kind, in order to produce a satisfactory effect. As soon as I changed the line of the path in agreement with this principle,—see *x*,—the matter was arranged satisfactorily. It may take a practised eye to understand this point on the plan, but the advantages gained by the change may be perceived by any one on the ground.

"Drives should be laid out so that chief points of interest and the most noteworthy objects in the entire park may be visited one after another without passing the same object twice, at least not in the same direction, on the round trip. This problem is frequently a peculiar one to solve; I may say I have given a good example in my park and it has cost me almost as much labour as the building of labyrinths may have cost our ancestors. The footpaths also must run into one another with this end in view, affording many separate paths, apparently undesigned, which should be connected together so as to leave a wide latitude of choice. Where one or several of the main roads or paths through the park are intended to serve as an approach (as it is called in English) to the castle or dwelling house, it should be concealed for a time to make the road appear long and more extended; but once the destination has come into view it is not well to allow the road to turn off any more unless there be a mountain or lake or other palpable obstacle for which the road must deviate." [1]

In *Hints on Landscape Gardening*, Prince Pückler also gives instructions relating to the construction of paths and roads and it is surprising how much the principles of the method recommended resemble those in vogue at the present day. But the construction of roads is an engineering problem and should be left to the engineer just as the architecture should be under the control of the architect.

A primary principle of road and path designing is to approach the subject with an instinctive sense that all roads and paths should be left out of the scheme as much as the exigencies of landscape effect and convenience will allow. In themselves they have no beauty, rather otherwise, hence wherever grass walks, or rides, or drives will suffice they are preferable on account of their unobtrusiveness. For the same reason their width should be minimized as much as the actual limitations of the situation will permit. It is hardly possible to give advice on the question of width, or as to the employment of grass for walks and drives, it is so entirely a question of wear and tear, of the number of vehicles, horses, and human beings who will be likely to use them.

The question of the character of the gutters is an

[1] *Hints on Landscape Gardening*, Prince Pückler.

important one, because, as generally constructed of stone, they are one of the least attractive features in the lawn or park. The best form they can take is that of grass or sod gutters which can be made almost imperceptible by keeping the centre of the drive or walk high in relation to the surrounding lawn. In order to insure success with these grass gutters, the drainage of the road or walk needs skilful treatment. If good drainage be secured and the centre of the walk or drive kept high the sod gutter can be constructed so shallow as to be hardly perceptible in the grass.

Another important suggestion in designing a road or walk is to avoid leaving little triangles or islands of grass or trees or shrubs, or all three, at the junctions of their several courses. It seldom makes a desirable effect, and is usually the result of a hasty or unintelligent solution of the problem. An open space even for a turn in front of the house is better suited to the general effect than if the road is carried round a formal oval of grass. Such a space moreover is certainly better suited for turning all kinds of vehicles. The road should also always *pari passu* enter the estate or park at right angles. The scene opens out in better shape, and one enters the place with equal ease, without a sharp turn, from whatever direction one is coming. The straight part should continue at least fifty feet into the property before it curves at all.

It has been already shown that all reverse curves in a road or path should be avoided, unless obstacles exist like a tree or large stone or building to evidently require its deviation from its natural sweep, but a further caution should be given to be careful not to make the artifice of placing a rock to excuse a curve too evident. The recourse to such obvious devices would tend to make the road take on a formality and sameness which would very likely be much worse than the most rigidly formal design of walks with straight lines and circles. The latter would start out with a distinct and entirely defensible purpose if it were located in the right portion of the place. A badly related, incongruous design is possibly the worst kind of landscape gardening and yet it prevails largely because the person who really controls the layout of the place probably fails to appreciate the difficulties involved and the necessity of basing the work on well conceived and definite principles.

Because the road or path is not in itself beautiful does not prevent the most attractive rural incidents from clustering along the borders. Mr. Olmsted expresses the same idea when he writes as follows in the Mt. Royal Park Report:

> "Taking then, as an illustration, a road (because it is the most unavoidably conspicuous artificial thing that you must have), you will have been compelled at various points by the topography to so lay it out, [that] though slightly curving, its course is open to view and excessively prominent far ahead, dissecting, distracting the landscape. Planting trees close upon the road, they must either be trimmed too high

to serve as a screen to its course ahead, or their limbs will in time obstruct passage upon the road. Your resort then must be bushes of species chosen with reference to the heights and breadth of foliage they will ultimately develop, with a view to the range of vision of observers in carriages. If there is a walk following the road it should, in such cases, be so far divided from it as to give room for the required bank of low foliage between it and the wheelway."

Messrs. Olmsted and Vaux made a joint report to be found in the Sixth Annual Brooklyn Park Reports (page 97), and they thus express their ideas on roads and paths:

"To illustrate the practical application of these views, we will take one of the many classes of arrangements for the accommodation of the movements of the public through a park, the drives or carriageway, and consider what is required of it. A drive must be so prepared that those using it shall be called upon for the least possible judgment as to the course to be pursued, the least possible anxiety or exercise of skill in regard to collisions or interruptions with reference to objects animate and inanimate, and that they shall as far as possible be free from the disturbance of noise and jar. To secure those negative qualities, the course of the road must be simple; abrupt turns must be avoided; steep grades that would task the horses or suggest that idea must not be encountered. The possibilities of the road becoming miry must be securely guarded against; its surface must also be smooth and be composed of compact material. These being the first and essential engineering considerations, it is necessary, secondly, that they should be secured in a manner which shall be compatible with the presentation of that which is agreeable to the eye in the surrounding circumstances; that is to say, the drive must either run through beautiful scenery already existing, or to be formed, and for this purpose it may be desirable at any point to deviate from the line which an engineer would be bound to choose as that which would best meet the first class of requirements. It must also be remembered that although the drive can hardly be expected in itself to add to the beauty of the scenery, it must always be more or less in view as part of it, and it should, therefore, be artistically designed so as to interfere as little as possible with the views and to present at all points agreeable and harmonious lines to the eye. Moreover, as it is desirable that at some point in the course of a drive through every park there should be an opportunity for those in carriages to see others and be seen by others, some portion of the ground which by development of natural suggestions cannot be made readily attractive to the eye should be chosen for the purpose. And here it will be proper that the application of art to inanimate nature as in architectural objects and by festive decorations of the

A Winding Road in the Trosachs.

From a Photograph.

outlines of the drive itself should distinctly invite attention and aid to produce a general suggestion of sympathy with human gaiety and playfulness."

The device is a good one of arranging roads and paths so that they may make decided turns when they reach some tree, or group of shrubs and trees, and thus find an excuse for turning and securing that short curve followed by a long curve which Prince Pückler so much prefers to the exactly repeated reverse, "the line of beauty" as it has been termed. This advice is doubtless excellent when the object exists around which to turn, but some go farther and advise the placing of trees and shrubs at points where turns would be desirable; and this again is not bad advice, provided the trees would be well placed if the road did not run there.

The ideal line for a road to approach the house is in one single sweep, but the limitations of trees and shrubs, convenience, and the opening out to view other scenes which present themselves often prevent this. On the same principle the road should approach the house on the least attractive side, that of the outbuildings and farming territory, leaving the secluded and most beautiful outlook in front of the living-rooms of the house, the dining-room, and library. All things being equal, the drive should reach the house on the side where the flower garden and vegetable garden are situated, and give an undisturbed pastoral effect to the lawn on the far side.

The illustration "The Trosachs" shows why a

road winding away from the eye through park or wild woodland gives so much pleasure. The eye loses the drive around a graceful curve and as one moves along bits of road and scenery keep opening ahead and one wonders what is coming next. Change and surprise form important elements of pleasure in landscape gardening.

If conditions, however, force or strongly suggest the use of a straight road, there is no rule of good taste that should prevent its employment. The trees along its borders should be of a character and size that will give it dignity, but at the same time there should be a diversity of the grading or topography of the lawn nearby, and above all a pleasing variety of shrubs between a number, though not necessarily all, of the trees. To leave open spaces at intervals, provided the views there are attractive, would be an advantage.

The illustration shown of the straightaway road on the east of Central Park indicates how such an arrangement can be made agreeable in cramped and uninteresting conditions, and the same rule applies to paths or walks. Curving paths are the most agreeable to the eye, but if the dignity or exigencies of the place require it, there is no reason why the straight ones should not be used. It is well to remember that to make a straight path among curved ones may seriously disturb the harmony of the entire scene, but the straight path in the illustration of Lovers' Lane in Central Park shows that the scene can be so diversified by planting as to prevent the formality from marring the beauty of the scene.

A Straight Drive on the East Side of the Reservoir between 86th and 94th Streets, Central Park, New York City.

VIII

WATER

"EVEN if fresh and clear water (whether stream or lake) is not so indispensable to landscape as a rich vegetation, it greatly increases its charm. Eye and ear are equally delighted, for who does not hearken with delight to the sweet murmur of the brook, the distant plashing of the mill wheels, the prattling of the pearly spring—who has not been enchanted in quiet hours by the perfect calm of the slumbering lake in which the giants of the forest are dreamily mirrored, or the aspect of foaming waves, chased by the storm, where the sea-gulls merrily rock? But it is very difficult for the artist to conquer nature here, or to impose on her what she herself has not created on the spot.

"Therefore, I would advise rather to leave undone altogether a faulty imitation. A region without water can yet present many beauties, but a stinking swamp infects everyone; the first is only a negative fault, the second a positive, and with the exception of the owner himself nobody will take a cesspool of this kind for a lake, or a stagnant ditch overgrown with duckweed for a stream. But if one can by any means guide a running stream into the domain of one's own property, if the terrain gives any prospect of it, one should do one's utmost, and forego neither expense nor pains to acquire such a great advantage, for nothing offers such an endless variety to the beholder as the element of water.

"But in order to give the water, artificially obtained, whatever form it may take, a natural, unforced appearance, much trouble is necessary. In the whole art of landscape gardening, perhaps nothing is more difficult to accomplish.

"Several of the rules which I have given for laying out the roads and for the outlines of the plantations can be readily applied to the shape of the water effects. As in the former case one can, according to the requirements of the terrain and the obstacles that occur, bring in sometimes long and sometimes short, abrupt bends, making, for preference, rounded corners rather than semicircles, sometimes even quite sharp turns where the water is visibly diverted. Both banks of a stream or brook should follow fairly parallel lines, yet with various nuances, which must be decided not according to one's fancy, but by the laws determined by its course. Two rules hold good almost universally:

"1. The side towards which the stream turns should have a lower shore than the opposite, because the higher one diverts it.

"2. Where the current of the water suddenly be-

Lover's Lane, a Winding Walk Parallel with the South Side of the South Reservoir, Central Park, New York City.

From a Photograph by William Hale Kirk.

comes swift and yet needs to be turned aside lest it break bounds if left free, a sharp bend should be constructed rather than a round one and a steeper shore should signify the conflict. But never follow what our gardeners call 'noble lines.' I suppose the terrain to be the same in both cases. The old practice would give the line of the stream as illustrated in *a;* the student of nature will try to make it something like *b*.

"Frequently, larger and smaller promontories, as well as deep bays, tend to give the scene a natural appearance, and it is equally effective to vary the height and form of the crown or upper part of the shore. One must be careful to avoid high finish in constructing the slope of the shore in such a way as to betray the artificial work.

"An exception to this may be made in the case of the pleasure ground, but here also it would be well to strike a middle course between nature and cultivation. See *c* for the stiff and *d* for the more natural bare shore, *e* for the advantages of variety in the shores on both sides. The plantation supplies what is still lacking and completes the whole by the free play of the overhanging branches. It would hardly be possible to give an entirely natural appearance to an artificial shore without a plantation.

"If one would like a larger, more lakelike expanse of water, which is especially desirable in the view from the mansion, one should so treat it, partly by means of islands, partly by very deep bays, the limits of which are mostly concealed in shrubbery, that from no one point the whole mass of water can be overlooked, but that everywhere behind the thick shrubbery the water appears to flow onward; otherwise, every piece of water will appear small, even though it take an hour to walk round it. Open, grassy shores, single high trees, woods and thickets should vary the effect with broad spots where the sunlight can have full entry in order not to deprive the water of its transparency and brillancy by concealment. A lake whose shores are entirely in shadow loses much of its effectiveness, as the water reveals all its magic only under the full rays of the sun where the reflections from above appear to come from the bottom in transparent silvery clearness. I have frequently seen this very necessary rule quite ignored by unskilful gardeners. The projecting tongues of land must for the greater part run into pointed, not rounded, ends, for I cannot sufficiently dwell on the fact that no line in picturesque landscape is more unpropitious than that taken from the circle, especially in any great extent of space. A green shore which ends quite in a point and is at its termination almost in the same line as the water, and beyond which the water appears on the other side, makes quite a charming variety, especially when a few high-stemmed trees stand on it, and where one looks through under the foliage. If any important object is in the neighbourhood of a building, mountain, or conspicuous tree, plenty of room should be given for its reflection

An Artificial Lake at Skylands—a Country Estate in New Jersey.
From a Photograph by William J. Wilson.

in the water, and attention drawn to the picture shimmering in its depths by a path or bench placed there for the purpose.

"The form *f* is by no means the worst which I have seen carried out, nor will I say that *g* is the best for execution; but the latter will assuredly make a more picturesque effect, and from no point of view will the end of the water be visible, which is one of the chief considerations."[1]

The interesting part of the above dissertation is that Prince Pückler carried out his principles and directions, as they are here set forth, in an entirely successful manner on his own estate at Muskau, where the results can be seen to-day after the lapse of nearly a century.

Not long before the time of Prince Pückler we find Humphry Repton in *The Art of Landscape Gardening* expressing the following sound views on the subject of the use of water in the landscape:

"The general cause of a natural lake or expanse of water is an obstruction to the current of the stream by some ledge or stratum of rock which it cannot penetrate, but as soon as the water has risen to the surface of the rock, it tumbles over with great fury, wearing itself a channel among the craggy fragments and generally forming an ample basin at the foot. Such is the scenery we must attempt at Thorsby.

"When under the guidance of Le Notre and his

[1] *Hints on Landscape Gardening*, Prince Pückler.

disciples the taste for nature in landscape gardening was totally banished or concealed by the work of art. Now in defining the shape of land or water, we take nature for our model, and the highest perfection of landscape gardening is to imitate nature so judiciously that the influence of art shall never be detected."

However satisfactory we may find the words of Prince Pückler and Humphry Repton on the subject of the use of water in landscape gardening, the excellent and extended study of Thomas Whately on similar lines should not be overlooked. It conveys much valuable advice:

"So various are the characters which water can assume, that there is scarcely an idea in which it may not concur, or an impression which it cannot enforce: a deep, stagnated pool, dank and dark with shades which it dimly reflects, befits the seat of melancholy; even a river, if it be sunk between two dismal banks and dull both in motion and colour, is like a hollow eye which deadens the countenance; and over a sluggard, silent stream creeping heavily along all together, hangs a gloom, which no art can dissipate nor even the sunshine disperse. A gently murmuring rill, clear and shallow, just gurgling, just dimpling, imposes silence, suits with solitude, and leads to meditation: a brisker current which wantons in little eddies over a bright sandy bottom,

On the Shore of the Harlem Mere, Central Park, New York City.

From a Photograph by William Hale Kirk.

or babbles among pebbles, spreads cheerfulness all around; a greater rapidity and more agitation to a certain degree are animating; but in excess, instead of wakening, they alarm the senses: the roar and the rage of a torrent, its force, its violence, its impetuosity, tend to inspire terror; that terror which, whether as cause or effect, is so nearly allied to sublimity. . . . But it is not necessary that the whole scene be bounded: if form be impressed on a considerable part, the eye can, without disgust, permit a large reach to stretch beyond its ken; it can even be pleased to observe a tremulous motion in the horizon, which shows that the water has not there attained its termination. Still short of this, the extent may be kept in uncertainty; a hill or a wood may conceal one of the extremities, and the country beyond it, in such a manner as to leave room for the supposed continuation of so large a body of water. Opportunities to choose this shape are frequent, and it is the most perfect of any: the scene is closed, but the extent of the lake is undetermined: a complete form is exhibited to the eye, while a boundless range is left open to the imagination. But mere form will only give content, not delight; that depends upon the outline, which is capable of exquisite beauty; and the bays and the creeks and the promontories, which are ordinary parts of that outline, together with the accidents of islands, of inlets and of outlets to rivers, are in their shapes and their combinations an inexhaustible fund of variety. A straight line of considerable length may find a place in that variety, and it is sometimes of singular use to prevent the semblance of a river in a channel formed between islands and the shore. But no figure perfectly regular ought ever to be admitted; it always seems artificial, unless the size absolutely forbids the supposition. A semicircular bay, though the shape be beautiful, is not natural; and any rectilinear figure is absolutely ugly; but if one line be curved, another may sometimes be almost straight; the contrast is agreeable; and to multiply the occasions of showing contrasts may often be a reason for giving several directions to a creek and more than two sides to a promontory.

"Bays, creeks, and promontories, though extremely beautiful, should not, however, be very numerous, for a shore broken into little points and hollows has no certainty of outline, it is only ragged not diversified; and the distinctness and simplicity of the great parts are hurt by the multiplicity of subdivisions: but islands, though the channels between them be narrow, do not so often derogate from greatness; they intimate a space beyond them whose boundaries do not appear; and remove to a distance the shore which is seen in perspective between them. Such partial interruptions of the sight suggest ideas of extent to the imagination.

"The inlets and outlets of rivers have similar effects; fancy pursues the course of the stream far beyond the view—no limits are fixed to its excursions. The greatest composition of water is that which is in part a lake, and in part a river, which has all the expanse of the one, and all the continuation of the other, each being strongly characterized to the very point of their junction: if that junction breaks into the side of the lake, the direction of the river should be oblique to the line it cuts—rectangular bisections are in this, as in all instances, formal; but when the conflux is at an angle, so that the bank of the river coincides with one shore of the lake, they should both continue for some way in the same direction; a deviation from that line immediately at the outlet detaches the lake from the river.

"Though the windings of a river are proverbially descriptive of its course, yet without being perpetually wreathed, it may be natural; nor is the character expressed only by its turnings. On the contrary, if they are too frequent and sudden the current is reduced into a number of separate pools, and the idea of progress is obscured by the difficulty of tracing it. Length is the strongest symptom of continuation; long reaches are therefore characteristic of a river, and they conduce much to its beauty; each is a considerable piece of water and a variety of beautiful forms may be given to their outlines, but a straight one can very seldom be admitted; it has the appearance of a cut canal, unless great breadth, a bridge across it, and strong contrasts between the objects on the banks disguise the formality. A very small curvature obliterates every idea of art and stagnation; and a greater is often mischievous; for an excess of deviation from a straight towards a circular line shortens the view, weakens the idea of continuation, and though not chargeable with stiffness, yet approaches to regularity; whereas the line of beauty keeps at a distance from every figure which a rule can determine or a compass describe.

"A considerable degree of roundness is, however, often becoming, where the stream changes its direction, and if the turn be effected by a sharp point of land on one side, there is the more occasion for circuity on the other. The river should also be widened under that other bank; for it is the nature of water thus driven out of its course to dash and encroach upon the opposite shore; where this circumstance has been attended to, the bend appears natural; and the view ending in space gives scope to the imagination: the turn therefore ought generally to be larger than a right angle; if it be less, it closes immediately, and checks the idea of progress.

"Water is so universally and so deservedly admitted in a prospect, that the most obvious thought in the management of it is to lay it as open as possible, and purposely to conceal it would generally seem a severe self-denial: yet so many beauties may attend its passage through a wood, that larger portions of it might be allowed to such retired scenes, that are commonly spared from the view, and the different parts in different styles would then be fine contrasts to each other. If the water at Wotton (the seat of Mr. Greville, in the vale of Aylesbury

A View of the River as Arranged and Improved by Prince Pückler von Muskau, in his Park at Muskau, Silesia, Germany.

Redrawn from an Old Print.

The Boundary Fence on the Park of Prince Pückler von Muskau, Silesia, Germany.

Redrawn from an Old Print.

in Buckinghamshire) were all exposed, a walk of near two miles along the banks would be of a tedious length from the want of those changes of the scene, which now supply through the whole extent a succession of perpetual variety. That extent is so large as to admit of a division into four principal parts, all of them great in style and in dimensions; and differing from each other both in character and situation. The two first are the least; the one is a reach of a river, about a third of a mile in length, and a competent breadth, flowing through a lovely mead, open in some places to views of beautiful hills in the country, and adorned in others with clumps of trees, so large that their branches stretch quite across, and form a high arch over the water. The next seems to have been once a formal basin encompassed with plantations; and the appendages on either side still retain some traces of regularity; but the shape of the water is free from them; the size is about fourteen acres; and out of it issue two broad collateral streams, winding towards a large river, which they are seen to approach, and supposed to join. A real junction is, however, impossible, from the difference of the levels, but the terminations are so artfully concealed that the deception is never suspected; and when known is not easily explained. The river is the third great division of the water; a lake into which it falls is the fourth. These two do actually join; but their characters are directly opposite; the scenes they belong to are totally distinct; and the transition from one to the other is very gradual, for an island near the conflux, dividing the breadth, and concealing the end of the lake, moderates for some way the space, and permitting it to expand but by degrees, raises an idea of greatness, from uncertainty accompanied with increase. The reality does not disappoint the expectation; and the island which is the point of view is itself equal to the scene; it is large and high above the lake; the ground is irregularly broken; thickets hang on the sides; and towards the front is placed an Ionic portico which commands a noble extent of water, not less than a mile in circumference, bounded on one side with wood, and open on the other to two sloping lawns, the least of a hundred acres, diversified with clumps, and bordered by plantations; yet this lake when full in view and with all the importance which space, form, and situation can give, is not more interesting than the sequestered river, which has been mentioned as the third great division of the water. It is just within the verge of a wood, three quarters of a mile long, everywhere broad, and its course is such as to admit of infinite variety, without any confusion. The banks are clear of underwood; but a few thickets still remain; on one side an impenetrable covert soon begins; the interval is a beautiful grove of oaks, scattered over a greensward of extraordinary verdure. Between these trees and these thickets the river seems to glide gently along, constantly winding, without one short turn, or one extended reach, in the whole length of the way. The even temper in the stream suits the scenes through which it passes; they are in general of a very sober cast; not melancholy, but grave; never exposed to a glare; never darkened with gloom; nor by strong contrasts of light and shade exhibiting the excess of either; undisturbed by an excess of prospects without, or a multiplicity of objects within, they retain at all times a mildness of character which is still more forcibly felt when the shadows grow faint as they lengthen; when a little rustling of birds in the spray, the leaping of the fish, and the fragrancy of the woodbine denote the approach of evening; while the setting sun shoots its last gleams on a Tuscan portico, which is close to the great basin, but which from a seat near this river is seen at a distance, through all the obscurity of the wood, glowing on the banks, and reflected on the surface of the water."

Here are good words about flowers on the waterside:

"One beautiful way in which flowers can be used, especially those distinguished for the brightness and clearness of their colouring, or for their tall stalks, is to plant them in moss and among wild vegetation along the edge of a brook or some other piece of water. The reflections in the water and the play of their movements thus doubled clothed with a new charm this scene which is altogether natural."[1]

Throughout all these quotations, however, no one

[1] Hirschfeld's *Theorie der Garden Kunst*, Leipzig, 1777.

dwells on the importance of the margin, the lip of the shore of a stream, or a lake, or a pool. Landscape gardening can display no greater skill than the work that can be done in varying the line which touches the water with myriads of changes even in small ways so that the eye is continually diverted. It is so that nature works, and we will see it, if we observe with seeing eyes. Here a secret cove with pond lilies and water plants, there a point on which grows, with its roots in the water, a fine tree, a scarlet maple or a willow, or perhaps it is a rock all moss-grown. The grass—not cement under any circumstances—on the edge of an open lawn coming down to the water may sink its feet directly in the pool or stream, where its green will be reflected in the most charming manner. There is no end to the effects; all kinds of drooping shrubs may hang the ends of their curving branches in the water, and trees and shrubs redouble their beauty by their reflected images. Rushes may gather along the banks, and irises thrust themselves beyond the margin. Beaches of sand and gravel should also find places where they would naturally assume shape and remain quiescent until some freshet comes along. It is the end, the margin, the border, the tip of everything that counts above all things in the landscape picture. The margin of the shrub groups, the shore line we have termed it, gives the lawn its true value in the scene: the tips of the branches of the shrubs and trees mark their character in most cases more than anything else, and make much of their charm and beauty. It is for this reason, if for no other, that shearing of shrubs seems an unkind proceeding.

In the same way, we should seek to touch and beautify the very edge and margins of our water spaces on nature's lines, with all the devices of horticulture. Such refinements of landscape gardening are after all the supreme result to be sought, for it is these seemingly minor things, these small touches, that make for perfection. Again the warning should be reiterated that all sense of effort, all fussiness, should be avoided, and simple and relatively large effects alone sought. Above all, any attempt to exhibit variety of plant forms as horticultural curiosities is specially objectionable.

Water used in the form of fountains should find no place on an estate or park except in the midst of some architectural development, among trees if possible, in a portico, a court, a plaza or esplanade, or in some stately garden in connexion with buildings. Waterfalls, cascades, rapids, that dash and resound and trickle and murmur, and swing and sweep, and in so many ways delight the eye and ear, are desirable above most landscape-gardening effects; but the attempt to produce such effects had better be limited to places where water features already exist, and dash and trickle of their own volition. A rock can be added here, and a plant there, or a shrub and tree, and greatly increase the attractions. Water, plants, rocks, and soil can undoubtedly be gathered together in distinctly natural forms that will not insult the surrounding scenery by their incongruities, but it will be a difficult undertaking and should not be attempted except after due consideration and the full recognition that failure is quite likely, and that the work may have to be done over more than once. Landscape gardening affords more temptations than most occupations to dream dreams the practical realization of which will be found almost if not quite impossible.

In order to form some idea of what the construction of an ideal lake means the accompanying illustration is given of Prof. C. S. Sargent's artificial lake on his estate of Holm Lea, Brookline, Boston, Mass.

> "It was formed by excavating a piece of swamp and damming a small stream which flowed through it. In the distance toward the right the land lies low by the water and gradually rises as it recedes. Opposite us it forms little wooded promontories with grassy stretches between. Where we stand it is higher, and beyond the limits of the picture to the left it forms a high steep bank rising to the lawn on the farther side of which stands the house. The base of these elevated banks and the promontories opposite are planted with thick masses of rhododendrons, which flourish superbly in the moist peaty soil, protected as they are from drying winds by the trees and high ground. Near the low meadow a long stretch of shore is occupied with thickets of hardy azaleas. Beautiful at all seasons, the pond is most beautiful in June when the rhododendrons are ablaze with crimson and purple and white and

An Artificial Lake Bordered by Rhododendrons, Irises, and Other Water Plants at Holm Lea, the Estate of Professor Charles A. Sargent, Brookline, Mass.

From a Photograph by Thomas E. Marr & Son. (Reproduced by Permission.)

when the yellow of the azalea beds—discreetly separated from the rhododendrons by a great clump of low-growing willows—finds delicate continuation in the buttercups that fringe the daisied meadows. The lifted banks then afford particularly fortunate points of view: for as we look down upon the rhododendrons, we see the opposite shore and the water with its rich reflected colours as over the edge of a splendid frame. No accent of artificiality disturbs the eye despite the unwonted profusion of bloom and variety of colour. All the plants are suited to the place and in harmony with each other; and all the contours of the shore are gently modulated and softly connected with the water by luxuriant growths of water plants. The witness of the eye alone would persuade us that nature unassisted had achieved the whole result. But beauty of so suave and perfect a sort as this is never a natural product. Nature's beauty is wilder if only because it includes traces of mutation and decay which here are carefully effaced. Nature suggests the ideal beauty, and the artist realizes it by faithfully working out her suggestions."[1]

The two views of castle and moat at Muskau are full of suggestions. The ancient moat has been enlarged in one case to a small lake with charming plantations of trees and shrubs on its borders, and the other, with the moat disappearing from the eye, appeals to the imagination and takes the memory back to ancient days.

[1] *Garden and Forest*, vol. i., p. 8.

The view which shows a pool in Central Park on the west side near 77th Street might well be the moat of a feudal castle like that of Muskau, but its background which makes it so picturesque is simply the south-east tower of the Natural History Museum. There is a winding path that goes down to the water for the benefit of horseback riders who may be passing on the bridle path nearby.

The view of Durham Cathedral is somewhat familiar. The reason for its introduction is to show how much water adds to the value of the view of a noble building.

The water-soaked margins of our ponds and lakes furnish a home for many graceful, fine foliage and flowering plants. Necessary variations of height and impressiveness are made with the great Gunnera and the lesser heights with irises or daffodils or the little water-lily (*Nymphæa pygmea*).

The question which we need to consider here is the way they should be used on the shores of the pools and streams of the landscape picture. We are again called to study the homes where such plants live nearby, on, or in the water, and to see where they appear to best advantage. An eye keenly alive to such opportunities for study will see many things along the banks of brooks and lakes that are suggestive and worth imitating in water planting. It will see first of all, especially in confined areas, pools and arms of a lake or stream, that there should be plenty of water surface left uncovered by planting. The level space is the *eye* of the

The Castle and the Moat, and a View of the Park on the Estate of Prince Pückler von Muskau, Silesia, Germany.

From a Photograph by Thomas W. Sears.

A Castle, Lake, and Moat on the Estate of Prince Pückler von Muskau.

From a Photograph by Thomas W. Sears, Providence, R. I.

leafage of the park,—the unbroken grass space; in the same way the open water is the eye of the water picture. It gives breadth and composition to the scene, allows play of sunlight and reflection of leaf and flower in the water and brooding of shadows on its surface. The principles of design are the same, if one will only pause to consider; whether it be a woodland grass patch in a recess, a stream, or a great park meadow with shrubs and trees receding in bays or boldly thrusting themselves forward in promontories with expanse and freedom of level space around them. It is all a matter of scale—the small and the large, breadth and height, colour and scent, they all aspire, reach upward, lift, feel their strength to conquer and then give way and yield, until finally there is an interval of peace, of rest, when the smooth space stretches out to bear on its liquid or green bosom the sun's rays and the drifting shadows, to give to the open water a little quiet to receive the sunset's last glowing touches and to settle down finally into the soft odorous gloom of evening. Then there are the battles of the seasons, heat and cold, freshet, and storm wind. Even the little waterside flower has to fight for its life, but it, too, gains its victory, and rest and happiness after all the disaster. The beauty and the modesty of the riverside flower is not to be gainsaid in the days of its victory. No stately plants of the palace garden can surpass it in loveliness. Can any denizen of the formal garden surpass in charm the subject of these beautiful lines:

The woodland willow stands a lonely bush
Of nebulous gold,
There the Spring Goddess comes in faint attire
Of frightened fire.

The golden willows lift
Their boughs the sun to sift,
Their sprays they droop to screen
The sky with veil of green,
A floating cage of song
Where feathered lovers throng.[1]

The beauty and the dainty charm of plants, trees, and shrubs and flowers on the waterside transcends description. What a fascination there is in the water-lilies, Nuphar, Nelumbium, and Nymphæa—and it is not easy to locate them rightly. It needs study and it should not be undertaken lightly, although easy enough if you know how to do it. Without much study and observation success in managing these little water plants is not easy to attain. The following lines of Robert Bridges show a fine knowledge of the common water-lily of lakes and streams, a knowledge of a kind that is often lacking in poets:

But in the purple pool there nothing grows,
Not the white water-lily spoked with gold,
Though best she loves the hollows, and well knows
On quiet streams her broad shields to unfold,
Yet should her roots but try within these deeps to lie,
Not her long-reaching stalk could ever hold her waxen head so high.[1]

[1] Robert Bridges, *Poems*, p. 307, 1912.

The Natural History Museum in Manhattan Square, and in Connection with it a Pool and Bridge in Central Park, New York City.

IX

ISLANDS

THE design and construction of islands in rivers and streams and lakes or ponds requires much study of the spot where they are to be made, and also the exercise of the memory to accumulate examples for consideration, which, though not exactly the same, will be helpful.

I recall for instance a wonderful afternoon, sailing through the upper reaches of Lake George, New York State. The day was showery and as the mists gathered and dispersed and the sun now came out and now disappeared, the illusions of light and shade were magical. Islands of all sizes from a few rocks to cedar-clothed hills loomed up on every side and then disappeared. Ever changing, it was like some scene in fairyland, unearthly, unreal—the mind seemed transported to a space between lake and sky where the islands had a realm of their own. There were thousands of them and the study of how many of them were growing from a few rocks into larger and larger masses of trees, rocks, soil, and grass was most instructive, most illuminating.

"Islands scattered in a large lake or judiciously arranged in the broad flowing river are of great assistance and add much to the beauty of the whole by their variety. Here, too, the example of nature must be very fully studied. It is remarkable how seldom this is the case and I can hardly remember having seen anywhere an artificial island which did not betray at first glance its forced, unnatural origin. Thus I recently found, even in the small celebrated royal gardens attached to Buckingham House, which I have highly praised elsewhere, one which represented more the picture of a pudding in its sauce, than an island built up by nature. It is true that nature sometimes indulges in peculiar freaks, but there is always *je ne sais quoi*, which cannot be attained by mere imitation, therefore it becomes us to follow her rules, not her exceptions.

"Generally, as I have said, artificial islands can be recognized at the first glance. Their shape is either oval or round, sloping down equally on all sides, (see Plate VII., *e*,) and they are planted at random in separate patches, see *i*. Nature forms them quite otherwise, seldom by building up, more frequently by erosion. For how is an island originated? First, either a piece of land has withstood the pressure of the flood by its height and solidity, see *a*; or secondly, it has been forcibly torn asunder, see *b*; or it may be an eminence has been quietly surrounded by a stream in its course; or finally accumulated soil, having been borne along by the stream, remains after the

Park Treatment of Water in the Neighbourhood of Durham Cathedral, England.
From a Photograph by F. Hovey Allen.

flood has receded, as an island standing above low water, see *c*.

"Where the water flowing swiftly into a basin forms an island at the inlet, it will take about the shape of *d*; following the outer banks, the swiftly flowing stream by its strong pressure on both sides will somewhat round the ends. But if the river widens into a lake by gently filling a deep basin, rather than rushing into it, then *e* may be assumed as the natural shape, for here the river doesn't round off both sides, but forms in a slow current on the right, a long spit on the left bank, beyond which the quiet water, no longer in a powerful stream, proceeds and gently flows round the higher ground. Very seldom, on the other hand, does a stream flow into such a basin as is generally made out, after the model of a bottle, see *f*.

"Let the surface and shelving of an island on the same principle be constructed in accordance with the probable effect of the terrain and the water which washes it. The equal shelving on all sides and the equality of height throughout is the commonest mistake. I fell into this error at first; *g* is bad and *b* is good.

"But even the best forms may be bettered by plantations skilfully arranged covering the spots that appear less satisfactory and giving more variety to the surface without disturbing the harmony, concerning which the right feeling certainly must again decide; united taste and experience, recognizing the proper course, knows what cannot be altogether taught by correct rule. Islands planted down to the water's edge cannot be quite failures, be their shape what it may, and if the spirit of the scene is to be followed it may be the only alternative. I should never recommend leaving the shores of the island entirely unplanted, see *i* and *k*, even if it is a very good form, since the bare outline of nature, if I may so express it, is the most difficult of all to imitate. Finally one must confess that with all our endeavours to emulate nature, she yet retains *in petto* something unattainable, and says to us poor human beings, 'Thus far and no farther.'"[1]

Prince Pückler in his *Tour in England* writes:

> "It is necessary to study the forms of water for the details, but the principal thing is never to suffer an expanse of water to be completely overlooked or seen in its whole extent. It should break on the eye gradually, and if possible lose itself at several points at the same time in order to give full play to the fancy—the true art in all landscape gardening."

The actual construction of an island should be done on solid foundations of earth or stone and good drainage secured. A rock here and there on the shores, if rocks already exist in the neighbourhood, will give a natural appearance and diversify the effect. Little miniature islands, outside of the main island, even a

[1] Prince Pückler, *Hints on Landscape Gardening.*

few bits of stone with a little earth and a shrub or two, or just a few bare rocks jutting out on the surface of the water, tailing off as if they were small islands in the train of a big one, are found in thousands of places in the lakes of the country and are suggestive of this kind of landscape gardening that should be undertaken.

The clothing of islands with trees and shrubs should be in harmony with the growth of the shores nearby. If young plants are selected almost any of the woodland types can be used; elms, maples, alders, white willows, birches can all be used, but the kinds similar to those on the neighbouring shore should predominate. Where the mainland is free from woods, it is a good idea to throw across the water on the shore a mass of similar island growths. The repeating of a note of foliage in this manner is always effective and should be used in various ways throughout the neighbourhood as well as on the islands. All formalism in the planting should be avoided and the trees and shrubs grouped in many sizes, but for the sake of a considerable mass of colour, masses of one sort should be used together. If a small valley or cleft in the crest of an island occurs, it should not be planted, except with low shrubs or undergrowth, so as to emphasize the variety of surface and increase the contrast or contradiction of parts which contributes so much to the beauty and picturesqueness of the landscape.

It takes almost a special gift to compass these natural effects, but the above simple hints or suggestions will place one on the right road. It sometimes almost makes one despair of trying to manage to create these natural-looking features. There are bits of views that have a beauty that cannot be imitated, and therefore it is often better to let a fine view alone when we can, because we can rarely improve it. Fortunate is any one who already has a natural and beautiful island. Best set out a water-lily or two or some other aquatic flower, but leave the trees and shrubs of the island untouched except a little cutting out of dead wood here and there or lopping off a rampant branch.

A landscape gardener learns above most artists to exercise restraint and humility. Nature is so much better an artist than he can hope to be. Many a place should never be planted at all except with vines and low shrubs and a tree or two immediately adjoining the house; nature herself having done the work so supremely well.

It has been already noted that to make an island after nature's standard, or type, there may well be more than one island, one in several and yet the whole constituting an island scheme, a unified effect. The most natural and beautiful island is one that is growing, one that has other small islands around it, emerging into sight, consisting, in some cases, of no more than a rock or a few square feet of earth and one or more small shrubs, an island very much like the larger one was at an earlier stage of its existence. To build such companion islands successfully, the controlling forces of the environment must be carefully studied and taken into account, the character of the current and the prevailing winds, from whence the soil drifts, even the source of the stones that may be conveyed by the ice. These factors will all work effectively in the natural development of an island, and in artificial constructions we should continually recognize their value.

If an island is large enough to require a bridge to connect it with the mainland, or to make the erection of some kind of building advisable, the simplest forms and material should be used, and generally it would be better to use stone alone. "Rustic work" as represented by the intricate arrangement of cedar, locust, or sassafras branches twisted into the strange conventional forms has become popular for bridges and summer houses on islands and elsewhere, but good taste should really bar it. It is neither defensible as architecture of a sort, nor suitable as material for use in the landscape.

The outline of the shore of the island is a feature that needs the most careful management to retain the infinitely varied contours and even indentations characteristic of the method of treating such places followed by nature. Nothing that nature does is accidental or haphazard and therefore it is always important to study her methods and see how and why she arrives at certain results. Something of the play of these natural forces is indicated in the diagrams and explanations contained in the quotations from Prince Pückler contained in this chapter.

X

ROCKS

THE employment of rocks in landscape gardening should be founded on study of the way similar fragments have naturally disposed themselves in the scenery of the territory where they are to be employed.

To complete the natural beauty and proper effect of rocks in the landscape, rock plants are required, plants that thrive in shallow soil and in the crevices, pockets, and nooks found in such places.

> "They (the rocks) may also occasionally be connected with a stretch of wall built of blasted field stone as if for some purpose, like reconstructing a bridge or supporting a steep bank, one had merely taken advantage of the rocks which had naturally accumulated and supplemented the rest with a wall for the same purpose. This also gives the opportunity to gather together plants which demand a rocky soil, and which are often very ornamental, especially near water where such rock work is most desirable for a bulwark, dam, strong wall, etc., and in a large park they are almost indispensable. A slight artistic

touch which can be recommended is to set the stones in a slanting direction as if they had been forced up in that manner and to make one or more of the edges stand out conspicuously, which gives the whole a more picturesque and bold aspect."[1]

There are few things more beautiful in a park or garden than an old wall treated with rock plants in an intelligent manner.

"A grand old wall is a precious thing in a garden, and many are the ways of treating it. If it is an ancient wall of great thickness, built at a time when neither was work shirked nor material stinted, even if many of the joints are empty, the old stone or brick stands firmly bonded, and, already two or three hundred years of age, seems likely to endure well into the future centuries. In such a wall wild plants will already have made themselves at home, and we may only have to put a little earth and a small plant into some cavity, or earth and seed into a narrow open joint, to be sure of a good reward. Often grasses and weeds rooting in the hollow places can be raked out and their spaces refilled with better things. When wild things grow in walls they always dispose themselves in good groups; such groups as without their guidance it would have been difficult to devise intentionally."[2]

[1] Prince Pückler, *Hints on Landscape Gardening.*
[2] Gertrude Jekyl, *Wall and Water Gardens.*

These walls, ancient or recently made, are valuable in many places, bordering roads and lanes, supporting steep banks, and making the main structures of bridges and their approaches; but it should be understood that, in order to have a rustic character, they should be made of stone collected in the fields near where they are to be used, or taken from a quarry where the rock shows a cleavage or lamination, a colour and grain which suit the character of the region where it is to be employed. Next in importance to the character of the stone is the size of the individual blocks used. These should be taken as large as possible and should not show any signs of the chisel, only a blow of the hammer here and there, to break off corners so that a rough fitting can be made. To this end, no chinking or thrusting little pieces of stone into the joints should be allowed. All these crevices or openings should be left exposed and then, by devising lips or pockets of cement, soil can be introduced and retained for growing plants. This will in a year or two, when the plants have grown, give an old weather-worn appearance to the wall, an ancient moss-grown look, and at the same time a great charm of leaf and flower. Any concrete that may be necessary should be set in the core of the wall where it is out of sight. There are few rock plants that will grow in America, or even elsewhere, in these dry crevices, and such plants are confined largely to the mossy-looking sedums of dwarf habit, preferably the stonecrop (*Sedum acre*). Besides these there are the wild cactus or prickly pear (*Opuntia vulgaris*), the houseleeks (sempervivums), which do well in these difficult places. Hardly any other kinds can be used for the purpose.

At the base of these walls ferns, iris, saxifrage, and other medium-sized herbaceous plants that bloom at different parts of the season may be grown, but the kinds should be selected so that only the base of the wall for a foot or two is covered, because the beauty of the grain and colouring of the wall is quite as important as the plant growth.

Judgment should be carefully exercised in the quantity of climbing plants used,—roses, clematis, Virginia creeper, euonymus, Japanese ivy, etc.,—because the growth of these vines is so luxuriant that without proper control they will soon cover the entire wall and hide the beauty of the stone itself and its moss-covered crevices and surface. The right way is to plant climbing vines nearly always at the back of the wall, in which case they will grow up to the top and then can be trained longitudinally along the coping. Unless this training is carefully followed up, the vines grow out in all directions and, more or less, droop down and cover too much of the beautiful surface of the front wall. The *Euonymus radicans* is a small evergreen vine of great beauty and has the advantage of growing in a moderate way in front of the wall, fitting itself into some of the large crevices which are difficult to cover with the sedums and sempervivums, but even this vine needs considerable attention to prevent its spreading too much over the picturesque wall surface.

The accompanying illustration shows the appearance

of a wall two years old. This wall extends in front of the estate of W. W. Cook, Esq., bordering King Street about two miles from Port Chester, N. Y. The stone, a heavy granite, is of striking beauty, having a warm pink colour shading into browns and yellows. Much of it is water worn and all of it was taken out of a quarry on the shores of the Sound a few miles from New Haven. The blocks vary in size from three feet to ten feet long and three feet wide and weigh some of them nearly a ton each. The coping has been carefully selected from the quarry and hammered somewhat to give it a comparatively uniform surface, but leaving the naturally rounded and curving contours.

Such a wall should neither look like a ruin, nor on the other hand like a neatly laid up structure made of small flat stones, but every foot of it should be studied with the object of harmonizing and contrasting the colour and form of the stones, grouping them and combining their colour in the most effective way. There are beautiful kinds of granite which are well suited to this purpose. Mica in stones should be avoided and only rock selected that will *weather* attractively. It is a good idea to consider that the function of rock plants and vines is simply to frame beautiful panels of stone in the wall. In that case it will be difficult to go far wrong. To pile earth on top of the wall and in banks against the sides and almost cover everything with flowering plants is to miss the chief object of rock gardening.

Mr. William Robinson in the *English Flower Garden*

A Granite Wall Made of Large Blocks of Stone with Interstices Filled with Earth and Rock Plants.
On the Estate of W. W. Cook, Esq., Port Chester, N. Y.

From a Photograph by William Hale Kirk.

well expresses the way in which such work should be done:

> "No burrs, clinkers, vitrified matter, portions of old arches and pillars, broken-nosed statues, etc., should ever be seen in a garden of alpine flowers. Never let any part of the rock garden appear as if it had been shot out of a cart. The rocks should all have their bases buried in the ground, and the seams should not be visible; wherever a vertical or oblique seam occurs, it should be crammed with earth, and the plants put in with the earth will quickly hide the seam."[1]

All suggestion of artificiality of any kind should be carefully avoided in using rocks in landscape gardening. The least appearance of the hand of man is more injurious to the charm of the place than it is anywhere else in the landscape scheme. To imitate, or better to simulate the natural surface of a meadow by grading is difficult and is a work of art, the management and disposition of trees and shrubs is not easy, but to place rock work so that the presence of the mason is not dominating, nor the careless method of the teamster in dumping his load of stone, is the most difficult of all. This latter form of dumping down rock is by some wrongly deemed natural and well designed, provided the interstices be filled with plants.

Thomas Whately writes as follows on the same subject:

[1] *English Flower Garden*, chapter xi., p. 144.

"But too strong a force on the nature of the place always fails; a winding path which appears to be worn, not cut, has more effect than a highroad, all artificial and level, which is too weak to overbear, and yet contradicts the general idea; the objects therefore to be introduced must be those which hold a mean betwixt solitude and population; and the inclination of that choice towards either extreme should be directed by the degree of wildness which prevails; for though that runs sometimes to an excess which requires correction, at other times it wants encouragement, and at all times it ought to be preserved; it is the predominant character of rocks, which mixes with every other, and to which all the appendages must be accommodated; and they may be applied so as greatly to increase it: a licentious irregularity of wood and of ground, and a fantastic conduct of the streams, neither of which would be tolerated in the midst of cultivation, become and improve romantic spots; even buildings, partly by their style, but still more by their position, in strange, difficult, or dangerous situations, distinguish and aggravate the native tendencies of the scene. In the choice and application of these accompaniments consists all our power over rocks; they are themselves too vast and too stubborn to submit to our control; but by the addition or removal of the appendages which we can command, parts may be shown or concealed, and the characters with their impressions may be weakened or enforced: to adapt the accompaniments accordingly is the utmost ambition of art when rocks are the subject.

"Their most distinguished characters are *dignity*, *terror*, and *fancy:* the expression of all is constantly wild; and sometimes a rocky scene is only wild, without pretension to any particular character.

"Art may interpose to show these large parts to the eye, and magnify them to the imagination, by taking away thickets which stretch quite across the rocks, so as to disguise their dimensions, or by filling with wood the small intervals between them, and thus by concealing the want, preserving the appearance of continuation. When rocks retire from the eye down a gradual declivity, we can, by raising the upper ground, deepen the fall, lengthen the perspective, and give both height and extent to those at a distance: this effect may still be increased by covering the upper ground with a thicket, which shall cease, or be lowered, as it descends.

"A thicket on other occasions makes the rocks which rise out of it seem larger than they are; if they stand on the bank overspread with shrubs, their beginning is at least uncertain, and the presumption is that they start from the bottom.

"Rocks are seldom remarkable for the elegance of their forms; they are too vast and too rude to pretend to delicacy; but their shapes are often agreeable; and we can affect those shapes to a certain degree, at least we can cover many blemishes in them, by conducting the growth of shrubbery and creeping plants about them. For all these purposes mere underwood suffices, but for greater effects larger trees are requisite; they are worthy of the scene, and not only improvements but accessions to its grandeur; we are used to rank them among the noblest objects of nature, and when we see they cannot aspire to the midway of the heights around them, the rocks are raised by comparison. A single tree is therefore preferable to a clump; the size, though really less, is more remarkable; and clumps are besides generally exceptionable in a very wild spot from the suspicion of art that attends them; but a wood is free from that suspicion, and its own character of greatness commends it to every scene of magnificence."

No chisel should be allowed to touch the stones except to break off chunks. The stone or rock masses should be laid lengthwise in the wall, not with the narrow parts up and down, and naturally the larger pieces should rest on the ground. Where the stones rest on the ground, the point of junction of the stone and soil should be at least two or three inches above the actual rock base. There is a principle involved in the idea. Concealment serves to suggest that the rocks have not been brought to the spot, but have grown there, and the soil gradually gathered about them. In this way it looks, and should look, as if the position of these rocks was the work of nature. Sometimes it is well to have a few small rocks at the foot of the wall, as if nature had dropped them there broad side down. It ought, however, to be a stony region where this is done. Wherever no visible rocks exist, nothing but the upright stone wall should be constructed, and above all, only stone should be used the appearance of which has considerable resemblance to those native to the region. In most places there are some indications of native stone cropping out of the surface of the ground. Should the estate or park be located in a distinctly sandy territory like some parts of New Jersey, there would certainly be found somewhere within a few miles sandstone that would suit the purpose. Stones loaded with mica should be avoided as already noted, for time fails to weather them satisfactorily; for the same reason pudding-stone, conglomerate, lava-like material, slaty stone, and anything of the nature of fine-grained marble are unsatisfactory. Rough-grained stone is required generally, whether granite, limestone, sandstone, or even a nondescript material which is difficult to classify. The same instinct for simplicity and rugged strength would suggest in connexion with such stone walls that gates with their hinges and fastenings, lamps, and braces of all kinds be made of the roughest kind of hammered wrought iron, strong looking and quaint and grotesque in design. Such rough-looking metal may be cast so as to look like hammered wrought iron, in which case its use may be admissible, although strictly speaking it is hardly in good taste. It is generally wise to design such features either yourself or with the aid of some special artist. Hardly ever can you get a design from books or samples that really fits the scheme of treatment suitable for your wall. The proportions of the wall are also a consideration of great importance. Whether the wall should be three feet high or four feet or a mere border of a few inches or a foot, depends naturally on existing conditions, but there should always be plenty of proportionate thickness and something of a batter, that is a narrower top than base, and always at intervals wide stones running through the wall and tying the mass together. The coping should be equally proportionate and lie comparatively level or sloping regularly down. Stepping down with the coping at intervals should be avoided if possible. It is not natural looking.

The construction of the cave and rough stone archway in the Ramble in Central Park forms one of the best examples of rock work to be found anywhere. Two enormous masses of rock near each other, with recesses forming a cave, were bridged over with large masses of stones laid so as to make rough parapet walls and rough stone side pieces, and then sloping off in two directions are steep banks bordering the path and planted with masses of rock and vines and shrubbery. The rocky incident originally existed, but its essential nature was seized and improved on right lines.

Many are the forms which rock work may assume, besides a wall. There are steps, caves in hillsides, bridges, and even houses, and very often there are rocks to be discovered in the neighbourhood whose beauty can be enhanced by locating other and smaller stones in their neighbourhood and ornamenting the entire mass

The Rustic Bridge Adjoining the Cave in the Ramble,
Central Park, New York City.
From a Photograph by William Hale Kirk.

with vines, sedums, etc. Moreover, wherever rock crops out in the lawn, alongside a path, on a hillside or on the level, there is an opportunity to add similar pieces of rock half buried with the interstices between them filled with earth and then with plants. To do this there are chances in many parts of the country and the possibilities of thus creating natural effects of the greatest beauty are endless and scarcely realized at the present time. The very selection of the stones with their beautiful grain and contour invites study of the most delightful sort. Think what could be done if the same attention were given to this study as to the collecting of curios or gems or to the use of stained glass. After all there are few things finer than these marvellous effects of nature that belong to the countryside and which are generally overlooked as commonplace and not specially interesting.

The bridge over the pond in Central Park indicates the rustic effect without plants in the interstices of the stones, and the Lombardy poplars and shrubbery emphasize and screen the entrance of the footway.

Here is an example of a stone bridge of the type we have been considering, which illustrates the idea of simplicity and natural dignity and charm. To *Garden and Forest*, vol. i., p. 52, we owe the illustration and the following description:

"This very ancient bridge spans one of the small streams on Dartmoor in the south-west of England. Its construction is sufficiently explained by the picture—two land piers and one stream pier are connected by long spanning stones which carry parapets made up of large irregular blocks. It is hardly necessary to point out the degree to which this bridge combines picturesque beauty with durability, or to explain the fitness of such bridges for rural situations in our own country. In the immediate vicinity of a very dignified house so rude and unarchitectural a bridge would perhaps be out of place, and the same is true of those portions of an urban park where formality rules or where architectural works of importance are in view. But in the sequestered naturally treated portions of parks a bridge of this sort would be entirely appropriate; and carrying a road or footway near a country home of modest character or in a village suburb it would be a most charming feature. Naturally we have no wish to suggest that this bridge be copied either in its special form or in the size and disposition of its stones, although in both these respects it would be an excellent model. It is illustrated merely to show how very simply a stone bridge may be built and how incomparably better in effect it is than the ugly constructions in iron or the rough assemblage of planks with which in this country we are so familiar. Weather-beaten boulders as old as those in this bridge at Leatherton, and as appropriate for bridge building, lie by every New England stream, and it would need no high degree of skill to put them to service. But we seem to have thought the bare straight lines of

The Rough Stone Bridge, over an Arm of the Pond in Central Park, near 59th Street and 5th Avenue, New York City.

From a Photograph by William Hale Kirk.

iron more beautiful than the infinite variety of form and surface and colour of our moss-grown stones. It is full time we changed our minds."

The bridge on the estate of Muskau as shown in the illustration is attractive because it spans a brawling stream and because it is simple and unassuming, but the stones of which it is constructed are too small and the entrance to the footway is bare of foliage.

Another fault to be found with this admirable method of bridge building, is that there is little or no moss, or sedums which would take the place of moss, to be seen.

There are other illustrations of the proper use of rocks in landscape architecture which are shown in some of the views of the chapters of this book. They have been taken from sketches, made by A. F. Bellows fifty years ago, of Central Park, New York, in the early state of its development. It is not easy to find examples of rock work anywhere equal to those in Central Park. Unfortunately the study of these examples does not seem to have commended itself to many people, for there is little evidence to be seen on country places of endeavour to excel in this branch of landscape architecture.

XI

GRADING AND SHAPING GROUNDS

"ON meadows as a rule, here and there, the little ups and downs must be levelled, for practical purposes as well as appearance: but larger undulations of the terrain must by no means be unnecessarily disturbed. But if nevertheless it is desirable for other reasons to remove and level any considerable height, and any fine trees happen to be standing there which should not be removed, then I advise leaving them standing on single small hillocks, which gives the meadow still more variety, for which reason I have often deliberately planted in this way and with good results.

"Although in general a certain undulation of the terrain is advisable at times, an excellent effect is brought about by making the bottoms of little valleys, having steep surroundings, quite level. We often find such formations in nature which charm us by the contrast." [1]

It is remarkable to find these wise reflections recorded

[1] Prince Pückler, *Hints on Landscape Gardening.*

A Bridge at Leatherton, Dartmoor, England.
From a Photograph Taken from *Garden and Forest.* (By Permission.)

A Rough Stone Bridge in the Park on the Estate of Prince Pückler von Muskau.
From a Photograph by Thomas W. Sears, Providence, R. I.

nearly a century ago. The feeling for nature is strongly evident, and the whole tendency of the views expressed is to confirm the fundamental ideas which I propose to discuss for the grading and shaping the earth surface for landscape gardening.

The problem, here as elsewhere, is to humour and conquer nature and yet, to all appearance, still keep her character intact. Before the planting of trees and shrubs and flowers, before, usually, even the final disposition of the paths and roads, comes this modulation of the surface of the earth, for it really amounts to this, for not only existing natural conditions should be harmonized and overcome without losing the characteristic topography of the place, but due regard should be given also to the general appearance of the scenery immediately outside of the place, and even miles away, and thus the keynote of the scenery of the region be kept continually in mind.

To do this work in the proper spirit, and in a really skilful manner, is perhaps the most difficult undertaking that the landscape gardener will have to master. There are niceties in the details of shaping the ground, the execution of which will not be easy of accomplishment. An active movement of the surface will have to be maintained that is not expressed by either of the words rolling or levelling, and yet both have their value in describing the process. The higher portions are made, or become, lower, overcome by the reaction of the next swell. Nothing is regular. There should be conflict and contrast, and for a moment or longer, harmony and restfulness. The lawn should be like the waves of the sea or a lake beating on the shores of varied coast lines of trees and shrubs, with the flowers acting like the foam and spray, thrusting themselves forward on much the same lines of contrast, conflict, and yielding. The chief art, however, lies in keeping the essential spirit of the scenery pervasive and recurrent at irregular intervals throughout.

It is hardly possible to convey any adequate idea of how this grading is to be done under all circumstances, conditions vary so continually, but there is a way of doing this, depending on existing relations of things that can only be attained by long training and much observation; and yet this is the very thing that is generally left to the ordinary day labourer.

We have cited Prince Pückler's wise suggestions on grading, but going back quite half a century earlier we read in the pages of Thomas Whately a really profound and illuminating dissertation on the subject. Thomas Whately is a well-known and highly respected authority on landscape gardening both in his own day (1770) and at the present time. The weight of his advice therefore will excuse the following extended quotation from his principal work:

> "A plain is not, however, interesting, and the least deviation from the uniformity of its surface changes its nature; as long as the flat remains, it depends on the objects around for all its variety and all its beauty, but convex and concave forms are

The Waterfall South of, and near, the Boulder Bridge, Central Park, New York City.

The Waterfall near the Lock, Central Park, New York City.

generally pleasing; and the number of degrees and combinations into which they may be cast is infinite, those forms only in each which are perfectly regular must be avoided; a semicircle can never be tolerable: small portions of large circles blended together or lines gently curved which are not parts of any circle, a hollow sinking but little below the level; a swell very much flattened at the top, are commonly the most agreeable figures. In ground that lies beautifully the concave will generally prevail; within the same compass it shows more compass than a swell; all the sides of the latter are not visible at the same time, except in a few particular situations; but it is only in a few particular situations that any part of a hollow is concealed, earth seems to have been accumulated to raise the one, and taken away to sink the other. The concave, therefore, appears the lighter, and for the most part it is the more elegant shape; even the slope of a swell can hardly be brought down unless broken now and then into hollows to take off from the heaviness of the mass. In made ground the connexion is, perhaps, the principal consideration. A swell that wants it is but a heap, a hollow but a hole; and both appear artificial. The one seems placed upon a surface to which it does not belong; the other dug into it. Trees, too, without being connected with those within, and seeming part of a clump or a grove there will frequently obliterate every trace of an interruption. By such or other means the line may be, and should be hid or disguised; not for the purpose of deception (when all is done we are seldom deceived), but to preserve the continued surface entire.

"If where no union is intended, a line of separation is disagreeable, it must be disgusting when it breaks the connexion between the several parts of the same piece of ground. That connexion depends on the *junction of each part to those about*, and *on* the *relation* of *every part to the whole.* To complete the former, such shapes should be contiguous as most readily unite, and the actual division between should be anxiously concealed. If a swell descends upon a level; if a hollow sinks from it, the level is an absolute termination and a little run marks it distinctly. To cover that run, a short sweep at the foot of the swell, a small rotundity at the entrance to the hollow, must be interposed. In every instance when ground changes its direction, there is a point where the change is effected and that point should never appear. Some other shapes, uniting easily with both extremes, must be thrown in to conceal it. But there must be no uniformity even in these connexions; if the same sweep be carried all around the bottom of a swell, the same rotundity all around the top of a hollow, though the junction be perfect, yet the art by which it is made is apparent, and art must never appear. The manner of concealing the separation should itself be disguised, and different degrees of cavity or rotundity, different shapes and dimensions to the little parts, thus dignified by degrees; and those parts breaking in one place more, in another less, into the principal forms that are to be united, produce that variety with which all nature abounds, and without which ground cannot be natural.

"The relation of all the parts to the whole when clearly marked, facilitates their junction with each other: for the common bond of union is then perceived, before there has been time to examine the subordinate connexions; and if these should be deficient in some niceties, the defect is lost in the general impression. But any part that is at variance with the rest, is not barely a blemish in itself: it spreads disorder as far as its influence extends; and the confusion is in proportion as the other parts are more or less adapted, to point out any particular direction, or to mark any peculiar character in the ground.

"If in ground all descending one way, a piece is twisted across another, the general fall is obstructed by it, but if all the parts incline in the same direction, it is hardly credible how small a declivity will seem to be considerable. An appearance even of steepness may be given to a very gentle descent, by raising hillocks up on it which shall lean to the point, whither all the rest are tending, for the eye measures from the top of the highest to the bottom of the lowest ground; and when the relation of the parts is well preserved, such an effect from one is transfused over the whole.

"But they should not, therefore, all lie exactly in the same direction; some may seem to point to it directly, others to incline very much, others but little, some partially, some entirely.

"If the direction be strongly marked on a few principal parts, great liberties may be taken with the others, provided none of them are turned the contrary way. The general idea must, however, be preserved, clear even of a doubt. A hillock, which only intercepts the sight, if it does not contribute to the principal effect is, at the best, an unnecessary excrescence, and even an interruption in the general tendency, though it hide nothing, is a blemish. On a descent, any hollow, any fall, which has not an outlet to lower ground, is a hole: the eye skips over it, instead of being continued along it; it is a gap in the composition.

"There may indeed be occasions when we should rather wish to promote than to check the general tendency. Ground may proceed too hastily towards its point; and we have equal power to retard or accelerate the fall. We can slacken the precipitancy of a steep by breaking it into parts, some which shall incline less, than the whole before inclined, to the principal direction, and by turning them quite away, we may even change the course of the descent. These powers are of use in the larger scenes, where the several great parts lie in several directions; and if they are thereby too strongly contrasted, or led to points too widely asunder, every art should be exerted to bring them nearer together, to assimilate and connect them. As scenes increase in extent, they become more impatient of control: they are not only less manageable, but ought to be less restrained; they require more variety and contrast. But still the same principles are applicable to the least, and to the greatest, tho' not with equal severity: neither ought to be rent to pieces; and though a small neglect, which would distract the one, may not disturb the other, yet a total disregard of all the principles of union is alike productive of confusion in both.

"The style also of every part must be accommodated to the character of the whole, for every piece of ground is distinguished by certain properties: it is either tame or bold, gentle or rude; continued or broken; and if any varieties inconsistent with those properties be obtruded, it has no other effect than to weaken one idea without raising another. The insipidity of a flat is not taken away by a few scattered hillocks; a continuation of uneven ground can alone give the idea of inequality. A large, deep, abrupt break, along easy swells and falls, seems at the best but a piece left unfinished, which ought to have been softened, it is not more natural because it is more rude; nature forms both one and the other but seldom mixes them together. On the other hand, a small, fine, polished form, in the midst of rough misshapen ground, though more elegant than all about it, is generally no better than a patch, itself disgraced, and disfiguring the scene. A thousand instances might be produced to show, that the prevailing idea ought to pervade every part, so far at least indispensably as to exclude whatever distracts it; and as much farther as possible to accommodate the character of the ground to that of the scene it belongs to. On the same principle the *proportion* of the parts may often be adjusted; for though their size must be very much governed by the extent of the place; and a feature, which would fill up a small spot, may be lost in a large one; though there are forms of a particular cast which appear to advantage only within certain dimensions and ought not, therefore, to be applied, where they have not room enough, or where they must occupy more space than becomes them; yet independent of these considerations, a character of greatness belongs to some scenes which is not measured by their extent, but raised by other properties, sometimes only by the proportional largeness of their parts. On the contrary, where elegance characterizes the spot, the parts should not only be small, but diversified with subordinate inequalities, and little delicate touches everywhere scattered about them. Striking effects, forcible impressions, whatever seems to require effort, disturbs the enjoyment of a scene intended to amuse and please. In other instances similar considerations will determine rather the number than the proportion of the parts. A place may be distinguished by its simplicity, which many divisions would destroy; another spot, without any pretensions to elegance, may be remarkable for an appearance of richness: a multiplicity of objects will give that appearance, and a number of parts in the ground will contribute to the profusion. A scene of gaiety is improved by the same means; the objects and parts may differ in style, but they must be numerous in both. Sameness is dull; the purest simplicity can at the most render a place composed of large parts placid; the sublimest ideas only make it striking; it is always grave; to enliven it, numbers are wanting.

"But ground is seldom beautiful or natural without variety or even without contrast, and the precautions that have been given tend no further than to prevent variety from degenerating into inconsistency and contrast into contradiction. Within the extreme nature supplies an inexhaustible fund; and variety thus limited, so far from destroying improves the general effect. Each distinguished part makes a separate impression; and all bearing the same stamp, all concurring to the same end, every one is an additional support to the prevailing idea: that is multiplied; it is extended, it appears in different shapes; it is shown in several lights; and the variety illustrates the relation. But variety wants not this recommendation: it is always desirable when it can be properly introduced; and the accurate observer will see in every form several circumstances by which it is distinguished from every other. If the scene be mild and quiet, he will place together those that do not differ widely; he will gradually depart from the similitude. In ruder scenes the succession will be less regular, and the transition more sudden. The character of the place must determine the degree of difference between forms which are contiguous. Besides distinctions in the shapes of the ground, differences in their situations and their dimensions are sources of variety. The position will alter the effect, though the figure be the same; and for particular effects, a change only in the distance may be striking. If that be considerable, a succession of similar shapes sometimes occasions a fine perspective; but the diminution will be less marked, that is the effect will be less sensible if the forms are not nearly alike; we take more notice of one difference, when there is no other. Sometimes a very disagreeable result, produced by too close a resemblance of shapes, may be remedied by an alteration in the size. If a steep descends in a succession of abrupt falls, nearly equal, they have an appearance of steps; and are neither pleasing nor wild, but, if they are made to differ in height and length, the objection is removed: and at all times, a difference in the dimensions will be found to have a greater effect, than in speculation: we should be inclined to ascribe to it, and will often disguise a similarity of figure. It also contributes perhaps more than any other circumstance, to the perfection of those lines which the eye traces along the parts of a piece of ground when it glances over several together. No variety of form compensates for the want of it. An undulating line, composed of parts all elegant in themselves, all judiciously contrasted and happily united, but equal one to another, is far from the line of beauty. A long straight line has no variety at all; and a little deviation into a curve, if there be still a continued conformity, is but a trifling amendment. Though ground all falling the same way requires every attention to its general tendency, yet the eye must not dart down the whole length, immediately in one direction, but should be insensibly conducted towards the principal point with some circuity and delay. The channels between hillocks ought never to run in straight, nor even regularly curved lines; but winding gently among them, and constantly varying in form and in dimensions should gradually find their way. The beauty of a large hill, especially when seen from below, is frequently impaired by the even continuation of its brow. An attempt to break it by little knolls is seldom successful, they seem separate independent hillocks artificially put on. The intended effect may indeed be produced by a large knoll descending in some places lower than in others, and rooted in several points in the hill. The same end may be attained by carrying some channel or hollow on the side upward till it cut the continued line; or by bringing the brow forward in one place, and throwing it back in another, or by forming a secondary ridge a little way down the side, and casting the ground above it into a different though not opposite direction to the general descent. Any of these expedients will at least draw the attention off from the defect; but, if the break were to divide the run into equal parts, another uniformity would be added without removing the former; for regularity always suggests a suspicion of artifice, and artifice detected no longer deceives: our imagination would industriously join the broken parts and the idea of the broken line would be restored.

"Whatever break be chosen, the position of it must be oblique to the line which is to be broken. A rectangular division produces sameness; there is no contrast between the forms it divides; but, if it be oblique, while it diminishes the part on one side, it enlarges that on the other. Parallel lines are liable to the same objection as those at right angles: though each by itself be the perfect line of beauty, yet, if they correspond, they form a shape between them, whose sides want contrast. On the same principle forms will sometimes be introduced less for their intrinsic than their occasional merit, in contrasting happily with those about them: each sets off the other, and together they are a more agreeable composition than if they had been beautiful, but at the same time more similar. One reason why tame scenes are seldom interesting is, that, although they often admit of many varieties, they allow of few, and those only faint, contrasts. We may be pleased with the number of the former, but we can be struck only by the force of the latter. These ought to abound in the larger and bolder scenes of a garden especially in such as are formed by an assemblage of many distinct and considerable parts thrown together; as when several

A View of the North Meadow, with a Noteworthy Vista on Either Side of a Small Group of Trees, Central Park, New York City.

From a Photograph by William Hale Kirk.

rising grounds appear one beyond another, a fine swell seen above a slanting swell which runs before it, has a beautiful effect which a nearer effect would destroy: and (except in particular instances) a close similarity in lines which either cross, or face, or rise behind one another, makes a poor, uniform, disagreeable composition."[1]

No better illustration of the truth of these remarks of Thomas Whately can be found than the north meadows in Central Park and the meadows of Prospect Park, Brooklyn, N. Y. They are not only rolling but ridged up in long mounds at places as if fences had been removed from pasture fields and the headlands left unlevelled. See illustration of north meadow, Central Park. There is not a level spot on this meadow to all appearance; and when one thinks of it, the meadow or pastureland, the fundamental idea of a park, lawn, or meadow is not level. A cricket, tennis, or bowling court is, but not a pasture field. Farms do not produce level meadows, and sheep and cows do not wander on such places. It is the swell and swing of the surface coming now and then to a small ridge and then dying away into space that is almost level; it is the rise and fall, the becoming and dying away into the soft effect of the almost level. The same idea or type of treatment is evolved here as in the plantations and lines of walks and roads and rock work and water and islands; all start from the same idea. Let any one try, on the

[1] Thomas Whately, *Observations on Modern Gardening.*

other hand, to make a level meadow. He can with difficulty make a level cricket bowling streak, or a level tennis court—much less a large meadow a mile long like the one in Prospect Park. The eye will deceive one, and the place will never look level from every point of view. It will seem convex or concave and, worst of all, it will look as if an attempt had been made to produce a level territory and had failed. The sense of that kind of failure is always trying to any one who can understand the end which is sought.

Many people's sense of these niceties of landscape art is so obtuse and imperfect that they will at "one fell swoop" destroy these fine "nuances" of grading. This has indeed been done in Central Park through ignorant and, therefore, unintentional treatment of one of the most beautiful meadows near 59th Street, a meadow which has been spoken of as the most expensive piece of work of the same size in the area of the park; all spoiled by unintelligent grading. Of all undertakings of the landscape gardener, grading is the last to be left to the skill of the common day labourer. It would be just as sensible a proceeding to set the quarryman who hews and blasts out the stone from the hillside to carve a copy of some great statue. Yet the landscape gardener at his best can never hope to create work like nature when she is at her finest. He can only work in what he believes to be the same style, but never quite in the same style as she presents when she works in her best mood. He can enter into her spirit, but never quite reach her heart.

The illustration of Mr. Agar's estate is introduced to show how the shape of a lawn can be graded so as to give the impression of no change of surface whatever, just a retention of the natural character of the place by blending and moulding the contour lines of the ground.

The centre of the lawn to the north has been greatly depressed, and still further to the north it has been raised considerably and trees and shrubs planted to shut out an unattractive view.

XII

PLANTATIONS

"THE first requirement of a landscape is the vigorous growth of all plants. The finest forms of mountains and lakes, all the brilliancy of the sun and sky, combined with the naked rocks and bare lakes cannot replace the luxuriant growth of various forms of trees, and the diversified pleasing green and rich foliage and meadows. Fortunate the man to whom his forbears have bequeathed lofty woods, old oaks, beeches, and lindens, these proud giants of our Northern clime, standing there still untouched by the woodman's murderous axe. He should never regard them without veneration and delight, he should cherish them as the apple of his eye, for neither money nor power, neither a Crœsus nor an Alexander, can restore an oak a thousand years old in its wonderful majesty after the poor labourer has felled it. Terrible and swift is the destructive power of man, but poor and weak is his power of rebuilding. May an ancient tree be to you, kind reader, who love nature, a holy thing. And

A View of the Lawn of John G. Agar, Esq., Premium Point,
New Rochelle, N. Y.

yet, here also, the individual tree must be sacrificed, if need be, to the general group.

"It may happen that a tree which, taken alone is most beautiful, does really disturb the effectiveness and harmony of the whole, and then it must be sacrificed. Such occasions however are very rare, and I unfortunately know from my own experience that a slight alteration of my plans would often be sufficient to spare a precious veteran whose execution at first seemed unavoidable. At all events, before applying the executioner's axe, be sure to deliberate not once but many times. It may be that the importance which I give to this matter may appear exaggerated, yet a true lover of nature will understand me, and excuse the qualms of conscience that half a dozen trees murdered without reason continue to cause me. On the other hand, my only consolation is that by boldly cutting down other trees I have made such great improvements, that the gain outbalances the loss. Besides, there is no denying that more can be accomplished in one day by the removal of a few big trees, than by planting thousands of specimens in a hundred years, and that the loss of a couple of these is not to be regretted if their number is increased a hundred-fold to the eye by making so many others visible which had previously been quite obscured. This is so certain, that, although I have not been blessed with a surplus of ancient trees in my park, yet I have succeeded in apparently multiplying tenfold the number of them left standing. These are visible now from all points, by the removal of some eighty others. One is often struck by the fact in such cases that 'One cannot see the woods for the trees.' The great art in laying out a park consists in making use of comparatively few objects in such a way that a great variety of different pictures result, in which the recurrent elements are not recognized, or at least produce novel and surprising effects."[1]

A tree: a live organism, a unit in the landscape scheme of the park, country place, or garden; a unit that may live six months or a hundred years, working out its own peculiar nature and office in the service of the general artistic life that should inform every scheme of landscape gardening. It is a living, individual member of the whole conception, differing entirely from the blocks of wood or stone in the architectural design of a building. It is not only a life, but innumerable lives within its life to the very core of its being. It is for this reason that a tree or a flower may readily take on apparently something of the personality of a human being. The birch becomes the dainty, delicate, airy, graceful lady of the woods, the oak a monarch among his subjects.

Where is the line that can be taken to mark the separation of the life of the plant from that of man and define its essential difference? At what point of development does personality come into being in the

[1] *Hints on Landscape Gardening*, Prince Pückler.

A Diagram Showing Arrangement of Trees and Shrubs.

Diagrams Showing Arrangements of Rivers, Lakes, and Islands.

From Pückler's Atlas, 1834.

plant and in the animal and for that matter in man? Do they not break through boundary lines and overlap? Does not something of a personality, a spirit or soul, appear in the widely differing forms of all three of them?

Aristotle says in explanation of this line of thought:

> "Now all things in the universe are so somehow ordered together, whatever swims in the sea, or flies in the air, or grows on the earth, but not all in like fashion; nothing exists apart and without some kind of relation with the rest, for all things are ordered in relation with one end."

Hegel writes as follows in *Philosophy of Religion:*

> "it belongs to the very nature of unity that it should thus break up into parts,"

and that each of these parts should have distinct relations of its own, which become eventually one complete scheme or whole, and with

> "this individuality goes in each case the natural impulse of self-preservation—what Spinoza calls the *conatus in suo esse perseverandi,* the effort to"

maintain its own being; but why should not we say of the tree as of man, only in different degree, that here

> "the *conatus in suo esse perseverandi* swells into a demand for happiness, for a perfect completion and manifestation of its special being in which nothing shall be left to be wished or hoped for?"

> "It has taken a long process of evolution before man could conceive the idea of a rational organic order of the universe, in which each particular element, though rejected as an end in itself, might be reinstated as a necessary element of the whole, and all with justice done to their special characteristics might be united in"[1]

an all-embracing scheme, whether it be a landscape or a whole world. Further we may say that even in the consciousness of an animal (and why not in that of a plant?) there is such a universal unity that it would be absurd to treat its different appetites as isolated or standing in merely external relations to each other. Each animal and plant we may believe

> "feels *itself* in all it feels, and this gives an individual unity to its life through all its changes," "indeed three fourths of our own actions are governed by memory and most frequently we act like animals: plants also act, and if they do not think, at least feel (which is still thought), though more dimly than animals." [1]

As Goethe profoundly observes:

> "the material world (animal or vegetable, animate or inanimate) can only be truly realized as the living garment of Deity."

John Henry Newman was a poet and his instinct had

[1] Leibnitz.

Diagrams Showing Arrangement of Trees and Shrubs.

A Diagram Showing Different Arrangements of Islands.
From Pückler's Atlas, 1834.

an element of truth in it when he wrote as follows in his *Apologia sua Vita:*

> "Again I ask what would be the thoughts of a man who when examining a flower, or an herb, or a pebble, or a ray of light, which he treats as something so beneath him in the scale of existence, suddenly discovered that he was in the presence of some powerful being who was hidden behind the visible things he was inspecting,—who though concealing the wise hand, was giving them their beauty, grace, and perfection, as being God's instruments for the purpose,—nay, whose robe and ornaments those objects were, which he was so eager to analyse?"

Following the idea of a plant possessing a distinct personality, it will be found that it is not altogether fanciful. Some trees and shrubs and flowers in the landscape have, in a way, a liking for each other, a kind of kinship, that is not of the botanical sort, but simply an apparent wish to grow side by side. A bush honeysuckle naturally likes to live with a highbush cranberry or an arrowwood bush (*Viburnum dentatum*); the lilac, on the other hand, belongs by itself in the garden in a more civilized sophisticated state of existence; the beautiful hawthorns, both American and English, belong by themselves in the wilder and more outlying portions of the park or estate. So we might go on with shrubs and trees of all kinds and find always that there was one spot and one kind of companionship where any particular tree or shrub looked especially happy and behaved especially well. Considering plants as live creatures, whose strange idiosyncrasies are often seemingly almost past finding out except by the most sympathetic and penetrative study, we should start first to dispose certain of them in the landscape design as if we were blocking in the outlines of a picture indicating the main and controlling features of the group or place. To mark this distinctive character only a few kinds of trees, shrubs, and flowers are really necessary, the ones that assume such forms that the eye instinctively singles them out in any group. It may be said, with truth, that a park could be planted effectively with twelve trees, twelve shrubs, and twelve herbaceous plants. This means that if such kinds as an oak or elm, a linden, a maple, a plane tree, a birch, a spruce, a pine, a yew, an iris, a hollyhock, a phlox, a chrysanthemum were chosen, it would be quite possible to make a great place, perfectly designed in all essential ways. Of course, it would not be the greatest effect possible, because it would lack the fine, more recondite intermediate gradations of colour and form that would come in a less distinctive fashion from the employment of a large variety of hardy ornamental plants. It is not only necessary to punctuate, as it were, with marked trees and shrubs, the outlines or articulations of each member of the group, but of the group within the group, so that the lineaments of these familiar constructive features may direct the eye to the actual composition of the design.

Further than this, it is necessary to go on to the

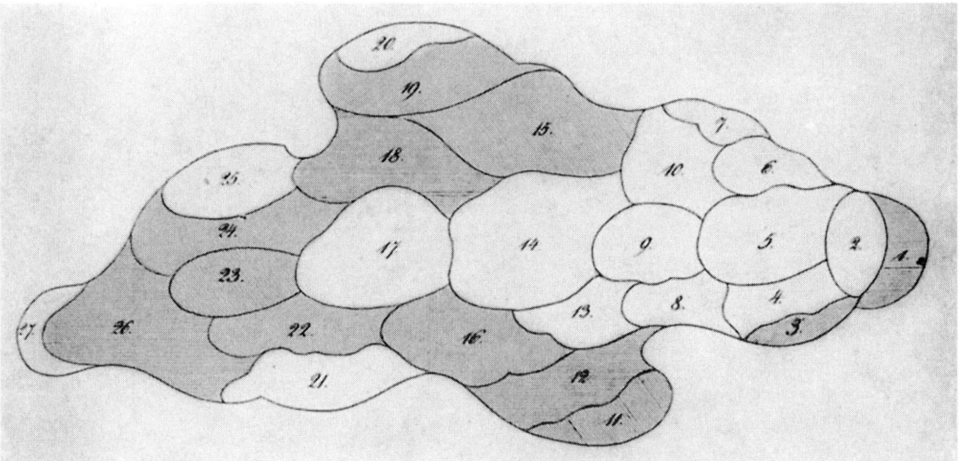

No.	Plant	Colour	Time
1	Lÿchnis Vesiaria fl. pleno	roth,	spat
2	Sÿringa perfica	lila,	früh
3	Campanula medium	dunkelblau,	spät
4	Cÿtifus elongatus	gelb,	früh
5	Sÿringa vulgaris fl. coeruleo	hellblau,	früh
6	Lilium bulbiferum	orange,	früh
7	Rubus odoratus	roth,	spät
8	Spiraea hÿpericifolia	weiss	früh
9	Lonicera tartarica fl. rubro,	roth	früh
10	Ribes aureum	gelb.	früh
11	Lunaria vederiva		spät
12	Rosa centifolia	rosa,	spät
13	Sÿringa chinensis	blassroth,	früh
14	Sÿringa vulgaris fl. albo	weiss,	früh
15.	Rhus Cotinus	braun,	spät.
16.	Potentilla fruticosa	gelb.	spät.
17	Sÿringa vulgaris fl. rubro	blauroth,	früh
18.	Spiraea falicifolia fl. rubro	blassroth,	spat
19	*Verschiedene Rosen*	rosa,	spät.
20	*gelbe und rothe gefüllte Tulpen*		früh und spät
21	Papaver bracteata	hochroth,	früh
22	Phÿladelphus coronarius	weiss,	spät
23	Craetaegus oxia cantha fl. pleno rubro	dunkelblau,	spät
24	Colutea, arborefiens	gelb,	spät.
25	Papaver bracteata	hochroth,	früh
26.	*Verschiedene Rosen*	rosa.	spat
27	*Gefüllte Tulpen*	gelb und roth,	früh
	Die nachher durch andere Sommerblumen ersetzt werden	bunt,	spät.

A Diagram Showing Arrangement of Shrubs and Herbaceous Plants.

From Pückler's Atlas, 1834.

establishment of a type of tree grouping, as well as shrubs and flowers, and make units of effect which may be used with variations over and over again, as far as their combinations of high and low size and contradictions or contrasts of colour and form will permit. One mass will now for a moment conflict with another and then flow over and blend with it. There will be sharp contrasts and then gradually the smoothest blendings. It is difficult to convey the idea of just how this can be done. It takes long practice and the study of nature in many moods. The observant eye well recognizes in fields and forest glades wonderful exhibitions of how such work can be accomplished. It will be discovered how the black alder grows among its native companions; who are these companions, how they behave when associated together, what soil and what exposure they like. An intimate knowledge of each should be acquired.

The types of growth should be allowed to assert themselves freely. Instead of a group of high and low growths, a single tree, or three specimens, may stand out almost alone with a few attendant shrubs trailing along in the neighbourhood. Perhaps farther on there may be a different kind of tree standing on the very edge of a solid group with a few scattering shrubs around it. Then again there will be one noble specimen of tree form standing entirely alone as if it were sufficient unto itself and brooked no companion, or there might be several in a grove. Such trees are, whether out in the middle of the lawn, or in a grassy glade near a path, the one most valuable feature of the picture. They lend dignity and character more than any other member of the association of trees and shrubs growing on the lawn, and, when combined with the loosely planted shrubs in the neighbourhood, a mystical and enlarged effect in the distance is often thus produced which is of the greatest value in the landscape. The following quotation may give some suggestion of how such a difficult grouping should be managed:

> "[A newly planted group] or a natural woods properly thinned out seems to show an inlet into a wood that has been cut, if the opposite points of the entrance tally, that gives a show of art and depreciates its merit; but a difference only in the situation of those points, by bringing one more forward than the other, prevents the appearance though the forms be similar. Other points which distinguish the great parts should in general be strongly marked; a short turn has more spirit in it than a tedious circuity; and a line broken by angles has a precision and firmness which in an undulated line are wanting: the angles should, indeed, commonly be a little softened; the rotundity of the plant which forms them is sometimes sufficient for the purpose; but if they are mellowed down too much they lose all meaning. Three or four large parts, thus boldly distinguished, will break a very long outline; more may be, and often ought to be, thrown in, but seldom are necessary: when two woods are opposed on the sides

of a narrow glade, neither has so much occasion for variety in itself, as if it were single: if they are very different from each other, the contrast supplies the deficiency in each, and the interval is full of variety. The form of that interval is, indeed, of as much consequence as its own; though the outline of both the woods be separately beautiful, yet if together they do not cast the open space into an agreeable figure, the whole scene is not pleasing; and the figure is never agreeable when the sides too closely correspond; whether they are exactly the same, or exactly the reverse of each other, they equally appear artificial.

Every variety of outline hitherto mentioned may be traced by the underwood alone, but frequently the same effects may be produced with more ease, and with much more beauty, by a few trees standing out from the thicket, and belonging to, or seeming to belong to, the wood so as to make a part of its figure. Even where they are not wanted for that purpose, detached trees are such agreeable objects, so distinct, so light, when compared to the covert about them, that skirting along it in some parts, and breaking it in others, they give an unaffected grace, which can no otherwise be given to the outline. They have a still further effect, when they stretch across the whole breadth of an inlet, or before part of a recess in the woods; they are themselves shown to advantage by the space between them, and that space seen between their stems they in turn throw into an agreeable perspective. An inferior grace of the same kind may be often introduced, only by distinguishing the boles of some trees in the wood itself, and keeping down the thicket beneath them. Where this cannot be well executed, still the outline may be filled with such trees and shrubs as swell out in the middle of their growth and diminish at both ends; or with such as rise in a slender cone; with those whose branches tend upwards; or whose base is very small in proportion to their height; or which are very thin of boughs and of leaves. In a confined garden scene which wants room for the effect of detached trees, the outline will be heavy, if these little attentions are disregarded. As for the kind of trees to be used, good taste and experience must be left to make the selection."[1]

The following words of Richard Jefferies will perhaps be found helpful as explaining how the character of trees counts in the landscape:

> "I listened to the sweet Briar Wind; but for weeks and weeks the dark black oaks stood straight out of the snow as masts of ships with furled sails frozen and ice-bound in the haven of the deep valley."
>
> "Thick are Hawthorn leaves, many deep on the spray; and beneath them there is a twisted and interentangled winding in and out of boughs, such as no curious ironwork of ancient artist could equal; through the leaves and metal work of boughs the soft west wind wafts us at his ease."

[1] Thomas Whately, *Observations on Modern Gardening.*

"The bark of the beech is itself a panel to study, spotted with velvet moss brown green, made grey by close-grown lichens, stained with its own hues of growth and toned by time. To these add bright sunlight and leaf shadow, the sudden lowering of tint as a cloud passes, the different aspects of the day and of the evening, and the change of rain and dry weather. You may look at the bark of a beech twenty times, and always find it different. There is another spirit among beech trees; they look like deer and memories of old English Life."

The sense of distant space outside of the estate is always desirable. If these single trees and scattering shrubs can seem to lose themselves over the crest of a hill into the sky it increases the mystery and sense of largeness, the feeling that one might own the Universe. Richard Jefferies expresses this idea when he writes as follows in *Field and Hedgerow:*

"Still higher and as the firs cease, and shower and sunshine, wind and dew can reach the ground unchecked, comes the tufted heath branched heather of the moorland top. A thousand acres of purple heather sloping southward to the sun, deep valleys of dark heather, further slopes beyond of purple, more valleys of heather—the heath shows more in the sunlight, and heather darkens the shadows of the hollows—and so on and on, mile after mile, till the heath bells seem to end in the sunset. Round and beyond is the immense plain of the air—you feel how limitless the air is at this height, for there is nothing to measure it by. Past the weald lie the south Downs, but they form no boundary, the plain of the air goes over them to the sea and space."

It is really a case of simplicity in variety, a type repeated and varied, becoming something new continually, evolving new charms, yet keeping in view a definite and foreordained unified beauty that is active and changing, but unlike a river that flows on and on, the type is ever returning on itself, melting together and anon conflicting, contrasting, dominating one over the other, and all the time actively advancing to new conquests of beauty, to new charms of blended form and colour. It is like the way the association of mother and child actively helps to develop the beauties of the characters of each person, bringing out the charm more and more the longer they live together, or if mismanagement of their relations occurs, the same tendency to discord and deterioration will reveal itself. The trees and shrubs are worked into a scheme, type within type making the picture fuse together after presenting different degrees of contrast, and finally wooing it to enter into a union where the parts are hardly perceptible to the general sweep of the eye. The play of forces ends in a picture, which in every way continues to change day by day while remaining of the same general character. If the woodland glades and the fields and hedgerow are studied in the light of these suggestions, their value will be more and more verified. The only difference is that there will be then a conscious recognition of the truth, whereas in the many cases that have already happened in the past, the best kind of such landscape work has been done on instinctively right lines. The best work is usually done by a man who cannot tell you why he did it.

The experience of thinning out forest trees in connection with a park or country place will teach many things if it is done seriously. Most people do not carry it on seriously. It is really almost as difficult an undertaking as to create a new place. It will be found that all the above ideas enunciated should be controlling in the management of this work, and its combination with new planting is the most difficult task of all. Thomas Whately gives the following advice, which is good as far as it goes but it does not go quite far enough:

> "It is not however foreign to the subject to observe, that the effects that have been recommended may sometimes be produced by wood alone, without any alteration in the ground itself: a tedious continued line may by such means be broken; it is usual for this purpose to place several little clumps along a brow; but if they are small and numerous the artifice is weak and apparent: an equal number of trees collected into one or two large masses, and dividing the line into very unequal parts is less suspicious, and obliterates the idea of sameness with more certainty. When several similar lines are seen together, if one be planted, and the other bare, they become contrasts to

each other. A hollow in certain situations has been mentioned as a disagreeable interruption to a continued surface; but filled with wood, the heads of the trees supply the vacancy; the irregularity is preserved; even the inequalities of the depth are in some measure shown, and a continuation of surface is provided. Rising ground may, on the other hand, be in appearance raised still higher, by covering it with wood, of humble growth toward the bottom and gradually taller as it ascends. An additional mark of the inclination of falling ground may also be obtained by placing a few trees in the same direction, which will strongly point out the way; whereas plantations athwart a descent, bolster up the ground, and check the fall; but obliquely crossing it, they will often divert the general tendency; the ground will in some measure assume their direction, and they will make a variety not a contradiction. Hedges, or continued plantations, carried over uneven ground, render the irregularities more conspicuous, and frequently mark little inequalities which would otherwise escape observation: or if a line of trees run close upon an edge of an abrupt fall, they give it depth and importance. By such means a view may be improved; by similar means in more confined spots, very material purposes may be answered.

"Though the surface of the wood when commanded deserves all these attentions, yet the outline more frequently calls for our regard; it is also more in our power; it may sometimes be great, and may always be beautiful. The first requisite is irregularity. That a mixture of trees and underwood should form a long straight line, can never be natural; and a succession of easy sweeps and gentle rounds, each a portion of a greater or less circle, composing altogether a line literally serpentine, is if possible worse. It is but a number of regularities put together in a disorderly manner, and equally distant from the beautiful both of art and of nature. The true beauty of outline consists more in breaks than in sweeps; rather in angles than in rounds; in variety, not in succession.

"The outline of a wood is a continued line, and small variations do not save it from the insipidity of sameness. One deep recess, one bold prominence, has more effect than twenty little irregularities. That one divides the line into parts, but no breach is thereby made in its unity; a continuation of wood always remains; the form of it only is altered, and the extent is increased. The eye, which hurries to the extremity of whatever is uniform, delights to trace a varied line through all its intricacies, to pause from stage to stage, and to lengthen the progress. The parts must not, however, on that account, be multiplied, till they are too minute to be interesting, and so numerous as to create confusion. A few large parts should be strongly distinguished in their forms, their directions, and their situations; each of them may afterwards be decorated with subordinate varieties; and the mere growth of the plants will occasion some irregularity; on many occasions more will not be required. Every variety in the outline of a wood must be a *prominence* or a *recess*. Breadth in either is not so important as length to the one and depth to the other. If the former ends in an angle, the latter diminishes to a point, they have more force than a shallow dent, or a dwarf excrescence, how wide so ever. They are greater deviations from the continued line which they are intended to break; and their effect is to enlarge the wood itself, which seems to stretch from the most advanced point, back beyond the most distant to which it retires. The extent of a large wood on a flat, not commanded, can by no circumstance be so manifestly shown, as by a deep recess; especially if that deep recess winds so as to conceal the extremity and leave the imagination to pursue it."[1]

It is not sufficiently realized by most people, even after hard experience, how difficult it is to grow plants in the shade among the roots of a piece of woodland. It would be easy to mention several trees and shrubs that have the reputation of doing well when planted in the woods, which in the final test generally fail. The presence of freshly cultivated and enriched soil, either on the ground or brought from elsewhere, will greatly encourage the growth of such plants, but to really succeed a great deal of light should be let in, and even under such circumstances too much confidence in the expected good results should not prevail.

[1] *Observations on Modern Gardening.*

Plants suitable for landscape gardening purposes naturally separate themselves into the following broad divisions: Deciduous trees, evergreen trees, deciduous shrubs, evergreen shrubs, perennial or herbaceous plants, and bedding or subtropical plants. There is no intention here of considering the habits, appearance, or methods of propagating these plants. Our subject is landscape gardening, not horticulture, not arboriculture or forestry, not soil culture nor grass culture. The principles and art of landscape gardening and its evolution in nature and history are the topics we are studying.

Evergreens occupy a position and perform functions that count greatly in the general purpose of the lawn. They produce the solid effects, the strong shadows, the enduring colours throughout the season. They shield the smaller, or less rugged plants, trees, or shrubs from the cold winds of winter, especially of March and April. In their alcoves and in the shelters behind their promontories they cherish and preserve alive many shrubs and perennials (flowers) that would otherwise wither under the cold winds and hot suns of early spring. Here again that strange instinct is felt which makes one like to see a great mass of evergreens intermingled with hardly any deciduous trees, stretching out in sweeping lines of form and colour, spirey and spreading, low or high, spruce, cedar, hemlock, pine, or juniper, blue, silver, green and fiery red, crimson and dainty pink, June and November, ever changing, boldly flaunting, or softly melting into delicate tender hues.

Evergreens form all the year round a very positive feature in the landscape, and require the nicest disposition of colour and form to establish pleasant and harmonious relations between different members of the lawn vegetation. There are colours of trees and shrubs that are offensive, why it is rather difficult to say. For one thing they are striped yellow or white and come at a time of the year which makes them look unnatural. It is not the maples and dogwoods to which we refer. Their clothing in June and October or November is always charming, and so are the silver firs and the larches in early summer:—but what is meant, for instance, is not the densiflora pine of Japan, grand in its panoply of green, but a sickly looking and slightly repulsive form of the same species which when striped and variegated with gold is called the sun ray pine. White may be of the highest value in the vegetation of a landscape, as witness the white birches finding a home in small numbers disposed against a background of dark evergreens, and yet the variegated ash-leaved maple (*Negundo acerifolium variegatum*) is of a sickly white hue. A single deciduous tree of light foliage standing out in front of a mass of evergreens will often look well, and so will a small grove of them. It is the evergreen type and the deciduous, properly related, and used over and over again, that pleases—conflicting, triumphing, and then trailing off or losing each other, in the midst of the blending always distinct and in some way each asserting its own individuality, but never carelessly mingling or failing to persist in an evidently preconceived, though ceaselessly varying, type or method of growing.

Besides the type of leafage, form, and colour, there is to be considered the still more positive character of the trunk, branches, and twigs, stark and bare in winter and early spring. The white birch already noted is one, and there are hosts of others. They stand out, the white oak, for instance, against a lurid winter sunset, or they glitter after an ice storm, showing their strange convolution of branches, like the oak and thorn described in another chapter by Richard Jefferies. There is also the fruit of the thorns and wild plums, chokeberries, black alders, viburnums, and roses, hanging in some cases all winter on their naked stems.

All these separate qualities in a tree or shrub need to be handled in a sympathetic way in the composition of a year round landscape. It may be asked how this is to be done. Certainly it is not easy, and few succeed in doing it. It can only be done by study, careful study, of the nature of the trees and shrubs and their behaviour in hundreds of instances on the lawn and in the field and woods, and some help can, of course, be had by reference to books and prints enabling one to pursue the trail of experience, and to finally attain to something really worth accomplishing. Did you ever hear of a man, a city clerk, who on a small city lot grew such flowers that finally his wonderful horticultural skill astonished his correspondents the world over. He did not accomplish these great triumphs by means of books, but books helped him.

Perennial plants need treatment in the scheme of the landscape gardener in the same general way as trees and shrubs, both deciduous and evergreen. They play a subordinate part, though a no less attractive one in the scheme. They should stand apart in colonies or in clusters at the feet of the shrubs and even of the trees; they should carpet the glades and borders of the shrub groups with trilliums and anemones, and even snowdrops in protected nooks. The iris and the daffodil and the water-lilies all have their places, one in the moist edge of the stream, the other a little higher up, and the last in two feet of water. There is always a way to associate them happily with their larger but not more beautiful companions, the trees and shrubs. This association is really necessary for the fullest development of the beauty of the perennial wild flower.

Of the annuals and the bedding and tropical plants nearly as good words can be said, for each in its way is just as beautiful and valuable as the other, provided it is set in its own appointed place, as designated by nature when her secrets have been revealed to the man who makes the landscape. In the chapter on Gardens is an illustration showing how this bedding should be managed and fitted into a natural scheme of this kind of planting, and so we leave the problem of bedding for each one to work out for himself, finding it on the whole one of the most difficult and perhaps most fascinating of any within the range of landscape gardening.

It has already been pointed out that the vegetation

of a new place should be conformed to already existing growths peculiar to the region. This does not mean that no trees save those that naturally grow in the neighbourhood should be used. There are many other trees and shrubs of kindred habit and hardiness and appearance but foreign in origin that suit a particular territory: in other words, the spirit and nature of the scenery of the country should be made the key to the harmony of the plantations. A quotation from the writings of the late Charles Eliot pertaining to this subject may make it more clear:

> "Within the area of the United States we have many types of scenery and many climates, but in designing the surroundings of dwellings, in working upon the landscape, we too often take no account of these facts. On the rocky coast of Maine each summer sees money worse than wasted in endeavouring to make Newport lawns on ground which naturally bears countless lichen-covered rocks, dwarf pines and spruces, and thickets of sweet-fern, bayberry, and wild rose. The owners of this particular type of country spend thousands in destroying its natural beauty with the intention of attaining to a foreign beauty, which in point of fact is unattainable in anything like perfection by reason of the shallow soil and frequent droughts. I know too many of these unhappy 'lawns.' Ledges too large to be buried or blasted protrude here and there. They are bare and bleached now, though they were once half

smothered in all manner of mixed shrubbery; the grass is poor and, wherever the underlying rock is near the surface, all is ugliness where once was only beauty. Moreover, if the lawn were perfect and truly English, how would it harmonize with the pitch pine and scrub birches and dwarf junipers which clothe the lands around? No, the English park with its great trees and velvet turf is supremely beautiful in England where it is simply the natural scenery perfected; but save in those favoured parts of North America where the natural conditions approximate those of the old country, the beauty of it cannot be had and should not be attempted.

"To be sure, the countries of the continent of Europe all have their so-called English parks, but the best of these possess little or none of the real English character and charm. The really beautiful parks of Europe are those which have a character of their own derived from their own conditions of climate and scene. The parks of Paulovsk near St. Petersburg, of Muskau in Silesia, of the villa Thuret on the cape of Antibes in the Mediterranean are none of them English, except as England was the mother of the natural as distinguished from the architectural in gardening. The Thuret park, if I may cite an illustration of my meaning, is a wonderland of crowded vegetation, of ways deep, shaded by rich and countless evergreens, of steep open slopes aglow with bright anemones. Between the high masses of eucalyptus and acacia are glimpses of the sea, and of the purple foothills and the gleaming snow peaks of the Maritime Alps. In the thickets are laurels, pittosporums, gardenias, etc., from the ends of the earth: but ilex, phillyrea, and oleander are natives of the country, and myrtle and pistacia are the common shrubs of the seashore, so that the foreigners are only additions to an original wealth of evergreens. The garden also has its palms of many species, with cycads, yuccas, aloes, and the like; but the agaves are common hedge plants of the country, and strange euphorbias grow everywhere about: moreover, the most monstrous of these creatures are given a space apart in the main garden, so that they may not disturb the quiet of the scene. M. Thuret saved the olives and the ilexes of the original hillside. He did not try to imitate the gardening of another and different country or climate but simply worked to enhance the beauty natural to the region of his choice.

"At the other end of Europe all this is equally true of Paulovsk. Here at the edge of the wet and dismal plain on which St. Petersburg is built, is a stretch of upland almost featureless, but which thanks to a careful helping of nature is now the most interesting and beautiful bit of scenery the neighbourhood of the Tsar's capital can show. Here is no futile striving after the loveliness of England or any other foreign land; no attempting the beauty of a mountain country or a rocky country or a warm country, or any other country than just this country that lies around St. Petersburg; here also is no planting of incongruous specimens and no out-of-place flower bedding. The park of Muskau teaches the same lesson, and under conditions closely resembling those of our Middle States.

"The lawns or open stretches or glades of turf are just as carefully considered, it will be noticed, in the semitropical park and luxuriant vegetation of the Antibes as in England or Russia. The open spaces with bordering foliage, the pastoral, the picturesque, have the same justification and interest given them here as in England or America."[1]

The philosophy of the development of lawn planting has come in the present day to mean far more than it did in the days of our fathers, in spite of the fact that the modern period appears to be one of fads and faddists, of Italian and old-fashioned gardens, of blue spruces and yellow Japan cypresses. In the eighteenth century there was little difference between the landscape architect and the architect; indeed it was the architect and gardener who generally designed the entire place. The name *landscape architect* was unknown.

To-day we have an outdoor art of many cultures, notably architectural and horticultural, the antagonisms of which have produced a play of forces which has tended to break up into various parts the formal and rigid landscape rules of classic and mediæval times. Extravagances of many kinds have naturally made themselves evident, yet these very antagonisms are

[1] *Garden and Forest*, vol i., April 4, 1888, p. 64.

doing good work; giving renewed and vivid life to landscape gardening and thrusting its roots deeper and deeper towards the heart of nature. Every part of outdoor art is coming to have its place, never quite its perfect place, but nearer and nearer to the highest standards. Antagonisms always lead to continually renewed activity and larger fruitfulness. Although antagonism sometimes means conquest and even defeat and death of a sort, it is only a case of dying to live and to reach heights of accomplishment previously inconceivable.

XIII

MAINTENANCE

"IT is quite impossible to plant a large extensive park so that it can present the same picture when full grown as it did at the beginning, only on an altered scale, and the objects in it are for ever after in the right relation to one another,—since nature cannot be calculated so accurately and it would also take too much time.

"Here we meet with the drawback of our art, in a certain sense—though it may also be regarded as an advantage. For it is impossible to create a finished, permanent work of art in landscape gardening, such as the painter, sculptor, and architect are able to produce, because our material is not inanimate, but living; we can say of the landscape gardener's art, as of all nature's own pictures, as Fichte said of the German language, "It is about to be, but never is." That is, it never stands still, can never be fixed and left to itself. Hence a skilful guiding hand is always necessary for works of this kind. If the hand is lacking too long they not only deteriorate, they become something quite different, but if the hand is present, beauties are continually being added without losing or sacrificing those already in existence. The chief tool which we use for construction, *i.e.*, our brush and chisel, is the spade, the chief tool for *maintenance* and improvement is the axe. It must not rest for a single winter, or it will happen to us with the trees as it did with the water-carriers in the Tale of the 'Wizard's Apprentice'—they will grow over our heads."[1]

It is more than a case of overcrowding a design which is always about to be but never is, in Fichte's phrase. It is also in other words always becoming, an ebb and flow, an unceasing evolution of skilled results, continually improvement, or retrogression, deterioration, and decay. Nature never stands still. It is ever increasing life or ever increasing decay, oscillation between the two, steadily or spasmodically, as the one gets the upper hand of the other. Consequently the maintenance and care must be unceasing and vigilant and based on penetrating study of new conditions as they arise. The seasons, cold, heat, drought, insect life, fungi, and pests of every sort, all need to be watched intelligently and continually.

It is a common saying that he, or she, knows how to make a plant grow. It thrives under his hand. A great propagator handles plants like a wizard. There is something, people think, uncanny in such successful operations. But, after all, it is chiefly a matter of

[1] Prince Pückler, *Hints on Landscape Gardening.*

maintenance. Seed is sown, a cutting or a small plant is set out, or a graft is set in a stock; one must know how to do it; but nine tenths of the success attained comes from an unceasing conflict with adverse conditions, eventually finding in the process of development the brief poise and equilibrium of a mature and successfully grown shrub or tree. Intimate, loving comprehension of the nature of the plant can alone do this. It would seem that love is actually necessary to achieve the greatest results even in growing a plant, but love without knowledge can accomplish little, as many an amateur horticulturist has learned to his cost. Knowledge generally comes from long, heart-breaking failure and diligent, oft-repeated effort. The man who hires such work done, even with practically unlimited means, seldom gets as good results as some enthusiastic amateur—crank his neighbours probably dub him—who works night and day whenever he has a moment to spare to give to his plants. And there is incessant work to do. There is planting to be done every little while throughout the seasons, spring, summer, fall, and winter, especially if the work is supplemented by a greenhouse. There is always pruning of some sort, pinching if nothing else, and warfare always on insects, weeds to fight and watering to be done, and cultivation, spading, hoeing, and mulching to be maintained.

It is difficult to realize what such maintenance means when it is faithfully carried out, unless one has been responsible for it himself. There are endless ways for maintenance to present its exacting demands. The lawn, for instance, grows bare in spots and needs rich soil spread over it and then to be reseeded, and, if the seed does not take on account of dry weather, then seeding again during a favourable spell. Few spots on an estate or in a park need more intelligent care than a lawn. The time apparently never comes when it can be forgotten any more than anything else on the place, although it is perhaps more neglected than almost anything. To mow the lawn every two or three weeks is often all that is done, whereas the weeds and rain will come at various intervals and thus make extra work. If the soil has been properly prepared and the right kind of clean seed used in making the lawn, there should however be little need of weeding. Pruning trees and shrubs may be done during nearly every month in the year, either in the old wood or the new, and there is hardly a time except in the depth of winter when noxious insects do not call for attention. And for each of these various operations, special knowledge and trained skill are needed. It is results obtained in this diligent way that have gained the unrivalled horticultural fame of the Chinese and Japanese. Verily! how do they do it? It is actually uncanny, and yet perhaps after all it is only intelligent maintenance, the skill of which, coming down through generations, is a possible explanation of it.

All the processes, however, all the knowledge that goes to the maintenance of a park or estate does not fall within the province of this book devoted chiefly to the discussion of ideas and illustrations. Reference is made in the bibliography to works on special subjects from which enough can be readily learned to enable any one to intelligently employ, if necessary, experts of sufficient knowledge and skill to do good work in the various departments of maintenance. In time, knowledge will doubtless come in this way to the owner of the place, and he will find the occupation of supervising such work a pleasure and even a delight. There will be failures and many accidents, but a fair degree of success will make the memory of the misfortunes soon grow dim in the joy of horticultural achievement.

The chief reason that this supreme excellence of maintenance is seldom attained is that few people acquire enough knowledge to know fine maintenance when they see it. Even if they have given long and what they consider diligent attention to their place, grown wonderful roses, or hothouse grapes, by means of a clever gardener, when they go about the world their kind of training hardly enables them to realize the quality of good maintenance. It would be well if more people prided themselves on the well-being of their whole estate, rather than some single feature of it, a rose garden, a greenhouse, a scheme of carpet beds or of foliage plants. By a well maintained place it should not be understood, however, that the standard of high excellence necessarily implies a swept and garnished and polished place such as one sees occasionally in Paris and elsewhere. Cleanliness and neatness are all very well, but they are overdone when the trees and shrubs are trimmed and trained until they hardly look like trees and shrubs, and the grass is mown till the roots are almost bare; where the presence of a stray leaf is profanation, and sand is spread over the walks and drives and raked and swept till they look like the sanded floor of a house. The thought at once protrudes itself how rich must be the man who can afford to do all this superfine work.

The kind of maintenance that is sane and sensible is not neatness and cleanliness only, but high development, not abnormal culture, but a happy condition of free, healthy growth with the accidents and defects and diseases always incident to life well looked after; otherwise, nothing extraordinary, just steady, easy growth that a sense of proper re-adjustment accomplishes without apparent effort, much as we find that the appearance of a well dressed man or woman is not noticed but unconsciously enjoyed. Such a place cannot be developed under the eye of a mere specialist even if he be multiplied many times. It needs the eye of a master, who appreciates its possibilities and loves to see the beauties of the place develop in an all-round manner. It is interesting to observe how artistic designs conceived in the early construction of Central Park have been realized and that fifty years later the original intention of the work is more evident by means of persistent maintenance than when it was first constructed.

In the next quotation it will be seen how a conception of natural scenery, a landscape poem, was carefully thought out in the beginning and constructed at great expense. At the present time, on a spring day especially, this conception is one of the most inspiring portions of the park and the most important trees are still there. The words of the landscape architects of the park are as follows:

> "As an important suggestion springs from this observation, we shall be pardoned for referring to a portion of Central Park, N. Y., where somewhat similar conditions formerly existed and where our views have been adopted and realized. Entering by the turn to the right at the Merchants' Gate (59th St. & C. P. W.) in a few minutes the visitor's eye falls upon the open space called the cricket ground where originally was a small swamp, enlarged at great expense in the construction of the Park in order to meet a similar artistic purpose to that above explained, by the removal of several large ledges of rock, and now occupied by an unbroken meadow which extends before the observer to the extent of a thousand feet. Here is a suggestion of freedom and repose which must in itself be suggestive and tranquilizing to the visitor coming from the confinement and bustle of crowded streets, but this is not all. The observer resting for a moment to enjoy the scene, which he is induced to do by the arrangement of the planting, cannot but hope for still greater space than is obvious before him and this hope is encouraged first by the fact that though bodies of rock and foliage to the right and left obstruct his direct vision, no

The Umpire Rock and the Ball Ground, Lower End of Central Park, near 59th Street and 8th Avenue, New York City.

From a Photograph by William Hale Kirk.

limit is seen to the extension of the meadow in a lateral direction, while beyond the low shrubs which form an undefined border to it in front there are no trees or other impediments to vision for a distance of half a mile or more and the only distant object is the wooded knoll of Vista Rock nearly a mile away, upon the summit of which it is an important point in the design not yet realized, to erect a slight artificial structure, for the purpose of catching the eye and the better holding it in this direction. The imagination of the visitor is thus led instinctively to form the idea that a broad expanse is opening before him, and, the more surely to accomplish this, a glimpse of the slope of turf beyond the border of the shrubs in the middle distance has been secured. As the visitor proceeds, this idea is strengthened and the hope which springs from it in a considerable degree satisfied, if not actually realized, first by a view of those parts of the cricket ground which lie to the right and left of his previous field of vision, afterwards by the broad expanse of turf on either side and before him, which comes into view as he emerges from the plantations at or near the marble archway.

"The carrying out of this most important purpose in the scenery of Central Park, owing to the rocky and heterogeneous character of the original surface, involved much more labour and a larger expenditure than any other landscape feature of that undertaking."[1]

[1] Olmsted and Vaux, Sixth Annual Report to Prospect Park Commission, 1866.

In considering this type of maintenance which aims at perfection, but which is neither superfine or affectedly natural, we should always remember that on estates and parks *pastoral* and *picturesque* are the terms that best express what we should seek to create and by maintenance to retain. There should always be a revealing day by day of a new scene, ever picturesque, always renewing itself by the help of a ceaseless and intelligent maintenance which retains all the essential elements that make landscape gardening grateful and sufficing.

The scene in Central Park in the Ramble well illustrates this idea of the picturesque. The trees are large and shadowy, with a quaint old weeping beech in their midst and a peaceful lawn extending away from them. The grass and the trees show evidence of good maintenance and the rocks and masses of the foliage have all the qualities of the picturesque.

Isaac Taylor in *The Spirit of Hebrew Poetry* has beautifully and truly expressed the essential qualities of the picturesque, and to create such qualities and to retain them in the landscape by sympathetic and skilful maintenance does certainly compass the highest reach of the art of landscape gardening. He says:

> "The poetry of all nations has conserved more or less of these elements of the primeval repose; and in fact we find them conserved also, and represented in that modern feeling—the love of and the taste for the picturesque. Modern undoubtedly is this taste, which has not developed itself otherwise than in

A Picturesque View in the Ramble, Central Park, New York City.
From a Photograph by William Hale Kirk.

connexion with pictorial art in the Department of Landscape. What is the picturesque? A question not easily answered; yet this is certain, that any attempt that may be made to find an answer for it must bring us in contact with the very elements which already have been named; and which are assembled in the idea of patriarchal repose.

"The picturesque is not simply beauty in nature—it is not luxuriance; it is not amplitude and vastness; it is not copiousness; it is not the fruit of man's interference: but rather it is the consequence of an indolent acquiescence on his part in things as they are or as they have become; the picturesque belongs to the foreground always, or to the stage next beyond the foreground—never does it take its range beyond the horizon. The picturesque claims as its own the cherished and delicious ideas of deep seclusion, of lengthened, undisturbed continuance, and of the absence, afar off, of those industrial energies which mark their presence by renovations, by removals, and by a better order of things, and by signs of busy industry and of thriftiness and order.

"Within the sacred precincts of the picturesque, the trees must be such as have outlived the winters of centuries, and been green through the scorching heats of unrecorded sultry summers: they stoop and yet hold up giant gnarled branches, leafy at the extreme sprays; and their twistings are such that they look supernatural, seen against an autumnal evening sky. The fences that skirt the homestead of the picturesque must have done their office through the occupance of three or four generations. The dwellings of man must declare themselves such as have sheltered the hoary quietude of sires long ago gone to their graves. Inasmuch as the picturesque abjures change it rejects improvement, it abhors the square, the perpendicular, the horizontal, and it likes rather all forms that now are other than at first they were, and that lean this way and that way and that threaten to fall; but so did the same building threaten a fall a century ago! In a word, the picturesque is the *Conservation of Landscape Beauty.* It is where the picturesque holds undisputed sway that we shall find—or shall expect to find—secure and placid longevity—domestic sanctity and reverence; together with a piety that holds more communion with the past than with the busy and philanthropic present. Give me only the picturesque, and I shall be well content never to gaze on tropical luxuriance, or upon Alpine sublimities, nor shall ever wish to travel the broad walks that surround palaces: shall never be taxed for my admiration of those things which wealth and pride have superadded to nature."

The strange quality of charm may not and yet is likely to go with picturesqueness and certainly requires consideration in landscape gardening. But it may be asked what is charm? Who shall say? Arthur C. Benson describing a landscape writes that charm "seems to arise partly out of a subtle orderliness and a simple appropriateness and from a blending of delicate and pathetic elements of a certain unascertained proportion. It seems to touch unknown memories into life and to give a hint of the workings of some whimsical, half tenderly conceived spirit brooding over its work, adding a touch of form here, and a dash of colour there, and pleased to see when all is done that it is good."

This is fine, and in a way true, but after all it is only an attempt to express the inexpressible. The magic and mystery may be there, but the interpretation, who will give it? If the charm is there, all will recognize it, either consciously or unconsciously, in any bit of landscape as well as elsewhere. The best course to pursue is to keep the charm as far as possible untouched and to set anything like buildings or plants outside of its sphere of influence. Its inherent quality is strangely fragile. On the other hand, if one were so fortunate as to give something of this subtile charm to a bit of landscape work, one should never allow it to be marred by a too strict adherence to academic influences; and moreover, having once created a picture possessing this precious quality, it behooves the artist to cherish and maintain his work in the excellent way that has been briefly, and all too unsatisfactorily, suggested in previous parts of this chapter.

XIV

GARDENS

FROM the discussion of the relative nature of parks and gardens there emerges the idea that buildings and gardens and parks are in the scheme of landscape gardening only parts of a whole, units in one organized creation made up of natural and artificial features developed in various ways. The law of contradictions and contrasts may be made to act here as it may everywhere else in landscape gardening to produce the most happy effects. There should be no evident dividing line between the park and garden where one passes into the other. There should be, however, a distinct contrast established, it may be by plantations of trees or by changing frequently and radically the character of the flowers and shrubs, yet the division line should be nowhere formal and rigid. For this reason hedges as usually seen do not make an agreeable dividing line between the garden and the lawn or park. The transition is too sharp and sudden. In a word it is too unnatural, and fails to give the suggestion of blending as well as contrast found so characteristic of the natural scenes of field and forest.

There are two important elements of design found in nearly all parks and gardens; one of these is architecture and the other is "free nature" as the Germans term it. The law of contradiction or contrast necessarily comes into play here as elsewhere, and on the way it is applied and the way the spirit of one idea breaks into and overflows into the other depends the success of the scheme.

This scheme divides itself naturally into simple parts, contrasting and in a sense contradicting each other but capable of working out into beautiful pictures. Open spaces of grass and bordering plantations with paths and roads running through them are the two divisions the relations of which should be always kept in mind, whether the object be to design a park or a garden, which after all are fundamentally the same, only variations and combinations of the divisions already indicated. It is a question of the rhythm of low and high, of broad or narrow masses of vegetation, and the overflow of one arrangement into the other. For instance, single trees and small masses of shrubs may be used effectively out in the open lawn beyond the bordering shrubbery, or, on the other hand, the grass spaces may penetrate with good effect far into the shrubbery.

Then, moreover, these types of division may be applied to a group of small designs and a number of them combined into the main design, which, subject to the same law and presenting the same variety of types, constitutes the treatment of the estate, gardens, lawns, and everything within its bounds.

Approaching the house from the park and coming to the pleasure ground through plantations more or less indeterminate in height and breadth, we reach a sort of middle ground. This is the pleasure ground, and after that comes the garden, as it were, a part of the house.

> "The word *pleasure ground* is difficult to translate accurately into German, and I therefore consider it better to retain the English expression; it means a *terrain*, abutting on the house territory and decorated and fenced in, of far larger dimensions than gardens usually are, something that establishes a gradation between the park and the true garden, which should appear to be really a part of the house."[1]

Thomas Whately says in *Observations on Modern Gardening:*

> "If regularity is not entitled to a preference in the environs or approach to a house, it would be difficult to support its pretensions to a place in any more distant parts of a park or a garden. Formal slopes of ground are ugly, right or circular lines bounding water do not indeed change the nature of the element; it still retains some of its agreeable properties; but the shape given to it is disgusting. Regularity in plantations is less offensive; we are habituated, as has been already observed, to straight lines of trees, in cultivated nature; a double row

[1] Prince Pückler, *Hints, etc., on Landscape Gardening.*

The Arrangement of the Beds of Foliage Plants Such as Cannas, Coleuses, and Geraniums around the Arsenal, Central Park, New York City.

Another View of the Arrangement of the Beds of Foliage Plants Such as Cannas, Coleuses, and Geraniums around the Casino, Central Park, New York City.

From Photographs by Messrs. Charles Scribner's Sons. (Reproduced by Permission.)

meeting at the top, and forming a complete arched vista, has peculiar effect; other regular figures have a degree of beauty, and to alter or disguise such a disposition, without destroying a number of fine trees, which cannot well be spared, may sometimes be difficult; but it hardly ever ought to be chosen in the arrangement of a young plantation. Regularity was once thought essential to every garden, and every approach, and it yet remains in many. It is still a character, denoting the neighbourhood of a gentleman's habitation; and an avenue as an object in the view gives to the house, otherwise inconsiderable, the air of a mansion."

Here in the pleasure ground the sensation produced by the landscape is of more formality, elegance, and finish, in other words, a touch of the spirit of the architecture should appear, retaining still a predominance of the feeling of free nature belonging to the park. The shapes of the flower beds should be more irregular as well as the outlines of the grass spaces, and the walks should be more meandering than in the garden.

In the garden itself the architectural lines, ovals, straight lines, and circular, or any form that fits the architecture of the mansion or house are admissible. Prince Pückler says in this connexion in his *Hints on Landscape Gardening:*

"I might repeat here with some variation what I have said before: as the park is nature idealized within a small compass so the garden is an extended dwelling. Here the tastes of the owner may have free play, following his imagination and indulging even in trivialities. Everything should be decorative, designed for comfort; and as ornamental as the means permit. Let the lawns appear as a velvet carpet embroidered with flowers; gather together the rarest and the most beautiful exotic plants (provided that nature or art will enable them to thrive); polished benches, refreshing fountains, the cool shades of dense avenues, order and fancy, in short everything in turn to evoke the richest and most varied effect, just as one furnishes every salon in the interior of a house in a different style. Thus one may continue the suite of rooms on a greater scale under the open sky, whose blue vault, with ever-renewed cloud canopy, takes the place of the painted ceiling, and in which sun and moon are the perpetual illumination."

But everywhere the same laws of design should control—low, broad, or narrow plantations in contrast or contradiction with high ones. In the beds of flowers the heights of the plants should bear the same relation to each other in the garden as grass spaces and trees and shrubs in the park; alternanthera making, as it were, the grass space, and then coleus and canna, for the trees and shrubs. It is not so much a question of the kind of plants as their mode of treatment. The law, the principle, the type should be the same in all cases. The unity of effect is just as important as the variety.[1]

[1] See flower beds in Central Park, New York, designed by Calvert Vaux on this principle. See illustrations on p. 240.

Variety, moreover, in landscape gardening and particularly in the garden may assume the guise of mystery that may under some circumstances, prove magical in effect. One of the supreme feats of landscape gardening is to suggest surprise, to tempt question as to what is behind that bush or tree, or round the next turn of the road or path, or over the hill. Wonderful effects of the most charming natural character come to us in this way. A sweep of grass creeps around yonder point of shrubbery and we wonder what is just there in the recess.

> "The willow wren sings, but his voice and that of the wind seem to give emphasis to the holy and meditative silence. The mystery of nature and life hover about the columned temple of the forest. The secret is always behind a tree, as of old time it was always behind the pillar of the temple."[1]

The character of the appearance of trees and shrubs is so varied at different seasons of the year, in sunshine and shadow, rain and clear weather, that there is hardly any limit to the mysterious and magical results that can be accomplished. Some special tree or shrub may lend itself more than another to this mystery and magic, and the art of the landscape gardener may do much, but in the final result there should appear no sense of effort, no loss of easy naturalness, and the law of contradiction and contrast should be so applied as to

[1] See R. Jefferies, *Field and Hedgerow*, p. 107.

give the idea of continual change and at the same time of adherence to a generally pervading law of arrangement throughout the entire landscape scheme, for "an organic unified scheme is one in which the whole is in every part."

Does this seem hard to understand? If the accompanying plan taken from Prince Pückler's book showing how a group of shrubs and trees should be constituted or designed is studied the meaning may be clearer. Certain spaces it will be seen are occupied with shrubs and trees and flowers of various kinds; these kinds are made to produce a variation of high and low forms and masses of colour related to each other according to a definite scheme which also has its own relation as a mass to the surrounding grass space; the grass space has again its own special relation to its environment.

This type of treatment, with its overlapping and predominance of each part as the landscape may demand, should repeat itself over and over again throughout the space in the garden as well as the park. From this statement it is evident that there is no absolute garden, nor any park in the sense of wild nature. Unfortunately there is, however, an antagonism of two types or schools of landscape art existing, one *architectural* and one that may be termed *natural.* The architectural school held sway for centuries and produced a one-sided landscape art, but, in the renewed artistic life of the Renaissance and the followers of Rousseau, a violent love of pure nature developed and produced in the reaction many fanciful and ill-devised conceptions. One school reacted on the other and finally out of the two has developed an art that is like neither of the old conceptions, but is a new one which uses more architectural lines near the architectural features and freer nature farther off.

> "All these little paths were confined and crossed by a limpid and clear stream, sometimes circling amid the grass and flowers in almost imperceptible threads, now in larger streams flowing over a pure mosaic of gravel which made the water more transparent. I can imagine, said I unto them, a rich man from Paris or London master of this house, bringing with him an expensive architect to spoil nature. With what disdain would he enter this simple, mean place! With what contempt would he have all these weeds uprooted! What fine avenues he would open out! What beautiful valleys he would have pierced! What fine goose feet, what fine trees, like parasols and fans! What fine fretted trellises! What beautifully drawn yew hedges, finely squared and rounded! What fine bowling greens of fine English turf, rounded, squared, sloped, and ovalled! What fine yews carved into dragons, pagodas, marmosets, every kind of monster! With what fine bronze vases, what fine stone fruits he would adorn his garden!
>
> "The grand air is always melancholy, it makes us think of the miseries of the man who affects it. Amid his parterres and grand alleys his littleness does not increase.

"What then will the man of taste do, who lives for the sake of living, who can enjoy himself, who seeks real and simple pleasures, and who wishes to make himself a walk within reach of his house? He will make it so commodious and so agreeable that he can please himself there at all hours of the day and moreover so simple and natural that he seems to have done nothing. He will combine water, verdure, shade, and coolness, for nature too combines all these things; he will give symmetry to nothing that is the enemy to nature and variety; and all the alleys of an ordinary garden have so strong a resemblance, that you think you are always in the same one; he will level the soil to walk on it comfortably: but the two sides of the alley will not be always exactly parallel; its direction will not be always on a straight line, it will have a certain vagueness, like the gait of a leisurely man who sways as he walks."[1]

The entire scheme, however, as indicated above, is coming more and more (as in Central Park, New York, and in Germany and England and France) under the control throughout of unified laws of design. This has given and is giving increasing value for both park and garden in the minds of many.

People seeking to improve their places themselves realize in many cases hardly anything of this harmonizing of schools, but they will find the best development will be on these lines, and landscape architects and

[1] Jean Jacques Rousseau, *Julie, or the Nouvelle Héloïse.*

architects do, in many cases, fully realize it, for already the garden and the estate or park are frequently thus made to correlate themselves. There has been conflict, and there is still some between the "architectural" and "natural" schools, but "discord is the proof of vitality" for it is here as elsewhere, again and again, the conflict of elements which in spite of their apparently absolute antagonism are really each contained in the design of a harmonious landscape scheme, and which will therefore eventually be reconciled by further development. The making of a home suggests naturally at first the building of a house and so the architect and his school or party take control, but "A party first truly shows itself to have won the victory when it breaks up into two parties: for so it proves that it contains in itself the principle with which it first had to conflict, and thus it had to get beyond the one-sidedness which was incidental to its earliest expression."

Here are several examples of how the struggle between the *architectural* and the *natural* progresses and takes shape. Smollett gives the following account of a classical architectural garden Villa Pinciana at Rome; although the writer is doubtless a prejudiced observer, he was a keen and, on the whole, veracious one and his travels in 1765 are of great interest and value.

> "He who loves the beauties of simple nature and the charm of neatness, will look for them in vain amidst the groves of Italy. In the garden of Villa Pinciana, there is a plantation of four hundred pines,

which the Italians view with rapture and admiration: there is likewise a long walk of trees extending from the garden gate to the palace; and plenty of shade with alleys and hedges in different parts of the ground, but the groves are neglected; the walks are laid with nothing but common mould or sand, black and dusty; the hedges are tall, thin, and shabby; the trees stunted, the open ground, brown and parched, has scarce any appearance of verdure. The flat, regular alleys of evergreens are cut into fantastic figures; the flower gardens embellished with thin cyphers and flourished figures in box, while the flowers grow in rows of earthen pots, and the ground appears as dusty as if it was covered with the cinders of a blacksmith's forge. The water, of which there is a great plenty, instead of being collected in large pieces, or conveyed in little rivulets and streams to refresh the thirsty soil, or managed so as to form agreeable cascades, is squirted from fountains in different parts of the garden through tubes little bigger than common glyster pipes. It must be owned indeed that the fountains have their merit in the way of sculpture and architecture, that here is a great number of statues that merit attention; but they serve only to encumber the ground, and destroy that effect of rural simplicity which our gardens are designed to produce. In a word, here we have a variety of walks and groves and fountains, a wood of four hundred pines, a paddock with a few meagre deer, a flower garden, an aviary, a grotto, and a fish pond, and in spite of all these particulars it is in my opinion a very contemptible garden when compared to that of Stowe in Buckinghamshire, or even to those of Kensington and Richmond."

And yet Smollett says that of the gardens he has seen in Italy that of the Villa Pinciana is the most remarkable and the most extensive, including a space of three miles in circuit, hard by the walls of Rome, containing a variety of situations which favour all the natural embellishments one would expect to meet in a garden, and exhibit a diversity of noble views of the city and adjacent country.

Vernon Lee thus characterizes Italian gardens:

> "For your new gardens, your real Italian Gardens bring in a new element—that of perspective, architecture, decoration, the trees used as building material, the lie of the land as theatre arrangements, the water as the most docile and multiform stage property."

Walter Savage Landor writes thus on gardens:

> "We Englishmen talk of planting a garden, the modern Italians and ancient Romans talk of *building* one."

Thus you have the two schools contrasted and a contradiction established, the Latin or Southern against the North man, and yet out of this is emerging in all countries the natural parks including the garden which is co-ordinated with the different parts of the place and especially the house.

In order to realize how fifty years later the Italian villas assumed a different aspect from that noted by Smollett, read what William Beckford, the creator of Font Hill Abbey and therefore a competent observer, writes:

> "I dined in peace and solitude and repaired as evening drew on to the thickets of Boboli. What a serene sky! What mellowness in the tints of the mountains! A purple haze concealed the bases, while their summits were invested with saffron light, discovering every white cot and every copse that clothed their declivities. The prospect widened as I ascended the terraces of the garden. After traversing many long dusky alleys I reached the opening on the brow of the hill and seating myself under the statue of Ceres, took a sketch of the huge mountainous cupola of the Duomo, the adjoining lovely tower, and one more massive in its neighbourhood, built not unprobably in the style of ancient Etruria. Beyond this historic group of buildings a plain stretches itself far and wide most richly studded with villas and gardens and groves of pine and olive, quite to the feet of the mountains.
>
> "Having marked the sun's going down and all the soothing effects cast by the declining rays on every object, I went through a plat of vines to a favourite haunt of mine: a little garden of the most fragrant

The Boboli Gardens, Florence, with a View of the City.

From a Photograph Used by Permission of William E. Bliz-Zard, L.A.

roses with a spring under a rustic arch of grotto work fringed with ivy. Thousands of fish inhabit here of that beautiful glittering species which comes from China. This golden nation were leaping after insects as I stood gazing upon the deep clear water, listening to the drops that trickle from the cove. Opposite to which at the end of a green alley you discover an oval basin and in the midst of it an antique statue full of that graceful languor so peculiarly Grecian. Whilst I was musing on the margin of the spring (for I returned to it after casting a look upon the sculpture) the moon rose above the tufted foliage of the terraces, which I descended by several flights of steps with marble balustrades crowned by vases of aloes. . . .

"Then I plunged into a winding path which led me by a series of steep ascents to a green platform overlooking the whole extent of a wood, with Florence deep beneath, and the tops of the hills which encircle it jagged with pines; here and there a convent withering in the sun. The scene extends as far as the eye can reach.

"Descending alley after alley, and bank after bank, I came to the orangery in front of the palace, disposed in a grand amphitheatre with marble niches relieved by dark foliage, out of which sprung cedars and tall aerial cypresses. This spot brought the scenery of an antique Roman garden so vividly into my mind, that, lost in a train of recollections this idea excited, I expected every instant to be called to the table of Lucullus hard by in one of the porticoes and to stretch myself on his purple triclinium, but waiting in vain for a summons till on the approach of night I returned delighted with a ramble that had led my imagination so far into antiquity."

Arthur Symons in his book on "Cities" has given an excellent description of the Italian garden at its best. Considering the Villa Mattei he writes:

> "Around are broken walls rising brown and jagged against the sky, the walls of the baths of Caracalla; a desolate strip of country on the edge of the city; and beyond, seen from the terraces lined with the dead bluish green of cactus, the Alban Hills. All the garden walks, where not even the cypresses are funereal nor the sunlight itself gay, breathe an exquisite melancholy, the most delicate and seductive breath of decay. There are wandering terraces, slim vistas, an entanglement of green and wayward life, winding in and out of brown defaced walls fringed with ivy, and about white and broken statues shining from under this green coat of leaves; everywhere surprising turns of ways among the trees curving out here and there, as if instinctively, into a circle about a fountain where broad leaves shadow the heads of gods or emperors in stone. And everywhere there is the cool sound of water which rises in the fountains, and drips under water plants in a grotto; and everywhere as one follows the winding paths, a white hand stretches out from among the darkness of

ivy, at some turn of the way, and one seems to catch the escaping flutter of white drapery among the leaves. You will sometimes see the shy figure of an old Cardinal taking his walk there; and if you follow him, you will come upon a broad alley of ilexes, lined with broken statues, broken friezes, and arched over by fantastically twisted branches, brown and interlaced, on which the blue-grey leaves hang delicately like lace; an alley leading to what must once have been a sarcophagus, covered on the side by which you approach it, with white carved figures. On the other side you find yourself in a little trellised circle from which, as through a window suddenly opened, you see the Alban Hills; there is a rustic wooden seat against the stone of the sarcophagus, on which, roughly carved, two lions meet and seem to shake hands; and above is written: 'Qui San Filippo Neri discorreva coi suoi discepoli delli cose di Dio.'"

For a modern rhapsody or ideal picture of Italian gardens, a poetical dream, a quotation is given from Mrs. (E. V. B.) Boyle:

"A garden, the word is indeed a picture, and what a picture it reveals! All through the days of childhood the garden is our fairy ground of sweet enchantment and innocent wonder. They are all beautiful, these Gardens of Poetry! and through the midst of them flows the broad stream of Memory, isled with fair lilied lawns, fringed with willowy forests of whispering reeds. And not less beautiful than these ideal shades are the gardens which live unchanging in many a painted picture within the heart. Real and not less ideal, is the remembrance of the gardens we have seen; seen once, it may be, and never since forgotten, lovely as truth, crystal clear as a poet's thought are the earthly Edens our eyes have beheld in the years that are past. How can we forget the gardens of queenly Genoa in the days before she was discrowned of Florence, of Rome and Albano and Tivoli?

"In all Italy, the land of flowers, the garden of the world, there are no gardens more stately, nor any nobler cypress trees than at Villa d'Este of Tivoli. In the spring by the straight smooth ways under the ilexes and cypresses all sunshine, the golden day is made rosy wherever anon the red Judas trees shower down their bloom. Marble stairs lead up through terraced heights to paved walks under Palazzo walls. There, the air is faint with rich fragrance of the orange trees. The lofty spires of ancient cypresses reach up above the topmost terrace; far below in the garden between their dark ranks sparkle the upspringing fountains. Beyond, above the tallest cypresses rise brown crumbling walls of the old town, piled up with open loggia and arched gates and overshadowing roofs; and high over these, great barren hills crowned with ruined fortresses and shattered keeps. To the west rolls out the ocean of the wide Campagna, undulating far away where Rome is lost in the sunset. Dream on! until you sigh with the wondrous sweetness

The Villa D'Este, Tivoli, Rome, with the Casino at the Left, just out of Sight.

From a Photograph Used by Permission of William E. Bliz-Zard, L.A.

of Rome herself in the wild garden of the Vatican, where in April days ten thousand odorous cyclamen flowers flush with crimson all the moss beneath the trees. Dream on: till you see once more the swaying of the tall vines and bathe your steps with flowery grass in the green Pamphili Doria, and watch the mystic fountains, most like the form of an inconstant spirit, like a blue-robed Undine, uncertain if to leave her source, trembling betwixt desire and fear."

Pity it is that so many abortive attempts are made to restore these old gardens in the modern style. Ribbon beds and gay parterres of showy flowers can be rarely made to fit an Italian garden. The real Italian garden is simple and dignified and depends for its charm on a combination of trees and architecture that is *sui generis*. Far better would it be if the modern owner of an old Italian garden could be induced to restore and retain the old conditions as far as possible, and to add, if addition is felt to be necessary, some more Italian cypresses, a magnolia or two, and other trees that naturally consort with the surroundings; a little more grass would help, and grass could certainly be secured by the use of water; it would be no more difficult than growing coleus and geranium parterres. Imitation in these old Italian gardens is to be avoided. You can never give the new garden the old spirit, but you can design the new garden in a similar spirit, as may be seen by referring to the illustration of Mr. Beale's garden (see page ——). This will secure not the Italian garden of Italy, but the home garden of America.

Here is another intimate and suggestive description of a garden which might be applied to the best gardens the world over:

> "Forgotten beside some rosy palace by the Adriatic, its fountain overrun with maidenhair, its goldfish twinkling in the marble font, and grass growing gaily and wildly where it will, the garden that once was trimmest has a delightful spirit that it could not have without precisely that past of artifice and ceremony. No prosperity except that of summer, no order that is not sweetly made light of while it is carelessly fulfilled, and all access open by way of the sunny air, so that no seeds are denied an anchorage in this port and harbourage of the winds. A trim garden that is no longer trim is full of frolic. A trim garden that is still trim has a kind of comeliness as an accessory of architecture. It is at any rate a garden and not a landscape.
>
> "How has the world taken so much trouble to make less lovely things out of those fine materials—the blossoming earth and the fostering sky? Pity is it that the word garden should be so vulgarized by worldly gardens. It is an early word for all men, one of the earliest of words. It is an Orient word, fresh and perpetual from childhood and the Divine East."[1]

[1] Alice Meynell, 1900.

The Formal Garden on the Estate of R. Beale, Esq., Newburgh, N. Y.

Fountains are a special and most important feature of a garden and here is a suggestion made by Henry A. Bright in *The English Flower Garden:*

> "One of the greatest ornaments in a garden is a fountain, but many fountains are curiously ineffective. A fountain is most effective when it leaps high in the air, and you can see it against a background of green foliage. To place a fountain among new flower beds, and then to substitute small fancy jets that take the shape of a cup, or trickle over in a basin of goldfish, or toy with a gilded ball, is to do all that is possible to degrade it. The real charm of a fountain is when you come upon it in some grassy glade of the 'pleasaunce' when it seems as though it sought, in the strong rush of its waters, to vie with the tall boles of the forest trees that surround it."

Such was the fountain of Leigh Hunt's story of Rimini which shot up beneath the shade of darksome pines.

> And twixt their shafts you saw the water bright
> Which through the tops glimmered with showering light.

This is very pertinent to the subject, as it is seldom that a fountain is met which is both designed and located properly, particularly when used in the garden.

But turning from the spell of these Italian gardens and their unquestionable beauty and charm we must not forget to recall the natural effects we have been considering, and allow ourselves to yield once more to the call of the flowers in their homes in the nooks of the bushes and groves of lawns and forests, where

Thick on the woodland floor
Gay company shall be
Primrose and hyacinth
And frail anemone,
Perennial strawberry bloom,
Wood sorrel's pencilled veil,
Dishevelled willowweed,
And orchids, purple and pale.[1]

Richard Jefferies, although not a landscape gardener, observed and appreciated and interpreted nature in a wonderful way. Here is his criticism of gardening and free landscape:

"Happily this park escaped and it is beautiful. Our English landscape wants no gardening, it cannot be gardened. The least interference kills it. The beauty of English woodland and country is its detail. There is nothing empty and unclothed. If the clods are left a little while undisturbed in the field, weeds spring and wild flowers bloom upon them. Is the hedge cut and trimmed, lo, the blue flower, the more and a yet fresher green buds forth on the twigs. Never was there a garden like the meadow; there is not an inch of the meadow in early summer without a flower. Old walls as we saw just now are not left without a fringe; on the top of the hardest brick wall, on the sapless tiles, on slates stonecrop takes hold and becomes a cushion of yellow bloom. Nature is

[1] Robert Bridges, *The Idle Flowers*, 1913, p. 352.

a miniature painter and handles a delicate brush, the tip of which touches the tiniest spot and leaves something living. The park has indeed its larger lines, its open broad sweep and gradual slope to which the eye accustomed to small enclosures requires time to adjust itself. These left to themselves are beautiful, they are the surface of the earth which is always true to itself and needs no banks for artificial hollows. The earth is right and the tree is right, then either and all is wrong. The deer will not fit into them then."

Washington Irving, although not known as a horticulturist or landscape gardener, nevertheless showed fine discrimination in the method he chose for the improvements of the lawns around his home near Tarrytown. This is what he says about English landscape gardening in his *Sketch Book:*

"The taste of the English in the cultivation of land, and in what is called landscape gardening is unrivalled. They have studied nature intently and discover an exquisite sense of her beautiful forms and harmonious combinations. Those charms which in other countries she lavishes in wild solitudes, are here assembled around the haunts of domestic life. They seem to have caught her coy and furtive graces, and spread them, like witchery, about their rural abodes. Nothing can be more imposing than the magnificence of English park scenery. Vast lawns extend like sheets of vivid green, with here and there clumps of gigantic trees, heaping up rich piles of foliage; the solemn pomp of groves and woodland glades with the deer trooping in silent herds across them; the hare bounding away to the covert; or the pheasant suddenly bursting upon the wing; the brook taught to wind in natural meanderings or expand into a glassy lake; the sequestered pool reflecting the quivering trees, with the yellow leaf sleeping upon its bosom, and the trout roaming fearlessly about its limpid waters. These are a few of the features of park scenery, but what most delights me is the creative talent with which the English decorate the unostentatious abodes of middle life. The rudest habitation, the most unpromising and scanty portion of land, in the hands of an Englishman of taste becomes a little paradise. With nicely discriminating eye, he seizes at once upon its capabilities, and pictures in his mind the future landscape. The sterile spot grows into loveliness under his hand; and yet the operations of art which produce the effect are scarcely to be perceived. The cherishing and training of some trees; the cautious pruning of others; the nice distribution of flowers and plants of tender and graceful foliage; the introduction of a green slope of velvet turf; the partial opening to a peep of blue distance, or a silver gleam of water; all these are managed with a delicate tact, a pervading, yet quiet assiduity, like the magic touchings with which a painter finishes up a favourite picture."

Prince Pückler's description of the garden at Windsor and the landscape beyond forms a good illustration of the proper relation of these features:

> "The garden lay before us, a perfect paradise, lighted by the glow of the evening sun. Along the whole house, now projecting, now receding, were verandas of various forms and clothed with creeping plants. These formed a border to the gayest flower garden covering the whole slope of the hill. Close upon the edge of it was a narrow green valley, between which the ground rose again and formed a higher line of hill, the side of which was clothed with huge beeches."

That all is not perfect in English landscape work Prince Pückler indicates in the following quotation:

> "I found the garden (pleasure ground) much altered, but not I think for the better; for there is now a mixture of the regular and the irregular which has a very unpleasant effect. The ugly fashion now prevalent in England of planting the 'pleasure ground' with single trees or shrubs placed at a considerable distance, almost in rows, has been introduced in several parts of these grounds. This gives the grass plots the air of nursery grounds. The shrubs are trimmed round so as not to touch each other, the earth carefully cleared about them every day, and the edges of the turf cut in stiff lines, so that you see more of black earth than of green foliage, and the free beauty of nature is quite checked."

For the flower gardens of Cheswick he has nothing but praise.

> "On the other hand," he says, "the flower gardens are magnificent. The beds are so thinly planted that each separate plant has room to spread, excepting in those beds which are entirely filled with one sort of flower. In them, the chief aim is the perfection of the whole, and they are consequently by far the most beautiful."

To emphasize more fully the value of the broad, simple, and wholly natural idea of making a garden, an example is shown from Union College, Schenectady, New York State. There is no pretence here: plenty of trees and shrubs with peonies and other old-fashioned flowers springing abundantly at their feet; little stretches of turf between the flowers and the walk; then almost out of sight a brook running under a bridge of plain boards out into a small grassy hollow, lying in an amphitheatre under high overarching elms. The Professor of Mathematics and Natural Philosophy in Union College, Isaac W. Jackson, commenced to make this garden in the early thirties of the last century, and his daughter, Mrs. Benedict, still cherishes it with loving care.

> I doubt not the flowers of that garden sweet
> Rejoiced in the sound of her gentle feet;
> I doubt not they felt the spirit that came
> From her glowing fingers thro' all their frame.[1]

[1] *The Sensitive Plant,* John Keats.

ERRATUM

Page 262, footnote—*For* John Keats *read* Percy Bysshe Shelley.

An Old-Fashioned Garden Belonging to Mrs. Benedict, Union College, Schenectady, N. Y.
From a Photograph.

Prof. Jackson had also the "most delicate artistic feeling and he loved beauty with so true an instinct that one can imagine the very flowers and shrubs which he affectionately tended returning his affection,"—thus testified an old friend at the time of his death.

The garden is a simple affair, just trees, shrubs, and flowers and grass, nothing rare or specially unusual, only a gathering of congenial plant friends, who have been looked after for nearly a century by people who loved them. The sight of this garden might easily recall, to those who have seen it, the one at New College, Oxford, of which Nathaniel Hawthorne says it has

> "lawns of the richest green and softest velvet grass, shadowed over by ancient trees which have lived a quiet life here for centuries, and have been nursed and tended with such care, and been so sheltered from rude winds, that certainly they must have been the happiest of all trees. Such a sweet, quiet, stately seclusion—so age long as this has been and I hope will continue to be—cannot exist anywhere else."

Long may these lovely old gardens continue to exist in their academic shades and cloistered homes.

XV

PUBLIC PARKS

THE problem of creating public parks while, in many respects, the same as that of estates or even of gardens, should always be carefully correlated with the rights and desires of the public. Historically, the public park is modern. A hundred years ago there were few public parks in the strict sense of the term, either in Europe or America. People were simply allowed to use Kings' and Princes' parks. Naturally, such parks had not been designed in the beginning for the use of the people, although they were of great size and magnificence like Versailles. The first man we can find who really seemed to comprehend and present intelligibly the idea of a public park in America was Andrew Jackson Downing, and no better expression has been given of appreciation of what he did for people's parks in both America and Europe than the eloquent words of William A. Stiles in the pages of *The Garden and Forest.*

"No one," he says, "who has looked into the history of public parks in American cities and the development of the public sentiment which brought them into being, will deny that the strongest impulse which the movement received at the outset came from Andrew Jackson Downing. Mr. Downing was born with a strong love of nature, and as his father was a nurseryman he was brought up in a calling that increased his interest in trees and planting. Reared almost in sight of many of the old places on the Hudson which had been planned and planted by Parmentier and others of that older school, he learned while still young that a landscape could be made impressive by the simplest and most natural treatment. As he was to become our first authoritative writer on the art of landscape gardening, the whole country has occasion to be thankful that he was in this way led to adopt what was then called the English style of gardening, in which, to quote his own words, 'the spirit of nature, though softened and refined by art, always furnished the essential charm, thus distinguishing it from the French or Italian style, where one sees the effects of art slightly assisted by nature.' Downing was a man of catholic views, but while he realized the fact that vases and balustrades and studied symmetry might be mingled with foliage enough to make a garden, yet his ideal garden-scene was the primeval paradise, whose pervading beauty was found in the unstudied simplicity of nature. With his natural taste refined by travel and by study, Downing's *Treatise on the Theory and Practice of Landscape Gardening*, which was published in 1841, became at once the accepted text-book of rural art in this country, and this book, passing through many editions, and his *Rural Essays* and other works, are still classics in this branch of literature. It was his example and precept which inspired such men as Henry Winthrop Sargent, and they in turn kindled the enthusiasm of younger men, so that the best private gardens in America to-day owe what is best in them to his sound teachings.

"Downing was a graceful and forcible writer as well as an artist of the highest intelligence, and as he had been already recognized as an authority a timely series of letters which he wrote for the *Horticulturist* on the subject of public parks in 1849 had a marked influence in creating and moulding popular sentiment in this direction. These essays, which appeared month after month, and were widely copied by the press, marshalled in a convincing way the arguments which were then fresh and original, although many of them have since become a part of our common knowledge and belief. He began by showing that public parks were needed not only to educate the public taste, but because everybody at some time felt the necessity for this contact with nature. He showed that this communion was not only a delight to people who were as unsophisticated as children, but that the more thoughtful and educated a community became the stronger grew the passion for rural pleasures. When it was argued that the people would not visit parks, even if artistic ones were constructed, he pointed to the large cemeteries to prove how eager all classes were to avail themselves of an opportunity for a visit to anything resembling a park. Mount Auburn, Greenwood, and Laurel Hill had been already established for a quarter of a century, and that they had come to be places of resort was certainly not because they afforded opportunity for solemn meditation or for the artistic value of the monuments reared within them. He truly argued that it was because they contained bits of forest-land, hills and dales, copses and glades that they attracted throngs of visitors in cities which possessed no great public gardens, and that if thirty thousand people would visit Laurel Hill in one year many times that number would visit a public park in a city like Philadelphia. He set his argument on the highest plane at the very outset, and, while recognizing the use of parks as helping to furnish air and sunshine, he held that the fostering of the love of rural beauty was quite as important an end, and that such a love of nature helped to civilize and refine national character. Mayor Kingsland's proposed park of a hundred and sixty acres he pronounced altogether too scant, and argued that five hundred acres between Thirty-ninth Street and the Harlem was the smallest space that should be reserved for the wants of the city, since no area less than this could furnish a rural landscape or offer space enough for broad reaches of parkland with a real feeling of the breadth and beauty of green fields and the perfume and freshness of nature. It was argued by some who assumed to represent the labouring classes that the park would be monopolized by those who ride in their carriages, and, on the other hand, some of the wealthy and refined people of the city complained that a park would certainly be usurped by rowdies and low people. It is refreshing now to read Downing's replies to such objections. He stoutly asserted that these social horrors were nothing but phantoms of the imagination; his faith was, as the event has proved, that rich and poor could breathe the same atmosphere of nature and of art and enjoy the same scenery without any jealousy or any conflict.

"The actual work of constructing Central Park was not begun until six years after Downing's untimely death, but it was his stirring appeals that aroused the city to feel its need, and provision to meet it quickly followed. By rare good fortune, too, designers were found whose artistic temperament and training were akin to his own, so that our first great urban park was planned on such broad lines as he would have approved. The works which followed at once in Brooklyn, Buffalo, Chicago, San Francisco, and other cities were beyond question the result of this same inspiration, so that his keen foresight and conscientious devotion to an idea were the most powerful of the agencies which united to initiate the movement which has given to American cities their thousands of acres of parkland during the past thirty-five years. When we think of the health and comfort, the rest and the refreshment, the delight to the eye and the imagination which these smiling landscapes have given and will continue for ever to give to all the people, it is not too much to say that Downing takes rank among the greatest benefactors to his country which this century has produced."

Largely as a result of Downing's writings in the *Horticulturist* and in his books and letters elsewhere, the idea gradually secured recognition that New York needed a large public park. In selecting a site there was much discussion, and at first Jones's Woods on the East River in the neighbourhood of 66th Street was chosen. It is not sure that in view of later developments better boundary lines might not have been obtained at the time than those of the present Central Park; and that brings us to the importance of giving most careful and intelligent consideration to the choice of public park sites. Let us see what Mr. Olmsted says on this subject. No one could speak with greater weight of authority than he did. This is what he says in *Public Parks and the Enlargement of Towns*—in discussing two different types of grounds for park sites:

"We want a ground to which people may easily go after their day's work is done, and where they may stroll for an hour, seeing, hearing, and feeling nothing of the bustle and jar of the streets, where they shall in effect find the city put far away from them. We want the greatest possible contrast with the streets and the shops and rooms of the towns which will be consistent with convenience and the preservation of good order and neatness. We want, especially, the greatest possible contrast with the restraining and confining conditions of the town, those conditions which compel us to walk circumspectly, watchfully, jealously, which compel us to look closely on others without sympathy. Practically, what we most want is a simple, broad, open space of clean greensward, with sufficient play of surface and sufficient number of trees about it to supply a variety of light and shade. This we want as a central feature. We want depth of wood enough about it not only for comfort in hot weather, but to completely shut out the city from our landscapes.

"The word park in town nomenclature should, I think, be reserved for grounds of the character and purpose thus described. Not only as being the most valuable of all possible forms of public places, but regarded simply as a large space which will seriously interrupt crosstown communication wherever it occurs, the question of the site and bounds of the park requires to be determined with much more deliberation and art than is often secured for any problem of distant and extended municipal interests." Speaking further about promenades being "congregated human life under glorious and artificial conditions," with the natural landscape not essential to them, he thus speaks of the level compared with the rugged or picturesque type of park: "there is no more beautiful picture, and none can be more pleasing incidentally to the gregarious purpose than of beautiful meadows, over which clusters of level-armed sheltering trees cast broad shadows, and upon which are scattered flocks of black-faced sheep, while men, women, and children are seen sitting here and there forming groups in the shade, or moving in and out among the woody points and bays.

"It may be inferred from what I have said that very rugged ground, abrupt eminences, and what is technically called picturesque in distinction from merely beautiful or simply pleasing scenery, is not the most desirable for a town park. Decidedly not in my opinion. The park should as far as possible complement the town. Openness is the one thing you cannot get in buildings. Picturesqueness you can get. Let your buildings be as picturesque as your artists can make them. This is the beauty of a town. Consequently the beauty of the park should be the other. It should be the beauty of the fields, the meadow, the prairie, of the green pastures and the still waters. What we want to gain is tranquillity and rest of mind. Mountains suggest effort. But besides this objection there are others of what I may indicate as the housekeeping class. It is impossible to give the public range over a large extent of ground of a highly picturesque character, unless under very exceptional circumstances, and sufficiently guarded against the occurrence of opportunities and temptations to shabbiness, disorder, indecorum, and indecency that will be subversive of every good purpose the park should be designed to fulfil."

Mr. Olmsted in the Mt. Royal Park Report again follows out much the same line of thought:

> "The value of a city property is to depend on the design in which it shall be adapted to attract citizens to obtain needful exercise and cheerful mental occupation in the open air, with the result of better health and fitness in all respects for the trials and duties of life; with the result also necessarily of greater earning and taxpaying capacities so that in the end the investment will be in this respect a commercially profitable one to the city."

Mr. Olmsted also says in the Mt. Royal Park Report that

> "The possession of charming natural scenery is a form of wealth as practical as that of wholesome air, pure water, or sunlight unobstructed by smoke or fog, as practical as that of sewers, aqueducts, and pavements."

There is a more potent influence, however, than the mere bodily one, valuable as that is, namely the refreshment and uplift of the spirit that come from the poetical side of the nature of most men. Here is the way that Mr. Olmsted explains and illustrates this point:

> "Let us say that for the time being the charm of natural scenery tends to make us poets. There is a sensibility to poetic inspiration in every man of us, and its utter suppression means a sadly morbid con-

dition. Poets we may not be; but a little lifted out of ordinary prose we may be often to our advantage. 'To compare our small measures with larger let us take a recorded experience of a full-grown poet. Wordsworth, only greater in poetic sensibility than any one of us, not differently organized, not differently affected by medicine, came home from a painful experience in France after its great revolution, sick, broken down, unfit for business. Everything was going wrong with him. His sister Dorothy, of whom it was well said that she was the greater poet of the two, only that she was not a *literary poet*, watched his symptoms, saw the nature of his troubles, and divined their cure. She persuaded him to let her guide him into the midst of charming scenery, and subject himself for a time to its influence,' and thus, says Dr. Shairp, telling the story, 'began the sanative process which restored him to his true self and made that blessing to the world that he has become.' Commenting further on Wordsworth's case he writes, 'continuing the study of nature (not with the science of the botanist, or the florist, but the poet), he at last came to hold the conscious conviction, what he had at first felt it, hardly knowing that he felt it, that nature had a life of her own, which streamed through and stimulated his life, a spirit which, in itself invisible, spoke through visible things to his spirit.'[1] That the characteristics of this spirit were calmness, which

[1] *The Poetic Interpretation of Nature*, p. 249, Dr. John Campbell Shairp.

stilled and refreshed man; sublimity, which raised him to noble thoughts; tenderness, which, while stirring in the largest and loftiest things, condescends to the lowest: is with the humblest worm and weed as much as in the greatest movements of the elements or the stars. Above all, nature he now saw to be the shape and image of right reason,—reason in its highest sense embodied and made visible in order, stability, in conformity to eternal law. The perception of this satisfied his intellect and calmed and soothed his heart."[1]

The sanative and pleasurable effects of "rural incidents" and open grass spaces of comparatively large extent are continually emphasized in the writings of Olmsted and Vaux whether they have been indited jointly or individually. Of all the different country experiences the charms of which they proclaim, the great sweeping meadows and shadowing trees on their borders, and now and then in the midst, are considered the most important—the green pastures and still waters, the restful embrace and life-giving glance of nature, where the turf and lakes or streams give new vigour to exhausted human beings, and prove that of all the phases of park landscape, the best and happiest is the pastoral one.

Read what Olmsted and Vaux say on this subject of the pastoral landscape in the Tenth Annual Report to the Prospect Park Commissioners in 1873:

[1] Mt. Royal Park Report.

"The development of the pastoral idea in its most favourable aspects is possible in a large city park and it is the peculiar advantage of the ground under your control that it offers an unusually favourable opportunity for the purpose. A stretch of greensward a mile in length, surrounded by woods and unbroken by any carriage way, should certainly offer a field of ample dimensions for an illustration of the idea, and this we have in the Brooklyn Park. Thousands of people, without any sense of crowding, stroll about on the level or undulating sunny or shaded turf spaces that are to be found in this strip of pasture or woodland."

The report goes on to state that they made every effort to improve a large portion of the ground with special reference to the development of this element of pastoral effect in pursuit of which they say they have, at several points, made considerable changes in the surface of the ground so as to connect a series of dissevered and isolated patches of comparatively level ground into one sweep of grass land that is extensive enough to make a really permanent impression on the mind.

Again in an earlier report of 1866 to the Prospect Park Commissioners, Olmsted and Vaux when discussing initial ideas which should govern in judging the capabilities and limitations of a park site, with reference to the artistic purpose, strongly emphasize the importance of securing as much pastoral effect as the conditions will allow:

"The first process in the application of this art [landscape architecture] upon any given site is the formation of a judgment upon the capabilities and the limitations of that site with reference to the artistic purpose. It is obviously impossible, for instance, to produce in the vicinity of Brooklyn such scenery as will affect the mind as it is affected by the Alps or the Sierras on the one hand, or by the luxuriant vegetation of a tropical swamp on the other.

"Moreover there are certain kinds of scenery which experience shows to be most satisfactory in a town park, which require an extensive aggregation of their elements. It will be readily seen for instance that if all the wood, water, and turf within a certain area of ground were distributed in patches, strips, and pools, however extensive as a whole, and however varied in detail it might seem to those who should thoroughly explore all its parts, there would be no part which would not seem confined, there could be no large open single scene, and no such impression or effect on the mind would be produced as there would be if all the water were collected in a lake, all the trees in one grove, all the strips of grass in one broad meadow. Such aggregations, and consequently the degree of the impression intended to be produced by them, must be limited by consideration for two other purposes, the purpose of variety and interest, and the purpose to make all the scenery available to the satisfaction of the public by ways of communication. Other limitations upon the artistic purpose, again, are imposed by conditions of soil and exposure, by rock and springs. How far each of these can be overcome, as by blasting, grading, draining, screening, manuring, and other processes, has to be studied with care, and the artistic purposes of the plan must be affected in every part and particular by the conclusions arrived at.

"In the case before us, it is obvious that we should attempt nothing that is incompatible with, or inappropriate to, comparatively slight variations of surface and a climate of considerable rigour. On the other hand, there are no protruding ledges of rock, no swamps difficult of drainage, and there is no especial bleakness or danger to trees from violent winds to be apprehended. It is under similar conditions to these that we find in nature that class of scenery already referred to as the original and typical scenery of parks and which is termed pastoral. It consists of combinations of trees, standing singly or in groups, and casting their shadows over broad stretches of turf, or repeating their beauty by reflection in the calm surface of pools, and the predominant associations are in the highest degree tranquillizing and grateful. As expressed by the Hebrew poet: 'He maketh me to lie down in green pastures, he leadeth me beside the still waters.' We know of no other landscape effects that can be commanded within the limitations fixed by the conditions of this site which experience shows to be more desirable in a town park than these. Only so far then as we can without sacrificing anything that will contribute to the highest practicable ideal of pastoral scenery, should we endeavour to secure any degree of those other ideals, of which the best types are found under widely dissimilar circumstances.

"Although we cannot have wild mountain defiles, for instance, in the park, we may have stony ravines shaded with trees, and made picturesque with shrubs, the forms and arrangement of which remind us of mountain scenery. We may, perhaps, even secure some slight approach to the mystery, variety, and richness of tropical scenery by an assemblage of certain forms of vegetation, gay with flowers, and intricate and mazy with vines and creepers, ferns, rushes, and broad-leaved plants. All we can do in these directions must be confessedly imperfect and suggestive rather than satisfying to the imagination. It must, therefore, be made incidental and subordinate to our first purpose."

When it is fully recognized that the poetic, artistic quality of a public park constitutes one of its chief assets of value, and that the development of the features that lend this quality to the landscape is of supreme advantage, the following words of Mr. Olmsted are specially pertinent, giving an idea of the vast extent that a park development may reach. Speaking of Mt. Royal Park, Montreal, he writes:

"Among properties of its class your mountain park possesses one marked advantage over all others,

I mean that of noble views extending far beyond its borders. These are of such extent and so composed and their foregrounds within the property are so easily adapted to increase their value: their interest is so varied according to the direction of the outlook and the passing effect of clouds and atmospheric conditions, that it is not only impossible to speak of them in adequate terms of admiration, but trying to make a business estimate of them and seeking standards of comparison for the purpose, it will be found that what communities have been able to obtain by expenditures counting in millions of dollars is really too insignificant to be available for the purpose."

. . . .

"It might be a question whether the most valuable influence of properties of this class (mountainous) is to be found in such distinct sensational features, even though provided by nature, as are commonly most consciously felt, most talked about, and written about, or in more unobtrusive, pervading, homelike qualities of which the effects come to us less in a torrent-like way than as the gentle persuasive dew, falling so softly as to be imperceptible and yet delightfully invigorating in its results. Even this might be to some a question, but let any man ask himself whether the value of such views as the grandest that the mountain offers is greater when they are made distinct spectacles, or when they are enjoyed as successive incidents of a sustained landscape poem to each of which the mind is gradually, sweetly led up, and from which it is gradually and sweetly led away so that they become a consistent experience; let him ask this with reference to the soothing and refreshment of a town-strained human organization, and he will need no argument to lead him to a sound conclusion."

In other words it may be said of parks as of painting and poetry that they should suggest thoughts of potent and distinct influence on the mind. The thoughts suggested may vary with the point of view and mental condition of the individual, but they should in any case arouse the mind and uplift and vivify the spirit.

Olmsted and Vaux in their work in Prospect Park, Brooklyn, New York, and Central Park, New York, have produced noteworthy examples of pastoral scenery combined with woodland effects of the kind that not only inspires thoughts of a different kind but that enhances by contrast the beauty of the meadows. These thoughts are explained in the following extracts from another report made at the time the parks were commenced. How true and fine were these conceptions is shown by the supreme beauty of these parks at the present time some fifty years later.

"Two classes of improvements were to be planned for this purpose: one directed to secure pure and wholesome air, to act through the lungs, the other to secure an antithesis of objects of vision to those streets and houses which shall act remedially, by impressions on the mind and suggestions to the imagination.

"The latter only require our present attention and the first question with reference to them is: What class of objects are best adapted to the purpose?

"Experience should lead most men to answer that they are chiefly such as give the characteristic charm to gardens, pleasure grounds, and rural landscapes. But some consideration may be required to determine by what mode of selection from among these, and by what general principle of arrangement, the highest practicable degree of the desired effect is to be attained. It sometimes occurs that certain species of trees grow naturally under conditions which favour such a result, in forms of extraordinary symmetry, their heads each having the outline of a haycock set upon a straight perpendicular pose. Occasionally several such trees may be found in nature, growing together. Any number of objects of that character would have but limited value, if any, for the purpose of the park, because it is a character more nearly compatible in a tree than any other with the convenience of men when living compactly in streets and houses. Trees of that form might be, and in fact sometimes are, grown along the streets of the city, between rows of houses.

"A series of rosebushes, grown in pots, trained to single stakes, would have still less value. Trim beds of flowers, such as might be set on the drawing-room table, or in the fore court of a city dwelling, still less.

A cluster of hornbeams and hemlocks, the trunks of some twisting over a crannied rock, the face of the rock brightened by lichens and half-veiled by tresses of vines growing over it from the rear, and its base lost in a tangle of ground pine, mosses, and ferns, would be of considerable value, partly because of the greater difficulty of reconciling the presence of such an assemblage of objects with the requirements of convenience in the streets, but mainly because the intricate disposition of lights and shadows seen in the back parts of it would create a degree of obscurity not absolutely impenetrable, but sufficient to affect the imagination with a sense of mystery. A broad stretch of slightly undulating meadow without defined edge, its turf lost in the haze of the shadows of scattered trees under the branches of which the eye could range, would be of even higher value, and if beyond this meadow occurred a depression of the surface, and the heads of other trees were seen again at an uncertain distance, the conditions would be most of all available for the purpose in view, first because there would be positive assurance of a certain considerable extent of space free of all ordinary urban conditions, and in the soft, smooth, tranquil surface of turf, of immunity from the bustling, violent, and wearing influences which act upon the surface of the streets; and secondly because the imagination, looking into the soft commingling lights and shadows and fading tints of colour of the background, would have encouragement to extend these purely rural conditions indefinitely.

"Considering that large classes of rural objects and many types of natural scenery are not practicable to be introduced on the site of a park,—mountain, ocean, desert, and prairie scenery for example,—it will be found that the most valuable form that could have been prescribed is that which we have last indicated, and which may be distinguished from all others as pastoral. But the site of the park having had a very heterogeneous surface which was largely formed of solid rock, it was not desirable that the attempt should be made to reduce it all to the simplicity of pastoral scenery. What would be the central motive of design required of the rest? Clearly that it should be given such character as, while affording contrast and variety of scene, would, as much as possible, be confluent to the same end, namely, the constant suggestion to the imagination of an unlimited range of rural conditions.

"The pleasing uncertainty and mysterious tone which chiaro-oscuro lends to the distance of an open pastoral landscape certainly cannot be paralleled in rugged ground where the scope of the vision is limited; but a similar influence on the mind, less only in degree, is experienced as we pass near the edge of a long stretch of natural woods, the outer trees disposed in irregular clusters, the underwood mingling at intervals with their foliage. Under such circumstances, although the eye nowhere penetrates far, an agreeable suggestion is conveyed to the imagination of freedom, and of interest beyond the objects that meet the eye. While, therefore, elements of scenery of this class (which may, for the present purpose, be distinguished as picturesque, sylvan scenery) would both acquire and impart value from their contrast with the simpler elements of open pastoral landscapes; their effect, by tending to withdraw the mind to an indefinite distance from the objects associated with the streets and walls of a city, would be of the same character.

"The question of adjusting and localizing these two classes of landscape elements to the various elements of the topography of the park next occurs, the study of which must begin with the consideration that the park is surrounded by an artificial wall twice as high as the great wall of China composed of urban buildings. Wherever this should appear across a meadow view the imagination would be checked abruptly at short range. Natural objects were thus required to be interposed, which, while excluding the buildings as much as possible from view, would leave an uncertainty as to the occupation of the space beyond, and establish a horizon line composed as much as possible of verdure. No one looking into a closely grown wood can be certain that at a short distance back there are not glades or streams, or that a more open disposition of trees does not prevail.

"A range of high woods, or of trees so disposed as to produce an effect when seen from a short distance looking outwardly from the central parts of the park, of a natural woodside, must be regarded more nearly indispensable to the purpose in view—that of relieving the visitor from the city—than any other available feature. The site of the park being naturally very broken and largely composed of masses of rock, the extent to which the meadow-like surface of pastoral scenery could be introduced in the plan was limited. It was then, first of all, required that such parts of the site as were available and necessary to the purpose should be assigned to the occupation of elements which would compose a woodside, screening incongruous objects without the park as much as possible from the view of observers within it.

"Secondly, of the remaining ground it was required to assign as much as was available to the occupation of elements which would compose tranquil, open, pastoral scenes.

"Thirdly, it was required to leave all of the yet remaining ground to elements which would tend to form passages of scenery contrasting in depth of obscurity and picturesque character of detail with the softness and simplicity of the open landscapes."[1]

The artistic necessity in park landscape gardening of having types of effect persist in some kind of size and form and colour everywhere; the one general effect among many, the grass space, the lake or pool surface, trees, shrubs, and flowers around, even a colony of flowers, a flower bed, if you will, all repeating in a hund-

[1] Second Annual Report to the New York Park Department, Olmsted & Co.

red ways whatever makes pastoral and picturesque changes true to the nature of the place: this is well explained in the following words:

"It has been stated that this park [Central Park] differs from most English parks in substituting a multiplicity of small picturesque scenes for broad expanses of turf but it ought not to be forgotten that the park has the same pastoral charm of simple, natural scenery which is found in landscapes where the features are broader. When the site was selected not the slightest attention was given to its landscape possibilities, and the fact seemed only to be considered that it was in the centre of the island and that the ground was so broken and intractable that it would cost as much to construct streets throughout it on the established rectangular system as it would to re-form it into a pleasure ground. South of the reservoir the surface was so rugged and heterogeneous, traversed as it was diagonally by ridges of outcropping gneiss, with marshy hollows between them, that no opportunity for making a spacious meadow-like effect was offered. The upper half of the park could be treated in a somewhat broader way, as its natural features were larger, its slopes had a grander sweep, and its horizon lines were nobler. The only landscape effects which could be produced under these restrictions were such as could be controlled between the boundaries of a long narrow, rocky territory with no prominent points commanding extensive views. No doubt, if the same intelligent study could have been applied to the selection of a site which was given later to devising contrivances to remedy its defects, the park could have been made still more satisfying. Nevertheless it was the primary effort of the designers to make as large open spaces as were practicable. Two considerable stretches of greensward were procured in the lower part at great expense by blasting out protruding rock and filling the space with earth and mould. As it is the green contains about sixteen acres and the ball ground but ten acres, although they both seem much larger. The rolling surface of the green and its obscure borders where the limits of the grass are lost in the shady recesses among the trees through which glimpses of grassy slopes are seen at intervals beyond, all suggest indefinite distances to the imagination. All the roads are arranged so as to bring these spaces into view—several times from different points with varying effect. Of course, there is a greater sense of enlargement and freedom experienced in the north meadows, but even here only nineteen acres could possibly be secured. These small picturesque scenes, therefore, were not used because the designers considered them preferable to large expanses and simple groves, but because this was the only possible method of treating the ground. They were so used, however, as to produce the same effect upon the imagination as broad pastoral scenes. The small spaces are distributed through the park in such a way that they carry forward and emphasize the softness and simplicity of the meadow scenery. Even the Ramble, which is characterized by intricacy and picturesqueness and where there are places which have all the mysterious charm of a natural wildwood, there are many little grassy openings bordered with trees which repeat the meadows in a small way and carry the idea of pastoral quiet throughout the work. Indeed, the great value of Central Park is that it is a work with unity of design and that it is consistent throughout, and it still remains the best, as it was the first example of a pleasure ground designed to have the restful charm of natural scenery and yet completely enclosed by a compactly built city. . . .

"'Truly,' says an English writer, 'the transformation of a tract of swamp and rock into one of the most beautiful parks in the world is a striking monument of American skill and perseverance.' It is more than that, it is a work of genius, and the more it is studied, the more we wonder at the prophetic power of the designers in providing so far in advance for the wants of a city, which only existed at the time in imagination. Whenever any radical change in this design is proposed, the project should always be examined with reference to its effect on the fundamental character of the work as a whole. It is just as truly a unit in conception as if it consisted of one broad meadow."[1]

[1] *Garden and Forest*, William A. Stiles, New York Park Commissioner.

There are other elements yet to be considered; but those already classified and assigned to various quarters of the site, contribute directly to the general and characteristic purpose of the park and are therefore to be distinguished as its essential elements.

After studying the essential artistic elements, especially the poetic elements that mark and emphasize the difference between a playground, a farm, a field, and a park, we find these authors (Olmsted and Vaux) writing in illuminating phrase and warning against the employment in parks of features which, though possessing a value of their own, do not contribute to, much less enhance, their characteristic beauty:

> "Accessory elements by which walking, riding, driving, resting, eating, and drinking are facilitated, were also to be required in the design of the park, in so far as they would be instruments necessary to be used to obtain the benefit of its essential elements.
>
> "But if people were allowed to straggle at will anywhere upon the ground and if provision were made for their doing so comfortably and with cleanliness, all the ground would need to be specially prepared for the purpose; there would be no turf and no trees upon it, and it would afford no relief from the city. It will thus be seen that these accessory elements of the park are admissible only where and so far as the advantages they offer make its essential elements available, and compensate for any curtailment their introduction may involve in these essential

elements. They are desirable so far as they aid the essential elements in inviting the observer to rest or move forward in one way or another, as shall most conduce to his recreation. They are undesirable in so far as they tend to weaken, divide, blot, or make patchwork of the essential features of the natural landscape.

"The first consideration, then, in a truly critical study of the size, form, and place in the park of any required construction for the accommodation of visitors was originally, and always should be, that the degree of display which may be allowed in it should correspond, as nearly as other considerations will permit, with the importance of the need it is designed to meet: this being measured not only by its average value to each user, but with regard also to the number of those who will have occasion to use it."

Bridges in landscape gardening are in reality what Olmsted and Vaux term an accessory, and not an essential artistic necessity of the landscape design. As a feature of the landscape, their artistic necessity is not felt when compared with the elements of trees, shrubs, water and grass spaces;—but the accessory of first importance is the passageways that lead the observer to the different views of the landscape picture, and the bridge forms part of these passageways. There is no question, however, that more than most other accessories in the landscape, the bridge may be so used as to give a charm and variety which may be kept in harmony with the general scheme. The general features of its construction should be therefore blended largely with foliage, retaining the pervading idea of natural effect. But the fact that it is a bridge for people to use in passing that way, makes it important that it shall be safe and comfortable. For the same reason the bridge structure should be quite visible. Hence its location, form, and material of construction become important. It may consist of stepping-stones, of one solid arch, or of a series of arches. There may be many forms, but they should be as simple as possible and as unobtrusive: lines, proportions, all seemly and graceful, yet with as little pretension to architectural display as may be. It is naturally chiefly a question of choosing material fitted to special conditions, and usually, almost invariably, stone of rustic character is to be preferred for bridges in the midst of a landscape, but it might readily be that some spot would suggest the use of wood or even iron. Central Park has in its Bow Bridge a light iron structure of such grace that its loss would be irreparable (see illustration). Artificial stone or cement in any form or mixture should be barred. In the midst of trees and foliage its unnatural appearance is specially objectionable.

The entrance and exit of a bridge should be clothed and screened with foliage and above the shrubs should tower some large trees to emphasize the effect of coming on to the structure. Sometimes Lombardy poplars in clusters are effective in such places. The bridge should emerge from the foliage with a certain distinction and yet not obtrusively. The exact point of the course of the stream or arm of lake chosen for the location of the bridge should be carefully selected and the height and conspicuousness of the bridge adjusted to the landscape. Thomas Whately has written perhaps better than any one else on these and other points in relation to bridges:

> "The form of a lake, on the contrary, intimates that all the several shores are, by making a certain circuit, accessible. Bridges therefore are inconsistent with the nature of a lake, but characteristic of a river: they are on that account used to disguise a termination; but the deception has been so often practised, that it no longer deceives; and a bolder aim at the same effect will now be more successful. If the end can be turned just out of sight, a bridge at some distance raises a belief, while the water beyond it removes every doubt of the continuation of the river, and the supposition immediately occurs, that if a disguise had been intended the bridge would have been placed farther back, and the disregard thus shown to one deception gains credence for the other.
>
> "To give bridges their full effect, the connexion between them and the river must be attended to: from the want of it, the single wooden arch, now much in fashion, seems to us generally misplaced. Elevated without occasion so much above, it is totally detached from the river; it is often seen straddling in the air, without a glimpse of the water to account for it; and the ostentation of it as an ornamental object

The Bow Bridge over the Lake in Central Park, New York City.

From a Photograph by William Hale Kirk.

diverts all the train of ideas which its use as a communication might suggest. The vastness of Walton Bridge cannot without affectation be mimicked in a garden, where the magnificent idea of including the Thames under one arch is wanting, and where the structure itself, reduced to a narrow scale, retains no pretension to greatness. Unless the situation makes such a height necessary; or the point of view be greatly above it, or wood or rising ground, instead of sky behind it, fill up the vacancy of the arch, it seems an effort without a cause, forced and preposterous.

"A gentle rise and easy sweep more closely preserve the relation. A certain degree of union should also exist between the banks and the bridge that it may seem to rise out of the banks, and not barely to be imposed upon them. It ought generally to swell much above their level; the parapet wall should be brought down near to the ground, or end against some swell, and the size and the uniformity of the abutments should be broken by hillocks or thickets about them:—every expedient should be used to mark the connexion of the bridge both with the ground from which it starts, and the water which it crosses."[1]

The two views of the Boulder or Huddlestone Bridge should perhaps have been included in the chapter on Rocks, but they are so characteristic of the rugged wild scenery of the part of Central Park where they have

[1] Thomas Whately, *Observations on Modern Gardening.*

been employed that they have been used as illustrations of a park feature.

With the exception of the rough archaic arch that forms the bridge, the whole picture of its south side might be that of a cataclysm of nature. If the illustrations are carefully examined it will be seen that before bringing these stones together there has been careful study given to their selection and the way they would naturally come together under the impelling force of the elements brought to bear on them year after year.

But there are other features pertaining to a park or an estate that are more evidently accessories and therefore need intelligent adjustment, or, in some cases, for various reasons, abandonment.

The names of these features are numerous; a few of them are statues, busts, memorials of all kinds including tablets let into the rock, museums, libraries, bandstands of a permanent character, stadiums, restaurants (no strong liquors should be sold in a park on account of the women and children if for no other reason), merry-go-rounds, playgrounds, games of all kinds.

These things mar the harmony and injure the turf and produce a disturbance of the mind that lessens the pastoral and other sylvan charms of the park. It should be remembered also that important as it is that children should have all reasonable opportunity to amuse themselves in the park, yet as there are adults as well as young people who have the right to enjoy the scenery, their "due and privilege" should not be neglected. The remedy for the temptation to overcrowd the park

The Boulder Bridge near the Harlem Mere, North End of Central Park, New York City.

From a Photograph by William Hale Kirk.

with games for children and adults is the construction elsewhere of children's playgrounds and athletic fields on special reservations of their own. This has been done in Brooklyn, New York, with great success, entirely outside of the boundaries of Prospect Park.

Every one of the objects named, with many things of a similar type, should be barred from the park. If it were found absolutely necessary to have any such structures in the park, they might better be placed beneath the surface of the ground in a subterranean hall.

It may be conceded that there is another class of artificial structures that should find a place in the park, and that is architecture on the borders. A wall or fence or some boundary treatment should surround every park. A park boundary barrier, however, should have a simple, unobtrusive character and be made as low as safety will permit, but to preserve this character no special ornaments, such as statues or urns, should be inserted in the wall: a plain tablet with names carved on it might appear just at or about the entrance. On the plazas opposite the park entrances, fountains, statues, and other architectural and sculptural structures may properly find a place if they are not allowed to dominate the neighbouring park scenery. Gates and architectural adornment of the actual park entrances are not likely to be altogether satisfactory, and, as a matter of fact, have hardly ever been designed successfully. Unless the architecture is extremely modest, it will insist on imposing too dominant and alien an influence for the poetic or pastoral character which should be evident in the park, even from outside of the entrance.

The question of museums in the park is discussed by Park Commissioner W. A. Stiles, one of the most enlightened officials who has ever written on the subject:

> "All this (employment of museums) is very attractive, and not impracticable. But when Mr. H—— declares that a public park does not fulfil its highest function until it develops into a vast and multitudinous museum for popular instruction he plainly ignores the specific purpose for which pleasure grounds like Central Park have been created. Indeed one may read Mr. H——'s article attentively and fail to discover whether he has ever cared to inform himself precisely what that purpose is. The fact is that in popular language there is no well-defined group of ideas suggested by the word park, and it is applied to areas of ground which are used for the most varied and incongruous purposes. To one man it means a baseball field, to another a military parade ground, to a third a place where race horses are used to facilitate gambling. Indeed the danger of the assaults on the integrity of city parks is constant because of the lack of clear popular conception of their true functions, and they never will be safe from attacks until their primary purpose is universally understood, and until this purpose is admitted to be of sufficient importance to justify their existence and maintenance."[1]

[1] *Garden and Forest*, vol. ii., May 2, 1891.

Again the same author says:

"Scenery of a purely pastoral character is no doubt the most valuable element of a park within the limits of a great city like New York, for no stronger contrast to the constrained and artificial conditions of urban life can be imagined than meadow-like stretches of greensward which are not fenced in by rigid boundaries but fade away in obscure and shadowy distance. Broad open landscapes with spacious skies, and the sense of enlargement and freedom which they bring, offer the most pleasing contrasts to the hard confinement of city streets with their skyline of roofs and chimneys; the tranquillizing influence of soft, smooth, grassy surfaces is an unfailing refreshment from the wear and weariness, the strain and pressure of city life, with its strenuous effort and consuming ambition. The designers of Central Park plainly endeavoured to embody as much as possible within their limitations, and in a dignified way without resorting to affectations and deceptions, the quiet, pastoral idea. Within the narrow area of the park the broadest scope of open meadow that could be secured was considerably less than thirty acres. But the bordering woods were so depressed as to leave the boundaries uncertain and mysterious, and the turf was made to flow into sunny alcoves and about promontories of foliage until it was lost in hazy shadows which suggested indefinite extent of the same restful scenery. The view shown [see p. 197] is taken from a point overlooking the north meadow near 100th Street on the west side. The glimpse of distant turf seen under the branches of the group of trees in the centre of the opening in the wood border on the left, the skyline of trees in the distance, all suggest to the imagination a limitless extent of similar rural conditions. No object meets the eye of the observer to indicate that there is anything beyond but green pastures and tree-flecked meadows."[1]

This is a most beautiful and true description of a public park as it should be and continue to be, and no museum or similar alien structure should be allowed a place within its bounds.

In connexion with the subject of parks, the importance of civic planning naturally suggests itself. A park is, in reality, only a part of a civic scheme which should have a wide extension and give attention to all of the spiritual, mental, and physical needs of a community in the largest sense of the term. A city is like a body and its members. Each part has a definite relation to the others and a distinct function of its own to perform. In its truest sense, it is an organism that necessitates a constant interplay of functions of various kinds. The park exercises one of these functions, while the streets, squares, circles, and other features possessing use or beauty are other members that contribute to the enjoyment and well-being of the community. This adjustment of the existing conditions to the various uses of the community should be so managed as to recognize the

[1] *Garden and Forest*, vol. i., May 9, 1888.

valuable legacy of the past, to recognize the needs of the present and the immediate future and something of the potentiality of a more distant time and circumstance. Perhaps the retention of the valuable features is the most important because it has a definite and determinable value about which there can be no mistake. Let us not, therefore, lose our hold on the past when we study our civic designs. Moreover, while modifications will naturally suggest themselves in view of changed conditions and requirements, there will still be the possibility of retaining much of the old features in conjunction with the new, combined together in one unified whole. The difficulty with many city planning designs is that they are not sufficiently conservative of the old and valuable conditions already existing and show often indications of a willingness to let go too readily old-time features. There are, likewise, various dominant ideas of even contradictory characteristics which should pervade the whole city plan and co-operate together to make an ideal extension of the lives of individuals. It should be remembered that "men do not form a community . . . merely in so far as the men co-operate. They form a community . . . when they not only co-operate, but accompany this co-operation with the ideal extension of the lives of individuals whereby each co-operating member says, 'This activity which we perform together, this work of ours, its past, its future, its sequence, its order, its sense,—all these enter into my life, and are the life of my own self writ large.'"[1]

[1] Josiah Royce.

Dr. Harald Höffding thus expresses the idea of how feeling acts in passing from the old to the new, which always, consciously or unconsciously, contains more or less of the old: "The stream of feeling," he says, "is in general reluctant to quit the bed that it has worked for itself. It has accommodated itself to the traditional ideas, and a time of unrest and discord must be passed through before it can reaccommodate itself to the new ideas. During such a time of transition, the two streams of feeling, the one tending to flow on in the old bed, the other to expand, have a hard struggle with one another. Or, to express it more correctly, the tendency of the old feeling to spread itself over and colour the whole of consciousness struggles against the same tendency on the part of the new feeling, for the feelings that are bound up with tradition have also an expansive tendency and will always try, if they cannot altogether crowd out the new feeling, at any rate to colour and transform it; in extreme cases, where they can maintain themselves in no other way, the old ideas become transformed in correspondence with the new."

These remarks, although they are intended to apply specially to the feelings of an individual, have an even greater force when predicated of a community. For instance, the park idea of pastoral restfulness, an old one, should be extended and transformed in a new way from the park to the sidewalk and street by means of intervals of grass space between trees and shrubs all skilfully associated together. This park idea should be further extended to the lawns and dooryards of citizens, and a certain amount of formality and regard for convenience should, on the other hand, reach over from the street designs to that of the park as well as the lawn and dooryard. It should not be confusing to speak of a whole city as an actual park, or of a great park as, in a perfectly legitimate sense, the abode of a community, that is a city developed on comprehensive lines. The city planner, therefore, should make his standpoint of design that of the community and thus evolve a comprehensive plan that allows due regard to the limitations of the place and of the residents. On the other hand, the formality, as understood in common parlance, is required for its distinctly human quality to take its proper place in the park and on the street and in the city lawn or yard. The park idea should pervade the city everywhere throughout its streets, and particularly around its residences and public buildings. In other words, if I may be allowed to repeat the same idea in other words, a city should be looked upon, if ideally laid out, as a great public park in which a community is to live and move and have its being.

The city planner, therefore, should make his standpoint of design that of the community and thus evolve for his city a unified artistic creation realizing the ideal of both the architect and landscape architect. In order to illustrate the application of these ideas I will venture to refer to a plan for redesigning an important part of the city of Washington made in 1900 for the Chief Engineer of the United States and submitted to the Speaker of the House of Representatives by the Secretary of War.[1] The region under consideration in this plan as designated by the Act of Congress includes that section of the District of Columbia situated between B Street S. W., the Capitol, Pennsylvania and Delaware Avenues, and requires a connexion with the Zoölogical Park. It should be specially noticed in this plan that the original design of Major L'Enfant made one hundred years ago has been treated with due respect. Pennsylvania Avenue and all the boundary streets have been retained in exact accordance with the original design. Like L'Enfant's design also the main treatment of drives and lawns is kept on the axis of the Capitol and Washington Monument. Moreover, by setting apart the Botanical Garden and the grounds of the Smithsonian Institute and the Agricultural Department and the space around the White House, an actual park in the heart of Washington has been already secured. The design under consideration seeks as far as possible to retain and improve all this highly developed and desirable park effect and also seeks to enlarge and complete it by purchasing the necessary land to extend it to Pennsylvania Avenue and Delaware Avenue. Very few cities in the world have such a park development as already exists in the Washington of the present day, which is much of it in a peculiar degree really the Washington of the past and of L'Enfant's creation. The essential and underlying idea of the plan in question is that in place of a park crisscrossed by traffic streets

[1] The preparation of this plan was awarded to Samuel Parsons in 1900 by the Chief Engineer of the United States.

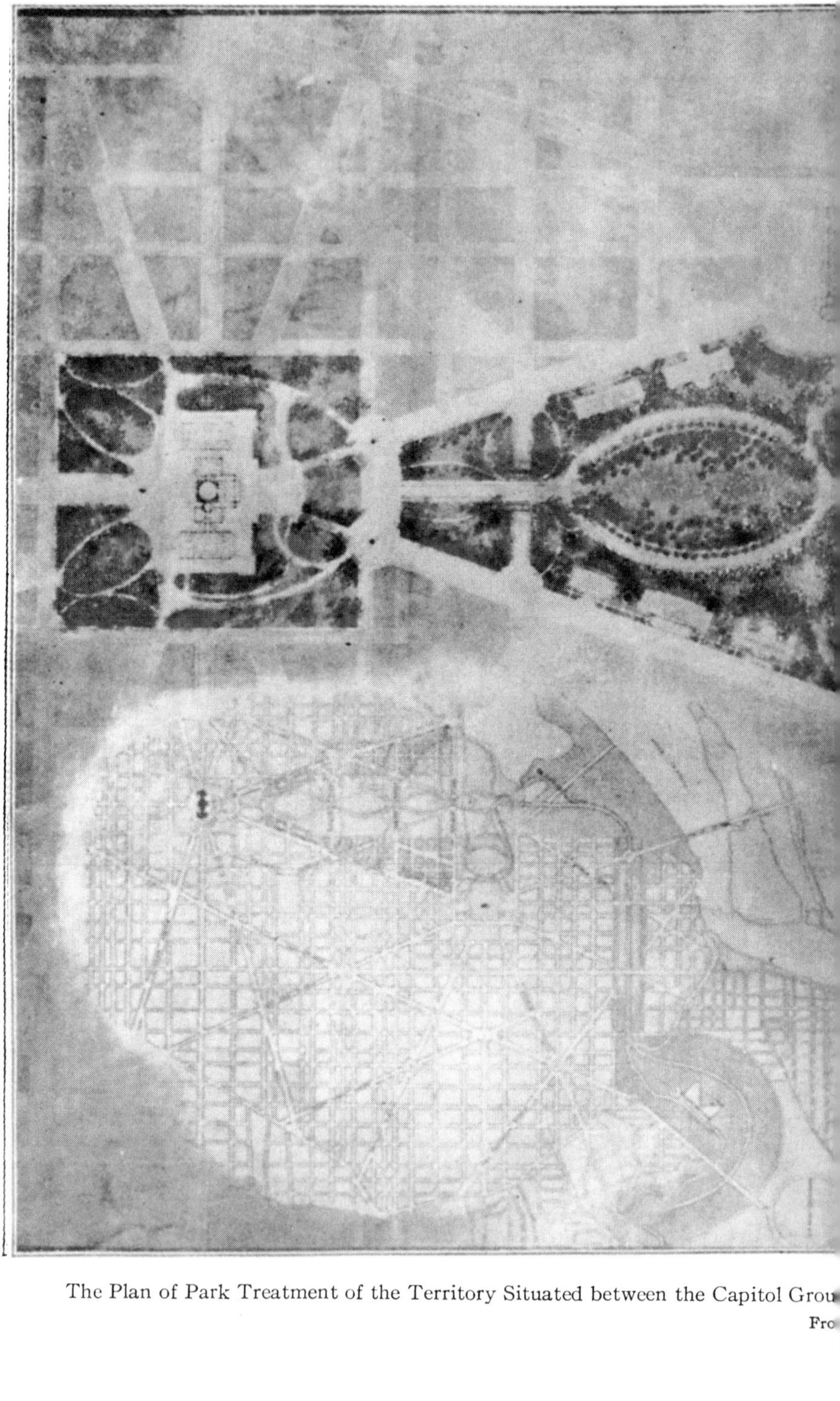

The Plan of Park Treatment of the Territory Situated between the Capitol Grou

Fro

hington Monument and Pennsylvania and Delaware Avenues, Washington, D. C.
gn.

and obstructed here and there by an inferior class of houses, the plan proposes to retain the half dozen important public buildings existing and lay out the grounds around them, or in other words *park* them. Broad lawns are arranged for pastoral effects and trees and shrubs are clustered along the paths and drives and on the borders of the lawns, and a series of longitudinal elliptical grass spaces leads the eye of any one standing in front of the Capitol down over a vista of green lawns to the Washington Monument.

By the employment of bridges over the transverse streets the entire territory of park space is brought into one unified whole, a park unit and yet correlated in the most intimate way with the neighbouring city. It is intended that the bridges shall be so screened and planted in the manner of those of Central Park, New York, that the sense of the close neighbourhood of the city shall not be appreciably felt as one wanders through the park. It is also proposed that in future all public buildings for the United States or the District of Columbia that may be erected here shall be kept strictly out of the main area of the park, and disposed along the borders of Pennsylvania and Delaware Avenues. It is not claimed that this arrangement of a great park in the heart of Washington City is entirely ideal, but simply that it does recognize and treat with due respect the original plan of L'Enfant, taking in consideration the needs and tastes of the present and future generations. Moreover, it may be said also that the admirable system of tree planting adopted long years ago on the streets of

Washington has given the city the appearance of a somewhat formal park, and this feature with the considerable lawns and dooryards of the citizens adorned with grass and shrubs and flowers helps to extend the park idea.

The main and most important principle, therefore, of city planning, to repeat in another form what has been already discussed, is for both architect and landscape architect to remember that, in the case of such work, they are designing for a community of various members having various needs and desires, and that they should always consider well traditions and peculiar inherited conditions. They should not design for individuals, or even groups of individuals, but for the whole community understood in the broadest and best sense of the term.

XVI

CHOICE TREES AND SHRUBS

ALTHOUGH it may seem to be a truism the reiteration of which is hardly necessary, it is well to keep in mind from the very start in this chapter that the problem of the proper use of plants varies with every spot where work is undertaken, and that the hardiness of trees and shrubs and fertility of soils will always be found relative to varying conditions.

Having emphasized these limitations, it has been deemed a good idea to bring together some notes on the peculiarities of certain choice trees and shrubs and flowers and suggestions as to their treatment. In doing this, ideas and facts may be set forth which will be familiar to many and yet it is believed they may possess a decided value for others.

It is important, first of all, to warn lawn planters not to make a museum of their lawns. Many trees and shrubs, and particularly perennials, or wild flowers, are interesting botanically and horticulturally, and yet do not count for much in the landscape picture, and are not specially controlling in the general effect. They, of course, may be used in their proper place duly related to their more important neighbours, but to have too many of them, or to locate them improperly, works often great injury to the picture and mars, in various ways, its harmony. The following remarks, therefore, will bear chiefly on this fitness of a plant for a landscape picture both in appearance and general habit.

To follow the seasons and make each one interesting as it comes forward in turn will always have much value for many people. One of the earliest things to come in leaf and flower is the willow, and as a lawn plant it has many good qualities. It will live and thrive in almost any soil, especially a wet one. The fresh-looking flowers it bears in early spring are always a kind of revelation or forestate of good things to come. Not all willows are of equal value in lawn planting although there are numerous species and varieties. The difficulty with the willows is that they are liable to become naked and bare of foliage as they grow older, and like most soft wooded trees their beauty is apt to be short lived. One of the best willows for its retention of beauty, bushiness, and general health is the common white willow, *Salix alba.* It is superior for this reason to the red-stemmed willow and the yellow, *Salix vitellina aurea*, and especially the weeping willow, *Salix babylonica.* The latter grows often into a fine tree with great spreading branches, but it is brittle and suffers much from ice storms, which, helped by windstorms, generally succeed eventually in destroying it. There seems to be little reason for using this willow along watersides. Its drooping habit is not specially attractive, being stringy and wanting in fulness. It is generally considered a sad-looking tree, suitable for graveyards and pools of water, why it would be hard to explain. The pussy willow (*Salix caprea*) is a fine bushy kind. It is important to remember that the members of the willow family need pruning strongly in order to keep them in good shape.

Other rapid-growing trees for the spring lawn are poplars, the oriental plane tree, alders, birches, and the forsythias, *fortuni* and *viridissima*. The latter kinds are excellent shrubs, blooming early with abundant yellow flowers and keeping a rich, compact, and in the case of *Forsythia viridissima* a graceful foliage throughout the summer and autumn. The *viridissima* looks well on the borders of shrub groups, because its branches droop close to the ground. There is another shrub, *Berberis thunbergi*, that is compact, of vigorous growth, and fine throughout the season with its glossy foliage, summer flowers, and autumn colour. It is one of the best shrubs for the lawn. Its relative, the common barberry, is also an excellent shrub, fine in masses with its bright flowers and fruit. The *Spiræa thunbergi* is perhaps the prettiest of spiræas with its light-coloured graceful foliage, early white flowers in great masses, and its lovely autumn colour.

The horse-chestnut is fine in May with its fresh green foliage and large white or red trusses of bloom, but later on in July it is apt to lose its leaves and look forlorn for the rest of the season. Hawthorns belong to spring, and the most celebrated and beautiful in flower is the English variety (*Cratægus oxycantha*) with its white or scarlet flowers, but this species is liable to blight in America and does not equal in beauty of foliage and size and brilliancy of fruit the numerous American species among which are the well-known cockspur (*Crus galli*) and coccinea kinds. These thorns are gems of beauty and of varied individuality; no soil or exposure seems too adverse for them. San José scale is an insect pest that troubles the American hawthorns as well as the English, but a little care will readily conquer it. The same may be said of the Japan quince and the flowering apple and peach and plum and almond. They are all most lovely in spring but are all liable to San José scale.

Magnolias make one of the choicest denizens of the lawn but are hard to transplant. One of the sights of Central Park, New York, is a large tree, a Chinese magnolia (*M. conspicua*), a perfect cloud of white bloom, with as yet no leaves, in the midst of a snowstorm in April.

But after spring come the summer effects, which really commence in May and linger on through the first and second weeks of June and later. This is the season of roses and with a little care they are beautiful, but with pruning at frequent intervals and also cultivating with plenty of manure and mulch, making a light mellow soil containing plenty of humus, they are unsurpassed for beauty. There are the climbing *Wichuriana* hybrids on the wall in mid-June and the regular June roses blooming freely once only such as the General Jacqueminot and similar kinds, and last and most important the ever-blooming roses, the hybrid teas, which flower repeatedly in the utmost profusion all summer until frost. A bed of these hybrid tea roses properly managed is a wonderful sight.

There is another summer rose blooming in late June and July, the prairie rose (*R. setigera*), already mentioned, that is very lovely in flower with small pink and white petals hanging in clusters. It is comparatively free from disease and grows to great size under the most unpropitious circumstances. The Japan rose (*R. rugosa*) is a shrub which has rich green foliage and large red and white flowers, and thrives on the seashore, and in autumn has large red fruit like small apples. It needs to be sharply pruned every year to keep it from becoming ragged and devoid of leaves.

If a general consensus of opinion were obtained among those who love and know something about flowers, I think the rhododendrons would, after roses, be declared most popular. Their rich dark evergreen foliage with red and purple and white trusses of flowers cannot be surpassed for massive and impressive beauty. The rhododendron is king of flowers as the rose is queen. Nevertheless they have their drawbacks, especially in this climate. Sometimes the spring hot suns and cold nights brown and even destroy the leaves. Even then the plant is seldom killed, only rendered unsightly for a time, and retarded in its growth. Usually it will be found in such cases that it has been weakened by disease or drought. A few of the best kinds that have proved hardy after many years of trial are as follows: Abraham Lincoln, rosy crimson, *Album elegans*, light blush fading white, Boule de Neige, white, dwarf, and very hardy, *Atrosanguineum*, blood red, Charles Dickens, dark scarlet, Charles S. Sargent, rich crimson, Charles Bagley, cherry red, *Everestianum*, rosy lilac, best and hardiest habit, General Grant, rosy scarlet, Kettledrum, rich purplish or crimson, bushy, excellent form, and very hardy, Lady Armstrong, pale rose, Lee's dark purple, Mrs. Milner, rich crimson, Old Port, rich plum colour, *Purpureum elegans*, *Parsons grandiflorum*, and Sefton, dark maroon. There are, however, others besides these kinds that are desirable for hardiness and beauty.

Of the hybrid tea, the ever-blooming roses, the following varieties ought to be mentioned as reliable and excellent, namely: Caroline Testout, bright satiny rose, Étoile de France, velvety crimson, large double, General MacArthur, large bright crimson, Gruss an Teplitz, bright rich scarlet, free bloomer, La France, clear silvery pink, large and full, Madam Abel Chatenay, carmine rose shaded with salmon, Madam Jules Grolez, bright China rose, Madam Cochet, deep rose pink, beautiful in bud and flower, Countess of Shaftesbury, silvery carmine, Juliet, vermilion red, reverse of petals, old gold, Bessie Brown, creamy white, Kaiserin Augusta Victoria, cream shaded lemon, Melanie Soupert, pale yellow, suffused carmine, Duchess of Portland, pale sulphur yellow, Richmond, bright, light crimson, Mildred Grant, creamy white, Dean Hole, pale silvery rose, deeper shaded on yellow ground, Arthur R. Goodwin, coppery orange red, Château de Clos-Vougeot, velvety scarlet, Duchess of Wellington, intense saffron yellow stained with crimson, Edward Mawley, velvety crimson, Entente Cordiale, capucine red with wide yellow base, and Farben Königin, imperial pink or salmon pink.

The azaleas are a charming family and do not receive as much attention as they deserve. They are, moreover, hardy, except the showy *Azalea mollis* whose unsatisfactory behaviour after cold winters has given the entire family a bad name. The colours vary between brick red, orange, and yellow white, while rhododendrons show white and purple and red and crimson, having a decidedly different key of colour. There are many species and varieties of azaleas but the best of them are native American species, especially *A. calendulacea* or *lutea*, and the *A. ponticum*, crossed with the *calendulacea*, which are always hardy and fine, while some of the varieties containing *ponticum* alone or mixed with tender kinds are not so hardy. These azaleas are all deciduous. Japan has given us some good kinds such as the deciduous form, *Azalea ledefolia narcissiflora* a mauve type and very hardy, and the evergreen *Azalea amœna* with glossy foliage and masses of deep red small flowers. The last is very beautiful, but occasionally it is touched with frost, though rarely killed. *Azalea kaempferi* is hardy and bears a fine red flower. The deciduous azaleas look well in the woods in nooks and corners where the shade is not too deep. Rhododendrons like similar places and in fact should be planted underneath or with a background of trees. If the trees are planted at the same time as the rhododendrons or azaleas the latter will do well, because everything can then grow up together. To plant them under old trees in dense shade where roots already occupy the ground and take up the moisture and fertility and to expect them to thrive is asking too much of any plant. The best soil for rhododendrons and azaleas is mellow loam with plenty of humus in it to retain moisture and lend fertility. If the soil is sandy with hard-pan, it should be well cultivated and some soil richer in clay and humus added to it; if it is a stiff clay it will doubtless need a good deal of sand. To the improper preparation of the soil of rhododendron and azalea beds may be attributed much of the failure of the plants.

Of all the members of the rhododendron family the best in the judgment of high authorities is the *Kalmia latifolia*, commonly called the mountain laurel. The splendid mass of the pinkish white flowers with the evergreen foliage make a most impressive combination; and the formation of the flower and the truss has an exquisite finish and elegance that should not be overlooked, and the colouring is delicate and lovely. There is nothing of its kind quite equal to the sight at the great Arnold Arboretum near Boston where thousands of kalmias or mountain laurels cluster in a glade and run up among the trees of a great hemlock-covered hillside.

Birch Woods on the Estate of Elon H. Hooker, Esq., Greenwich, Conn.

From a Photograph by Miss Frances Benjamin Johnston—Mrs. Mattie Edwards Hewitt. (Reproduced by Permission.)

There are many kinds of evergreen-leaved shrubs described in nurserymen's catalogues that are hardly to be depended on except in favourably situated spots, spots that are really quite difficult to find. In this country, evergreen trees and shrubs do not, as a rule, thrive as well as in England or in many parts of the Continent; but on the other hand, deciduous trees and shrubs thrive better here than in Europe. The deciduous shrubs bloom more freely and many trees and shrubs grow with more vigour and persistence, soil and other conditions being equal. We have been prone in the past to model our horticulture too much on that of Europe, forgetting how different the conditions are here from those abroad.

The glory of June and summer is the purple and golden leaved tree. The purple beeches, the purple maples, the golden oaks, the many-coloured Japanese maples, one type of which is well named polymorphum—all of these plants are rich and glowing with colour and their beauty on the lawn cannot be denied. Some abnormally coloured leaved trees have been referred to in the chapter on Plantations. These naturally need avoiding. The most delicate and charming of all summer or spring trees, the white birch, should be considered here in more detail. Its beauty is not easy to establish. The transplanting is difficult and can only be done successfully at one season of the year, unless by chance, namely in April just as the young leaves are pushing out. Even then it is necessary for success that the birch be young and recently transplanted so that it may have plenty of fibrous roots. The weeping cut-leaved form is the best variety for the lawn, its stem is so white.

June is the month of flowers. Later in midsummer, few blooms appear. There are the scarlet rambler roses and *Rosa setigera* or the prairie rose, and at this season, also, blooms one of the finest of all half trees or shrubs, andromeda, or *Oxydendron arboreum*, the sorrel tree. Its flowers are great white tassels like the plume on a helmet and the foliage is a rich glossy green. It grows slowly like the dogwood at first, but eventually it attains great size. This recalls the fact that the dogwoods have not been noticed. They are specially beautiful in summer after their spring bloom has passed. The foliage is fine and so are the branches, and they are fine at any age even when a ruin. It is a fact, when you come to think of it, there is no deciduous shrub of such great, as well as lasting, beauty to be found on the lawn, not even the andromeda. It is, however, shy in transplanting and takes some time to establish itself.

There is after all so much personality and individuality in plants that one never knows how to take them. They develop such queer freaks and odd divergence from ordinary habits. Dogwoods form an instance in point. Sometimes they will get away and grow at once after transplanting in spite of the fact that they are naturally slow in starting, so much so that dry weather and other causes kill many of them in the very beginning. It is often as hard to diagnose the troubles of plants

A Picturesque Effect of the Native Dogwood (*Cornus florida*) on the Estate of R. W. Deforest, Esq., Cold Spring, Long Island.

From a Photograph by Miss Frances Benjamin Johnston—Mrs. Mattie Edwards Hewitt. (Reproduced by Permission.)

as those of human beings. A rhododendron in good health usually termed hardy, will die and nearby a kind considered tender will survive. These surprises occur frequently with trees and shrubs and should not discourage any one. The dogwood, the birch, and the rhododendron are notable instances of the vagaries of plant nature.

The Virgilia lutea (*Cladrastis tinctoria*), the yellow-wood, is a beautiful tree in midsummer with its smooth bark like a beech and graceful branches bearing long racemes of sweet-scented, white wistaria-like flowers in June. Not unlike the Virgilia lutea, especially in its leguminous character, is the laburnum or golden chain. It is perfectly hardy, and though seldom seen in this country, is a favourite in Europe. Francis Thompson writes:

> Mark yonder how the long laburnum drips
> Its jocund spilth of fire, its honey of wild flame.

The catalpa has some good qualities for summer besides its rapid growth, which is sometimes an injury to it. The flowers are white and large and make a show in June. It is not a first-class shade tree any more than the silver maple, poplar, ailanthus (in some respects the toughest and finest of trees, barring the odour), the weeping willows, and the American ash. The beech is the shade tree *par excellence* for the lawn, but not for the street. Its unsurpassed beauty may not be gainsaid. The trunk and bark are wonderful, and the foliage is equally fine, especially the purple variety. A beech tree, in its prime, fifty or more years old, makes a feature on the lawn of inestimable value. Money value can hardly express it. Two or three such specimens will make an otherwise somewhat ordinary place a great and distinguished estate. The beeches are hard to transplant and slow of growth in youth, but they are well worth the trouble of establishing. The *Kolreuteria paniculata* (varnish tree) is fine in summer,has been long known, and but little used. Its showy panicles of yellow flowers are very welcome in July and it is hardy.

Of all native trees there is hardly any one that quite equals the tulip. To hear Henry Ward Beecher praise it—for he knew and loved trees—was a treat, especially to hear his grand voice roll out with sonorous accents its botanical name, *Liriodendron tulipifera*. The tulip makes a lofty tree with a fine stem and lovely foliage both in shape and colour, really quite curious in its way, and in June the yellow flowers nestle attractively among the leaves. It is not an easy tree to transplant, having fleshy roots somewhat like the magnolia: it should always be set out in the spring, not in the fall. The oriental plane is a notable tree in summer with its lofty form and thick spreading foliage. There are more beautiful trees but few that endure so well difficult conditions, especially in cities, or that grow faster and at the same time keep their beauty better in mature years, and they are not, moreover, difficult to transplant. It is a mistake to condemn any class of hardy trees, for they all have their value. Even poplars, whose beauty is apt to be short-lived unless skilfully pruned, have in some cases a decided advantage of their own. The Lombardy poplar, or better still the white-stemmed form (*Populus alba Bolleana*), with its narrow pyramidal growth has a distinct value for its colour as well as shape in the landscape, rising from the midst of other foliage. Employed as it often is, singly, or in lines, alongside a building, or in hedge effects bounding a garden or roadway, it is not satisfactory. The lower portions are, doubtless, apt to become unsightly, but a little pruning, intelligently and occasionally applied, will enable its towering form to show out from the general mass of foliage on the lawn for many years in the most attractive manner.

Something should be said for the oaks, for much can be said against them on account of their slow growth and generally crooked stems and tendency to failure in transplanting. All this may be said, and yet after all there is no family like the oaks. They are kings among northern trees. There is the white oak! What is there among trees like some specimens to be seen along roadsides throughout the country? Summer and autumn and winter all the oaks stand for the very ideal of strength and beauty, white oak, red oak, scarlet oak, pin oak, black oak, willow oak. They should be seen to appreciate them, for instance in Flushing, Long Island, near New York, the home of fine trees, where some of the avenues are lined with oaks. Look at those great pin oaks on Bowne Avenue, fifty or sixty feet high, with drooping shining foliage and trunks like masts of a ship black with age.

Another great tree for summer is the linden, the European linden in its various forms; the American linden or the basswood being a much inferior tree. The sweet-scented flowers and the deep shadowing foliage make it perhaps the most grateful shade tree in summer except the beech and Norway maple. The best three forms are the yellowish red kinds (*Tilia dasystyla*) and a specially drooping form, *T. petiolaris*, and the silver-leaved linden (*T. argentea* or *tomentosa*), which is the hardiest and most distinct of all. Nothing can be finer however, in its way, than a large tree of the old-fashioned linden (*T. petiolaris*). It should be remembered that the linden will not bear as much hardship as the Norway maple and certain other kinds of shade trees. The silver linden is the hardiest of the family.

What shall be said of the elms, American and English, both quite distinct in appearance as though they were not of the same genus? The American elm with its arching, Gothic form is quite familiar, for it may be seen everywhere in America, and the streets of the towns and cities of New England are greatly dignified by its presence. Of late years, however, the American elm has gained a bad name on account of the borers and other insects that infest it. This is no reason for giving up planting it, because horticulturists have learned to control these pests with a little care and skill. The old trees are hard to clean because they are so large, and there are also many of them so old as to be at the end of their natural careers, consequently it is no wonder they are dying in many old New England towns. The trouble is that nothing will quite take the place of the American elm. The wine-cup form is quite unique. It is to be hoped the use of the American elm will not pass away.

The English elm is very hardy and stands all sorts of difficult exposures, especially on the seashore and in cities. For instance, it suits the streets of Boston better than almost any other tree. It is not as beautiful as the linden and maple or even the American elm, but the massive dark green foliage is fine and the tree grows to great size and age. Its growth is quite rapid.

There is a tree, the ginkgo, which is so unique and excellent that it demands a few moments' attention. It is a strange looking tree. It might have come from another planet. Indeed, it is one of the oldest trees on earth, having been found in one of the lowest strata where fossil plant life appears. There is but one species and one variety and it is found native in the region of Northern China. The leaves are fan-shaped and weird and eastern looking. It is, moreover, hardy and free from disease to an extent that can scarcely be said of any other tree. The cones grow on the branches in a curious way, but it seldom fruits and then only if it stands near a female tree of the same kind, for it is diæcious. The great arms of these trees thrust themselves in the sky in strange fashion and yet some of the most notable specimens in America, in front of the Smithsonian Institute in Washington, District of Columbia, are broad and massive. The forms it assumes are myriad, and it is only apt to grow well after it is about ten years old. It is not a good shade tree. Its transplanting qualities are excellent.

Another tree of many interesting qualities is the deciduous cypress. Its form is picturesque as well as symmetrical. Delicate foliage and erect carriage give it dignity and elegance. There is a variety of it, the Chinese cypress (wrongly so-called, as it is a form of the American deciduous cypress), which is particularly refined and elegant. This tree naturally likes low wet ground, although it will grow well on high land. Fine specimens may be seen on the streets of Flushing, Long Island, on ordinary high land. One drawback it has, that of putting out its foliage very late in spring, as late as the middle of May.

The mountain-ash is a fine tree bearing beautiful berries. It is of moderate size and classes in that respect with the white birch. The *Sophora japonica* (the Japanese pagoda tree) is little used although it is excellent, and perfectly hardy, bearing quantities of yellow flowers in June in the midst of attractive foliage.

There are a few shrubs that have not been touched on which are well suited for summer bloom on the lawn. Very hardy and picturesque is the *Aralia pentaphylla.* It is somewhat low and compact in growth and altogether much superior to the *Aralia japonica*, the angelica tree from Japan, sometimes known as the devil's walking-stick, a great awkward, aggressive-looking object with large, ragged, tropical-looking foliage. The angelica tree is perfectly hardy, but so coarse looking that there are few places where it is acceptable. Some of the buddleias are fine and suited for summer effect, especially the variety *Buddleia veitchii.* The callicarpa is a good summer flowering shrub and so is the sweet-scented shrub calycanthus; and *Chionanthus virginica* is tall with fine, large, deep green foliage with fragrant, drooping, open clusters of white flowers, lace-like in appearance, hence its name, white fringe tree. The weigelas or diervillas make fine summer shrubs, especially *Weigela lavallee*, bearing deep crimson flowers all through the summer; of the same type is the bloom of the weigela, Eva Ratke, whose great masses of deep crimson make a rich effect in the summer.

The Elæagnus family is worth growing because it is so vigorous and has such silvery shades on the under sides of the leaves. It is called the silver-thorn or the oleaster, and although somewhat coarse, its great vigour and hardiness make it valuable for the lawn. The *Elæagnus longipes* is the best kind and is notable for its profusion of red berries in August and edible fruit in autumn. The rose of Sharon, althea or hibiscus, has its value for its brilliant midsummer flowering. The plant is vigorous and hardy and easily transplanted, but it is coarse and stiff looking in habit. *Potentilla fruticosa*, shrubby cinquefoil, bears on its low form bright yellow flowers in summer among narrow fuzzy leaves. The mock oranges (Philadelphus) are excellent shrubs, large, vigorous, and healthy, bearing showy flowers, somewhat like those of the orange; *Philadelphus grandiflora* and *Philadelphus coronarius* are two of the best kinds. *Rhamnus catharticus*, the buckthorn, is very hardy and suited to places where it is likely to have bad usage. It has good foliage and red berries in summer, turning black. *Rhamnus frangula* is, perhaps, the best species of the genus.

St. John's-wort, the hypericum, a July flowering shrub, is quite low in size with quanities of bright yellow flowers and compact foliage. The largest flower is, perhaps, that of *Hypericum moserianum* and the best kind *Hypericum kalmianum*. *Kerria japonica*, the globe flower, is another good summer blooming shrub. It is dwarf with bright yellow flowers and green branches. It is hardy, pretty, and rather refined. *Rhodotypus kerrioides* is a valuable shrub from Japan. The foliage is of a specially fresh and light green colour, making an excellent contrast to that of most other shrubs, and after all it is the foliage that counts; the flowers last such a comparatively short time. The flowers of the Rhodotypus are not specially conspicuous and the black berries are borne all winter. *Rubus odoratus*, the flowering raspberry, is pretty all summer with its clusters of beautiful pink or purple fragrant blossoms.

The spiræas are a numerous family and apt to look a little weedy on the lawn. *Spiræa Anthony Waterer* is one of the latest varieties, bearing bright-coloured flowers nearly all summer. *Spiræas bumaldi*, *callosa*, *billardii*, and *douglasi* all have red flowers, most all summer, and even though the flowers are gone, the delicate light green foliage of *Spiræa thunbergii* makes it a fine summer shrub. *Symphoricarpus vulgaris* (coral berry) is a humble little shrub, but it is useful with its red and yellow berries all summer in connexion with larger shrubs.

Stuartia pentagynia is a lovely shrub that is little known and not quite hardy in the Middle States. The flowers are strikingly large, of pearly whiteness, with orange-coloured anthers. The leaves are a bright rich green, reddish beneath. The whole shrub looks not unlike a camelia. *Styrax japonica* has a little the appearance of the dogwood, only its habit is not as good; it is, however, hardy, the flowers are pure white, bell-shaped, and arranged in pendulous groups, and bloom in May and early June.

The lilacs are the glory of spring. Few flowers are so popular both for odour and colour, and the foliage is massive and green throughout the summer and is specially suited to the garden. There are a number of tamarisks, both erect and spreading; some of them are naturally hardier than others. They all belong in exposed places near the shore or the brink of some feature of water, or in the seams of or near by rocks. They are wild looking and odd and graceful and bear bright red flowers in summer mingled with light feathery foliage. The tamarisk does not group well with other shrubs and should, therefore, be kept somewhat by itself. The best kinds are *Tamarisk africana*, *Tamarisk gallica*, *Tamarisk germanica*, and *Tamarisk indica*, and, perhaps, the hardiest and most generally useful is *Tamarisk africana*.

The snowballs (viburnums) are an important family

and include many species and varieties most valuable for grouping with other shrubs on the lawn. Their appearance is varied. The large-sized flowers of *Viburnum plicatum*, the well-known Japanese form, are much like *Viburnum tomentosum*, only the latter is more bushy, with less showy flowers, while on the other hand, the native *Viburnum acerifolium*, *Viburnum cassinoides*, and *Viburnum dentatum* are beautiful and valuable for their foliage, but not as much for their flowers, and they are different in almost every way from the Japanese or Chinese kinds, *plicatum*, *dilatatum*, and *macrocephalum*, while *Viburnum lentago* and *Viburnum lantana* are each beautiful in their way. The *Viburnum oxycoccus*, or *opulus*, and *opulus sterilis* have beautiful large white flowers, and in the case of the first, splendid red fruit in autumn. *Viburnum sieboldii*—if you have ever seen it, you have beheld the finest of the family. When mature, it is almost a tree, and has splendid large thick glossy foliage not easily described. The flowers are white and grow in more or less erect open clusters, and red berries decorate it in autumn. The little recognized *Viburnum prunifolium* (black haw or stag bush) comes a close second to the *Viburnum sieboldii*. Its foliage is glossy and fine and compact and picturesque and the autumn colouring is unsurpassed among shrubs except by the dogwood, andromeda, and *Euonymus alatus*.

And this leads to the consideration of the autumn coloured trees and shrubs. A list of some of them may be of value to induce study of catalogues and botanies to learn their habits; the best of them are maples (red and scarlet), the Japanese polymorphum, the striatum, the sugar, the circinatum, and *Tartaricum ginnali*, a brilliantly red kind. Then come the *Nyassa multiflora*, sour-gum or pepperidge, the red oak, the scarlet oak, the white oak (*Quercus alba*), the swamp white oak (*Quercus bicolor*), and the pin oak (*Quercus palustris*) and the liquidambar: these with the dogwoods, andromedas, the sumacs (*Rhus aromatica*, *Rhus glabra*, and *Rhus typhina*), and *Berberis thunbergi*, our excellent friend of the spring flowering kinds. In addition to the beautiful fall colour, there are the bright red berried kinds, Japanese *Rosa rugosa*, other roses, the barberries, and other hawthorns.

There is one shrub that is becoming deservedly popular and that is really in almost a class by itself, and that is the *Euonymus alatus*. Its red is unique. There is nothing just like it. The crimson is not exactly a fiery one, but there is a glow in the heart of it that is quite indescribable. You notice it afar off. Perhaps this red is not better than the velvety sheen of the dogwood autumn colour, but it is a surprise and a delight. The hydrangeas are a family which, while not noticeable for the colour of the leaf, make an important feature on the autumn lawn. They have large massive foliage and some species a silvery under surface, but their chief beauty is the flower. This grows in great trusses of a white colour which fade in September to pink, red, purple, and brown colour. Beside this flower which comes at a season when hardly anything else is in bloom, the foliage is somewhat uninteresting and a little coarse. On one kind, *Hydrangea paniculata grandiflora*, the flowers hang their heads in a somewhat heavy fashion. The *Hydrangea paniculata tardiva*, as it is sometimes called, has an erect spike of bloom which lasts much longer and is more attractive. Probably on account of this late blooming faculty the hydrangea has become very popular. It is a shrub that needs sharp pruning any time after it has bloomed in fall until it begins to put out leaves in spring. There is a way of pruning during the summer that induces growth of flower-bearing wood. *Hydrangea hortensia* is not hardy, but bears beautiful flowers. It is grown in tubs. The *paniculata* type is very hardy.

To the ornamental vines some consideration should be given. They are all fine: wistaria, Japan ivy (*Ampelopsis veitchii*), Virginia creeper, climbing roses, especially the Japanese kind *Wichuriana*, the trumpet vine (*Bignonia grandiflora*), and of less value *Bignonia radicans*, honeysuckles, climbers and half bush ones, *Sullivanti* and *Periclymenum belgica*, *Euonymus radicans*, the only evergreen climber of the lot, English ivy being of little value in this climate of America, the periwinkle (*Vinca minor*), matrimony vine, lycium in variety, the wild grape (the fox grape), *Vitis labrusca*, the *Dolichos japonica* (kidsu vine), fastest of growers, forty feet in one season, bitter-sweet, *Celastris scandens*, Dutchman's-pipe, *Aristolochia sipho*, a hardy, strong-growing, tropical-looking vine with large light green leaves; finally the Clematis family, the native kinds,

Clematis virginiana (the virgin's-bower), and *Clematis paniculata*, one of the most attractive and profusely blooming climbers with white flowers in August. The clematis hybrids are charming, purple, white, pink, red, and blue; only they are a little difficult to grow in this climate of New York State. *Actinidia polygama* is vigorous and picturesque.

There is one shrub that has not been mentioned and yet it is probably the most useful plant of all, and that is the privet. There are many kinds of privet, evergreen and deciduous, hardy and tender, and they are all interesting in their own way, but there are three that count a great deal in all lawn planting. The so-called California privet from Japan (*Ligustrum ovalifolium*) is used for hedges everywhere in Europe and America. Doubtless millions of plants are grown every year and it behaves well on all occasions except once in a few years a severe winter comes along and kills it, although it hardly ever altogether dies, but springs up the next season. It transplants well, grows fast, and if properly pruned will retain its beauty for many years. Perhaps it is felt to be a little stiff in form and monotonous, but it has glossy green foliage and if allowed to grow freely makes in time a good shape. Its stiffness probably persists in our minds on account of its frequent use as that abomination of vegetation, a hedge. The European privet has not so fine a shade of green, but in other ways greatly resembles it. The best privet is the *Ligustrum regelianum* from China, and this is rapidly being recognized. It has a graceful weeping, somewhat spreading habit and the leaves are grouped in a quaint, odd fashion. In time it grows to considerable size, but it always retains its graceful, quaint habit, and needs but little pruning. There are no shrubs perhaps that are so generally useful on the lawn as these unobtrusive privets.

Coming to the winter time our thoughts naturally turn to the evergreens. There are white-stemmed birches, red-stemmed dogwoods, yellow- and red-stemmed willows, and the berries that linger on them from fall, but the evergreens after all make the winter landscape and create by far the major part of its interest.

The Abies or firs are a numerous family, stately and of great size and beauty. There are firs and spruces in Europe one hundred and twenty feet high. The hemlock, *Picea canadensis*, or more properly *Tsuga canadensis*, is a beautiful, graceful evergreen that does not grow so rapidly as some others, but is easily transplanted and generally hardy, although it is apt to suffer from severe cold and winds in early spring, during the earlier years of its growth. There is a beautiful form of it called *Tsuga carolinianum* because it was found in the mountains of North Carolina. It is very symmetrical and has a drooping grace at the end of its branches and deep shadows in the inner spaces of its foliage in the case of a somewhat mature tree that is very lovely.

The white fir (*Abies concolor*) is, perhaps, after the hemlock, the finest of the firs. Its young growth is of unequalled beauty, light coloured, rich, and drooping, and there is the same beauty in its inner spaces which has been noticed in the Carolina hemlock. One of the finest evergreens to be seen anywhere is a specimen of *Abies concolor* in the Arnold Arboretum, Jamaica Plain, Boston, Mass. It stands forty feet high, is somewhat narrow compared to many other evergreens of the same size, but is compact and of perfect symmetry and unsurpassed colour. The colour is finer than that of the highly prized blue spruce, *Picea pungens*, but more of that hereafter. *Abies nobilis* (noble silver fir) is fine for its deep blue colour and picturesque form, but many of the silver firs that thrive in Europe do not in North America, and this is one. Noteworthy in this respect are the balsam firs, Nordman's fir, European silver fir (*Abies pectinata*), and Silver Spanish fir (*Abies pinsapo*). The Veitch's silver fir (*Abies veitchii*) and the Nikko fir (*Abies homolepis*, synonym *brachyphylla*) are, however, entirely hardy and satisfactory. The biotas or Chinese arbor-vitæ can hardly be said to be entirely hardy in the northern States of America. The biotas are a beautiful family with fine tints of blue and green and gold.

The cedars, so beautiful in Europe, Lebanon, deodara, and Atlas, are not hardy in the Middle States of the United States. The cryptomerias, especially the *lobbi*, which is certainly hardy, are strange, oriental looking trees that seem a little out of place in American or European landscapes. They belong, particularly, in a Japanese garden. The cypresses, especially

Lawson's, are very lovely in Europe, but they do not succeed in the Middle States of the United States. The junipers, on the other hand, are equally attractive and in many cases do well, though one of the best of them, the Irish juniper, does not succeed in the Middle States. Its narrow pyramidal form makes it a valuable plant in grouping. The American pyramidal forms, the red cedar and its varieties, are almost always hardy; yet what plant is absolutely hardy?

The red cedar is as effective in lawn planting as the celebrated Italian cypresses, which do not grow here. There are more or less trailing forms of juniper, *Juniperus canadensis*, the Savin juniper and its variety of great beauty, *tamariscifolia*, and also quite as trailing are *Juniperus squamata* and *Juniperus procumbens*, all excellent to use in connexion with rocks or along borders of streams. The Japanese and Chinese junipers are nearly all good and do not grow out of size. They have most picturesque and elegant forms. Some of them are *Juniperus chinensis*, *Juniperus pfitzeriana*, and *Juniperus japonica*. There is a blue Virginia cedar called *tripartita* that is excellent for planting near rocks. It has a wild and rustic look and is irregular and spreading in habit. The entire juniper family is most valuable on the lawn.

Among the spruces (the Piceas) the old *Picea excelsa*, the common Norway spruce, is not proving altogether satisfactory, as the years go on, but generally its proximity to the seashore will be found to be the cause of its failure, or it may have been grown too far south. The northern part of New York or Massachusetts suits it better than Washington, D. C. Moreover, when it becomes old, it is not always attractive in colour and form.

The white spruce is better and succeeds in more places, but even it has its favourite spots, and they are not so far north as those suited to the Norway spruce. The attractive lighter shades of the white spruce form another of its attractions, but for really fine blue tints it is necessary to go to the real blue spruces, *Picea pungens* or *Picea engelmani*. They are the richest of all the blue spruces. The most intensely blue are the grafted plants of *Picea pungens*, but seedlings are more symmetrical and make finer trees when fully developed, although some of them do not show as deep a shade of blue and silver. A hardy and picturesque dark fir is *Picea omorica*, and although there are many other firs, hardly any others than those mentioned can be said to be satisfactory in the climate of the Middle States of the United States. In many parts of Great Britain many others do well. The spruces (Piceas) have great value in landscape gardening. The Norway spruce is well known everywhere and its towering form and rapid growth are always fine. As already noted, it has not the beauty, however, of some other kinds and is a little more liable to disease in North America. An instance of a superior kind is the oriental spruce (*Picea orientalis*). This might be termed a highly refined Norway spruce. It is hardier, has richer, more closely set foliage, most beautiful colour, and often retains its beauty to great age. Though a little difficult to transplant and at first slow of growth it eventually attains great size and stateliness. *Picea omorica*, already mentioned, is somewhat like the last, only it has a very dark colour, darker than almost any evergreen except the yew. It is, unfortunately, little known and appreciated. Alcock's spruce (*Picea alcockiana*) has fine close set foliage, silvery underneath, and it is quite hardy. *Picea polita*, the tiger-tail spruce, is quaint with its dark rich foliage and shape of branches suggesting a tiger's tail. It is a very rugged kind. Of course, there are other fine spruces, but the ones mentioned are most useful for a lawn laid out on a well-conceived landscape design and not for a museum of evergreens.

The pines are always fine and the number of kinds is considerable. Some of the common American sorts, however, head the list for hardiness and usefulness, although they are, unfortunately, not much used. *Pinus resinosa*, red pine, is such a one and so is *Pinus regida*, pitch pine, though less beautiful. It is most useful, however, on poor, sandy land. The native white pine (*Pinus strobus*) is, on the other hand, fully appreciated though it is native. It is perhaps the most beautiful evergreen of North America. It attains a lofty size and is sometimes damaged by wind storms and ice, but it is lovely in its colouring. The Bhotan pine (*Pinus excelsa*) much resembles the white pine except the needles are a little longer and more graceful. It is not quite as hardy as the white pine. Then there is *Pinus parviflora* with its blue shades. Quite distinct, however, is the widely grown Austrian pine (*Pinus austrica*). This is the best of all evergreens for the seashore or very much exposed places. It grows fast, and is a positive feature in the landscape with its fine dark masses of foliage. In a dwarfer, more compact way, *Pinus mughus*, the Mugho pine, is about as hardy, and has a very decided and pleasing effect on the lawn. *Pinus cembra*, the Swiss stone pine (not the Italian stone pine which is tender in northern climates), is very hardy, has a pyramidal compact form, and grows slowly, although it attains considerable size.

The yews are a fine family of evergreens, one of the very best, but in America they are most of them not really hardy, that is, the winter is apt to destroy their beauty even if it does not kill them. There is a spreading yew, *Taxus repandens*, whose dark green foliage will sometimes cover a space fifteen feet square. Its chief value is its great hardiness. The last yew that will be mentioned is *Taxus cuspidata*, the best of the family for all purposes and in certain ways the best of all evergreens. The foliage is deep green and glossy; it grows as a rule compactly, but it takes on various forms, some low and even dwarf, and others pyramidal and of considerable size. All these forms are hardy and exceedingly effective in every way. The umbrella pine (*Sciadopitys verticillata*) looks like a yew, but it is not. Its form is symmetrical and its colour deep and glossy; a beautiful tree and a choice tree but no longer so very rare. The Japanese are sending them over in considerable numbers and they are grown in this country and

Europe. A large tree of this umbrella pine twenty feet high, as it can be seen in Europe, is a fine sight. It is quite hardy.

The Thuyas (arbor-vitæ) are most of them hardy, compact, and of pyramidal form. Their colouring is not as fine as the biotas, but they are hardier. Most of them are varieties of the American arbor-vitæ. There is a *Thuya standishii*, that is hardy and graceful with slightly pendulous branches. The Retinosporas are a beautiful family, but some of the kinds fall into a bad condition unless they are frequently pruned. This applies to the *Retinospora plumosa*, *squarrosa* and *psifera; Retinospora obtusa* and *filifera* are better. There is also a weeping hemlock (Sargent's weeping hemlock) which should have been noted before as a very beautiful evergreen, and also *Tsuga sieboldii*, a hemlock of very deep green colour, compact and hardy and a good tree though seldom seen on lawns. It should be understood that the term hardiness is meant in all cases to apply to the Middle States of the United States.

These notes are closed with the evergreens. Perennials and bedding plants of the tender kinds are too extended a subject to properly discuss within the limited space of this book. Moreover, such plants as the irises, phloxes, larkspurs, pinks, hollyhocks, peonies, the bedding plants, cannas, salvias, geraniums, and coleuses fill up the minor spaces of the landscape picture. They have great beauty, perhaps as much as anything on the lawn, but they do not count much in the general survey of the picture. It would not be unpleasant or a failure if they were not present; their presence would, on the other hand, lend a charm, a loveliness to the scene that can hardly be overstated. It would, therefore, be of great advantage to study diligently these plants.

Finally, in closing this chapter it should be noted that very many kinds have been left unconsidered not because they do not have value for the lawn in both this country and Europe, but because it was necessary in one short chapter to limit the purview to the most distinctive, easily obtained, and most important from a landscape gardener's point of view. If neglect or oversight is felt, it should be charged to lack of space and the desire to avoid the appearance of a nurseryman's catalogue.

NOTE.—The Douglas spruce is one of the best of evergreens for hardiness, vigour, and graceful symmetry, and for its beautiful bluish green colour.

BIBLIOGRAPHY

ANDRÉ, EDOUARD. *L'Art des Jardins.* Paris, 1879.
ALPHAND, A. *Promenades de Paris.* Paris, 1868.
BAILEY, L. H. *The Pruning Book.* New York, 1898.
—— *Nursery Book.* New York, 1896.
—— *Lessons with Plants.* New York.
—— *Cyclopedia of Horticulture.* New York, 1914.
BRITTON, N. L., and ADDISON BROWN. *Illustrated Flora.* New York, 1914.
BACON, FRANCIS. Essays "On Gardens."
CHAMBERS, SIR WILLIAM. *A Dissertation on Oriental Gardening.* London, 1772.
CORBET, C. L. *Pruning.* 1903.
COOK, E. T. *Gardening for Beginners.* New York, 1901.
DAVIES, CHARLES. *Surveying.* New York, 1883.
DOWNING, ANDREW JACKSON. *Landscape Gardening.* 1865.
DES JARDINS, GUSTAV. *Le Petit Trianon, histoire et description.* Versailles, 1885.
ELIOT, CHARLES. *Public Spaces of Boston.* 1892.
ELIOT, CHARLES W. *Life of Charles Eliot, Landscape Architect.* Boston, 1902.
ELY, HELEN RUTHERFORD. *A Woman's Hardy Garden.* New York, 1903.
FALCONER, WILLIAM. *A Historical View of the Taste and Laying out Grounds among the Nations of Antiquity.* London, 1783.
HAMLIN, A. D. F. *History of Architecture.* New York, 1909.
HAMERTON, PHILIP GILBERT. *Imagination in Landscape.* 1895.
HOME, HENRY, LORD KAIMES. *Elements of Criticism.* London, 1862.
HOWE, WALTER. *The Garden as Considered in Literature by Certain Polite Writers.* New York, 1892.
JEKYLL, GERTRUDE. *Wall and Water Gardens.* New York, 1901.
—— *Roses in English Gardens.* New York, 1902.
—— *Lilies in English Gardens.* New York, 1902.
KEMP, RICHARD. *How to Lay out a Small Garden.* London, 1858.
LARWOOD, J. *The Story of London Parks.* London, 1872.

LATHAM, CHARLES. *The Gardens of Italy.* London, 1905.
LE BLOND, E. A. F. *Old Gardens of Italy.* New York, 1912.
LEE, VERNON, and others. *In Praise of Old Gardens.* 1912.
LOBAT, J. *Plan Topographique du Bois de Boulogne.* Paris.
LODEMAN, E. C. *The Spraying of Plants.* New York, 1899.
LONGFELLOW, WILLIAM P. P. *Architectural History.* New York, 1891.
LOUDON, J. C. *A treatise on forming, improving, and managing country residences and on the choice of situations appropriate to every class of purchasers.* London, 1806.
LOUNSBERRY, ALICE. *A Guide to the Trees.* Introduction by N. L. BRITTON. 1902.
—— *Gardens near the Sea.* New York, 1910.
LOWELL, GUY. *American Gardens.* Boston, 1902.
MANSFIELD, M. F. *Royal Parks and Palaces of France.*
MILTON, JOHN. *Paradise Lost.* Book IV.
MALLING, E. A. *How to Grow Plants Indoors.* London, 1861.
MOREL, J. M. *L'Art de distribuer les jardins suivant l'usage des Chinois.*
MATHEWS, F. S. *Field Book of American Trees and Shrubs.* New York, 1914.
MAYNARD, S. F. *Landscape Gardening as applied to Home Decoration.* New York, 1914.
MACOUN, W. T. *Hardy Roses, Culture in Canada.* 1912.
MAXON, WILLIAM R. *A List of Ferns and Fern Allies of North America.* Washington, D. C., 1901.
METROPOLITAN PARK COMMISSION. *Flora of Blue Hills near Boston.* Boston, 1896.
MEYER, G. *Lehrbuch der Schönen Gartenkunst.* Berlin, 1895.
MICHAUX, F. A. *Histoire des Arbres Forestiers de l'Amérique,* translated by J. J. Smith. Philadelphia, 1852.
MIDDLETON, C. *Designs for Gates, Rails, etc.* 1835.
MILES, MANLEY. *Land Draining.* New York, 1914.
MILLER, C. H. *Making Paths and Driveways.* New York, 1912.
MILNER, HENRY ERNEST. *Landscape Gardening.* London, 1890.
MITCHELL, DONALD G. Rural Studies, 1884.
MORRIS, REV. F. O. *Country Seats of Noblemen and Gentlemen of Great Britain and Ireland.* London.
MUIR, JOHN. *Our National Parks.* New York.
NELSON, T. & SONS. *Famous Parks and Gardens of the World.* London, 1880.
NEVILLE, RALPH. *Old Cottage and Domestic Architecture.* New York, 1892.
NEWHALL, C. S. *Trees and Shrubs of N. E. America.* New York.
NICHOLSON, GEO. *The Illustrated Dictionary of Gardening.* London, 1891.

NORTON, J. B. S. *Rose Mildew.* Maryland Experiment Station, 1911.
NUTTALL, G. CLARKE. *Wild Flowers as they Grow.* New York, 1911.
OLMSTED, VAUX & Co. Preliminary Report, Prospect Park, Brooklyn, L. I., 1866.
—— Design for Prospect Park, Brooklyn, L. I., 1868.
PAGE, L. W. *Roads, Paths, and Bridges.* New York, 1913.
PANNELL, L. H. *Weeds of the Farm and Garden.* New York, 1914.
PARSONS, SAMUEL, JR. *Landscape Gardening.* New York, 1891.
—— *How to Plan Home Grounds.* New York, 1901.
—— *Landscape Gardening Studies.* New York, 1910.
PARSONS, SAMUEL B. *The Rose.* New York, 1888.
PAUL, WILLIAM. *Roses and Rose Culture.* London, 1883.
PEETS, E. *Practical Tree Repair.* New York, 1913.
PEMBERTON, REV. JOSEPH H. *Roses, their History, Development, and Culture.* London, 1908.
PETZOLD, E. *Der park von Muskau.* 1856.
—— *Fürst Herman von Pückler-Muskau.* Leipzig, 1874.
PINCHOT, GIFFORD. *A Primer of Forestry.* Washington, 1899.
PLATT, CHAS. A. *Italian Gardens.* New York, 1894.
POWELL, R. PAYSON. *The Country Home.* New York, 1894.
PRICE, SIR UVEDALE. *An essay on the picturesque as compared with the sublime and beautiful, and on the use of studying pictures for the purpose of improving real landscape.* London, 1810.
PÜCKLER-MUSKAU, PRINCE. *Andentungen der landschaftsgartnerei, verbunden mit der Deschreibung ihrer praktischen Anweidung in Stuttgart.* 1834.
RAND, EDWARD SPRAGUE. *The Rhododendron and American Plants.* Boston, 1871.
RAUCH, J. H. *Public Parks.* Chicago, 1869.
RIAT, G. *L'Art des Jardins.* Paris, 1900.
Report, New York Department Public Parks, 1871, 1872.
REPTON, HUMPHRY. *The Art of Landscape Gardening.* Edited by John Nolan. New York, 1907.
ROBERTS, H. *The Chronicle of a Cornish Garden.* New York, 1901.
ROBINSON, WILLIAM. *The English Flower Garden.* London, 1906.
—— *Wild Garden.*
—— *Garden Beautiful.* New York, 1907.
—— *Parks and Promenades of Paris.* 1878.
ROSS, JANET. *Florentine Villas.* New York, 1901.
ROUSSEAU, JEAN-JACÇUES. *The Nouvelle Héloïse,* Part IV., Letter XI. Paris, 1768.
SALTER, E. G. *Nature in Italian Art.* New York, 1912.
SARGENT, C. S. *Forests of Japan.* Boston, 1905.
—— *Trees of North America.* Boston, 1905.
—— *Garden and Forest.* New York, 1888–1897.

SCOTT, FRANK J. *The Palaces of America.* Boston.

—— *The Art of Beautifying Suburban Home Grounds of Small Extent.* New York, 1870.

SCHREINER, O., and others. *Lawn Soils and Lawns.* U. S. Agricultural Department, 1912.

SEDDING, JOHN D. *Garden Craft Old and New.* London, 1892.

SENNERT, A. R. *Garden Cities in Theory and Practice.*

SEXBY, J. J. *The Municipal Parks of London.* London, 1898.

SHALER, N. S. *American Highways.* New York, 1896.

SIEVEKING, ALBERT FORBES. *Ancient and Modern Gardens.* London, 1899.

—— *Praise of Gardens.* 1885.

STILWELL, SIR GEORGE (RERESBY). *On Making Gardens, being a Study of Old Italian Gardens, Principles of Design.* London, 1909.

SNYDER, HARRY. *Soils and Fertilizers.* New York, 1908.

SPRAGUE, ISAAC. *Wild Flowers of North America.* 1882.

STEP, EDWARD. *Wayside and Woodland Blossoms.* London, 1895.

STEVENS, DE T. *Chrysanthemums.* New York, 1912.

STILES, WILLIAM A. "Riverside Park," *Century Magazine,* New York, 1885.

STRUTT, JACOB GEORGE. *Sylva Brittanica, or Portraits of Forest Trees.* London, 1825.

TAYLOR, MRS. BASIL. *Japanese Gardens.* London, 1912.

THOMAS, HARRY H. *The Rose Book.* London, 1913.

THONGER, CHARLES. *The Book of Garden Design.* London, 1905.

THOREAU, H. D. *Excursions.* Boston, 1863.

THUNBERG, C. P. *Travels in Europe, Asia, and Africa.* London, 1794.

TRICKER, W. *Water Gardens.* New York, 1913.

TRIGGS, H. INIGO. *The Art of Garden Design in Italy.* London, 1906.

—— *Formal Gardens in England and Scotland.* London, 1902.

TUCKERMAN, W. P. *Die Gartenkunst die Italian Renaissance.* Berlin, 1884.

UNWIN, R. *Town Planting in Practice.* New York, 1910.

VACHEROT, J. *Parcs et Jardins au commencement du XXe. siècle.* Paris, 1908.

VAN RENSSELAER, MRS. SCHUYLER. *Art Out of Doors.* New York, 1894.

VAUX, CALVERT. *Concerning Lawn Planting.* New York, 1881.

WARNER, CHARLES DUDLEY. *My Summer in a Garden.* London, 1893.

WAUGH, F. A. *Landscape Gardening.* New York, 1914.

WATSON, WILLIAM. *Rhododendrons and Azaleas, Royal Botanic Gardens, Glasnevin.*

WEED, CLARENCE M. *Insects and Insecticides.* New York, 1914.

WEED, H. E. *Modern Park Cemeteries.* Chicago, 1912.

WEIDENMAN, J. *Beautifying Country Homes.* New York, 1876.

WHATELY, THOMAS. *Observations on Modern Gardening*. London, 1771.
WOODS, ALBERT FREDERICK. *Principles of Pruning*. Washington, 1895.
WOOLSON, G. A. *Ferns and How to Grow Them*. New York, 1914.
WRIGHT, MABEL OSGOOD. *Flowers and Ferns in their Haunts*. New York, 1901.
WROTH, WARWICK, and WROTH, ARTHUR EDGAR. *The London Pleasure Grounds of the 18th Century*. London, 1896.

INDEX